Constantine the Philosopher University in Nitra, Faculty of Arts, Nitra
Institute of Political Sciences of the Slovak Academy of Sciences,
Bratislava

Radoslava Brhlíková (Ed.)

SEEKING THE NATIONAL INTEREST

Slovakia after 15 Years of EU and NATO Accession

Bibliografische Information der Deutschen Nationalbibliothek

Die Deutsche Nationalbibliothek verzeichnet diese Publikation in der Deutschen Nationalbibliografie; detaillierte bibliografische Daten sind im Internet über http://dnb.d-nb.de abrufbar.

Bibliographic information published by the Deutsche Nationalbibliothek

Die Deutsche Nationalbibliothek lists this publication in the Deutsche Nationalbibliografie; detailed bibliographic data are available in the Internet at http://dnb.d-nb.de.

This publication was funded by the VEGA Scientific Grant Agency of the Slovak Academy of Sciences and The Ministry of Education, Science, Research and Sport of the Slovak Republic: The Image of the "Other" in post-1989 Slovak politics (Obraz "Iného" v slovenskej politike po roku 1989), No. 2/0046/19.

Authors: Radoslava Brhlíková, Juraj Marušiak, Lászlo Öllös, Norbert Kmeť, Radoslav Štefančík, Dirk Dalberg, Tibor Szentandrási, David Reichardt
Editor: Radoslava Brhlíková
Reviewers: Radoslav Ivančík, Lucia Mokrá

ISBN-13: 978-3-8382-1417-7
© *ibidem*-Verlag, Stuttgart 2019
Alle Rechte vorbehalten

Das Werk einschließlich aller seiner Teile ist urheberrechtlich geschützt. Jede Verwertung außerhalb der engen Grenzen des Urheberrechtsgesetzes ist ohne Zustimmung des Verlages unzulässig und strafbar. Dies gilt insbesondere für Vervielfältigungen, Übersetzungen, Mikroverfilmungen und elektronische Speicherformen sowie die Einspeicherung und Verarbeitung in elektronischen Systemen.

All rights reserved. No part of this publication may be reproduced, stored in or introduced into a retrieval system, or transmitted, in any form, or by any means (electronic, mechanical, photocopying, recording or otherwise) without the prior written permission of the publisher. Any person who does any unauthorized act in relation to this publication may be liable to criminal prosecution and civil claims for damages.

Printed in the EU

CONTENT

FOREWORD V

1. What is Slovakia's "National Interest" and Where is it Created? In Lieu of an Introduction 1
2. The Temptation of Underdevelopment 27
3. Security as a National Interest after EU Accession 45
4. National Interest and Politicians 69
5. Migration Policy as National Interest 89
6. The Importance of Political Culture for the Slovak National Interest in the Context of the Migration Crisis 113
7. Slovak National Interest and the Hungarian Minority in the Post-Integration Period 141
8. Slovakia's National Interests and Slovak-Russian Bilateral Relations in the Context of the Ukrainian Crisis (2013-2018) 155
9. Slovak National Interest: A Difficult Pursuit. The Three Key Blockages to the Attainment of National Interest 179

CONCLUSION 197

References 199

Authors 241

FOREWORD

This monograph analyzes the Slovak Republic's international relations in the post-integration period—that is, after the country joined the European Union and NATO in 2004. The authors examine how these memberships affected the discussion in Slovakia on the formulation of the country's national interests as well as related procedural aspects and political actors. The key research question of the publication is how Slovakia's integration into the European Union impacted the country's definition and subsequent enforcement of its national interests. The authors have primarily focused on the aspects contributing to the definition of Slovakia's national interests on a domestic level.

The individual chapters therefore explore the interaction between domestic, foreign, and transnational actors who take part in the development of Slovakia's national interests. While identifying these participants, the authors also examine the extent to which the role of non-state actors has strengthened in the formulation of Slovakia's national interests in the post-integration period. The authors work with the hypothesis that Slovakia's foreign policy preferences are to a considerable degree defined by political elites, while the role of civil society players remains largely passive.

When formulating their theses and conclusions, the authors have taken into consideration the fact that a state's definition of its national interest as a concept and as an integral part of its foreign policy is still a highly topical issue. The question of "national interests" is seen as one of the key areas of international relations. In Slovakia, the expression "national interest" has become a target of criticism especially because of the impossibility to delineate the terms "nation" and "state" in the multicultural Slovak society. This is why, besides "national interest" (*národný záujem*), the term "nation-state interest" (*národnoštátny záujem*) is also used. Slovak political and academic discourse operates with both terms, since there is no consensus on whether this problem should be analyzed from the perspective of the majority's interests—which implicitly suggests the exclusion of the minority population and the ethnicization of the term — or from the perspective of state interests, which are primarily understood as coinciding with the interests of the Slovak population as a whole. That is why the research team prefers to use in the Slovak version of this publication the term "nation-state interest," a much more consensual expression in the Slovak context. The question of migration, the position of autochthonous and allochthonous minorities, and minority policies are all comprised in the concept of national interest.

To what extent has its interpretation changed since 2004? And how is it being interpreted? These questions lie at the core of the individual chapters that examine the potential shift that might have occurred in the perception of the term "national interest" after 2004, acquiring a more transnational meaning. The research also explores the role bilateral relations and subregional cooperation structures play in this process.

The methodological framework of this publication is provided by case studies, the synthesis of individual outputs, and the analysis and identification of internal political factors that affect the creation of national interests. The authors have also attempted to classify the main actors and their role in society. The members of the research team analyzed the notion of "national interest" as the preferences of a state as a socially constructed reality. The authors based their observations on the concepts of liberal intergovernmentalism and Europeanization.

The authors of this publication have focused on several partial areas of Slovakia's national interests, such as security policy, the issue of ethnic minorities and human rights, the creation of Slovakia's public image, and the problem of migration. The chapters also examine the impact that the social and economic crises have on the formulation of Slovakia's national interests, and the coordination of political actors when it comes to enforcing them on a European level; that is, they scrutinize to what extent Slovakia's particular problem areas have become internationalized and how the country's national interests correspond (or not) with those of the EU and NATO.

In the chapter "The Temptation of Underdevelopment," László Öllös focuses on the objective and subjective causes behind this phenomenon in Central Europe, placing it in a wider European context. The author analyzes Central Europe's underdevelopment in the post-1989 period, which is characterized by the former socialist countries trying to "catch up" with Western Europe. Öllös furthermore notes that the EU is falling behind other world powers, posing the question of what such a gradual lagging behind would mean to Europe in its competition with other world powers. He concludes that in this globalized world (Kershaw 2016, 13-21) gradually falling behind its competitors would jeopardize Europe's belief in development and success. At the same time, Öllös believes this crisis would also affect the values of European democracy.

In the chapter "Security as a National Interest after EU Accession," Radoslava Brhlíková examines the connection between the concept of security and the concept of the state. In this methodological context, she compares the security interests of the European Union with those of the Slovak Republic. She defines the term "security" and analyzes it as the ultimate national interest. In the context of national interest and Slovakia's EU membership, she compares the interests of the European Union with those of Slovakia as a member of a wider community. Her premise is that with the gradual enhancement of the integration process (even in foreign policy matters), the national interests of Slovakia are gradually coming nearer and becoming more identical to the foreign policy interests of the European Union. She seeks to answer the question of whether upon joining a wider community of states in pursuit of a common policy, a state—a rather small one, considering its strength, capabilities, and skills—still has its own national interests. Brhlíková concludes that by being part of a wider community, a state seems to give up on its own interests, seeking protection—and therefore the fulfillment of its priorities and objectives—under the wings of a joint organization.

Norbert Kmeť arrives to almost the same conclusions in his chapter "National Interest and Politicians," where he analyzes the domestic political scene and its impact on the formulation of Slovakia's foreign policy. He comes to the conclusion that, as far as the external and internal policies of a state are concerned, whether one uses the term "state interest," "national interest," or "nation-state interest" is not the main issue. State interests should represent a society-wide consensus concerning matters such as a stable state economy, compliance with EU rules, the prevention of corruption, border protection, and state security. Slovakia's interests or strategic objectives should match those represented by the EU. In the pursuit of a common goal, individual interests must be pushed aside and cooperation between European and state institutions should be enhanced.

In the chapter "Migration Policy as National Interest," Radoslav Štefančík tries to define migration policy in relation to Slovakia's national interests. The author notes that in recent decades, migration policy has become a priority to every economically strong and modern state, as all of them now face the phenomenon of international migration. Štefančík claims that migration policy is an important part of politics which also affects the sovereignty of nation-states. He defines it as a set of arrangements a state makes to manage migration matters, such as regulating the admission of foreigners into its territory, determining the conditions of their stay, and arranging their integration into society. He emphasises that migration policy is not only about crossing borders and residing in the territory of another state, but it also concerns the integration of immigrants into the host society and ultimately dealing with the reactions of the resident population. He interprets "migration policy" as a term encompassing three areas of international migration: immigration, asylum policy, and the integration of immigrants. He differentiates between three basic models: the French assimilative model, the British (or Dutch) multiculturalist model, and the German model of social exclusion.

In the chapter "The Importance of Political Culture for Slovak National Interest in the Context of Migration Crisis," Dirk Dalberg also examines the phenomenon of migration. This chapter offers an interesting insight into a German researcher's view on Slovak political culture and the way it influences the perception and resolution of the migration crisis in the country. He opines that

Slovakia refuses the mandatory refugee quotas because of its negative perception of Islam, which is deeply rooted in its political and socio-cultural system. This negative image of Islam is nowadays much abused by national, conservative, and Christian-oriented parties such as the Slovenská národná strana ("Slovak National Party," SNS), the Ľudová strana—Naše Slovensko ("People's Party—Our Slovakia," ĽSNS), and Obyčajní ľudia a nezávislé osobnosti ("Ordinary People and Independent Personalities," OĽaNO) as well as by the left-wing Smer-SD ("Direction—Social Democracy") and the liberal Sloboda a Solidarita ("Freedom and Solidarity," SaS). This historically inherited and nowadays oft-articulated ideology has much to do with a fear of an asymmetric relationship between the EU and Slovakia. A considerable part of the Slovak population believes that the European Union is forcing the country and its citizens to accept "other" inhabitants, even though the Slovaks perceive them as a threat to their national and cultural identity. For this reason, the Slovaks have refused Muslim refugees in their territory. He also believes that there is another reason at play: Slovakia only has experiences with emigration. Slovaks primarily associate migration with emigrating abroad and not with immigrating to Slovakia. This Central European country differs from Western European states for this very reason.

In the chapter "Slovak National Interest and the Hungarian Minority in the Post-Integration Period," Tibor Szentandrási surveys the position of the Hungarian minority after 2004, which he sees as an important milestone in the research of minority issues. His core argument is simple: he claims that despite all their differences and contradictions, Slovakia's national and state interests have a lot in common with those of its neighbours, including the Hungarians, the alleged age-old enemies of the Slovaks. The European dimension brings new aspects into the research, nudging it in a different direction. Terms such as "ethnic conflict," "intolerance" and "antagonisms" are pushed into the background, while questions related to the region's development, the democratization of society, the development of civil society, and the comparison of these phenomena in the "old" and "new" member states of the EU. In the Slovak Republic, this approach is primarily implemented by an orientation towards European history, European regions, the category of citizenship, and the extent of democratization and the development of civil society in Central Europe. The current European debate on the further development of civil society focuses mainly on the topical issues of asylum policy and immigration; from this point of view, the constant revitalization of national questions is becoming anachronistic.

In the chapter "Slovakia's National Interests and Slovak-Russian Bilateral Relations in the Context of the Ukrainian Crisis (2013-2018)," Juraj Marušiak tries to identify how Slovakia's relations with Russia influence the formation of the former's national interests and to what extent Slovakia's discussion about its "Eastern policy" — and especially its relations with Russia — divide the Slovak political scene. Because of the complexity of the issue, Marušiak narrows his focus to the post-2013 period; that is, after the outbreak of the Ukrainian crisis. The author states that in the context of the Ukrainian crisis, Slovakia's national interests differ from Russia's policies in relation to Ukraine. Although Slovakia does not have a consolidated position regarding its relations with Russia — mainly because of the discrepancies between the Slovak political elite's words and actions, even within the EU — we can still conclude that Slovakia's key foreign policy priority (or more precisely, its national interest) remains integration into the EU, whereas establishing a dialogue with Russia is only secondary.

This publication is concluded by David Reichardt's chapter, "Slovak National Interest: A Difficult Pursuit. The Three Key Blockages to the Attainment of the National Interest," in which the author examines why Slovakia's promotion of its national interests slowed down after 2004 compared to the previous decade. The author argues that the reasons are largely three-fold and concern ideology, corruption, and short-term decision-making. Reichardt bases his hypothesis on the interpretation of the concept of "national interest" and the exploration of its application to Slovakia's political and social environment.

This publication wishes to make a contribution to Slovak discourse on foreign policy and the role of its individual participants. The authors try to outline a possible direction the discussion about Slovakia's national interests might take. Their studies aim to identify the conflicts that characterize Slovakia's national interests in relation to those pursued by the organizations in which Slovakia holds a membership, focusing mainly on the European Union. The authors believe this publication might be of educational use to universities, but could also be perused by a wider academic and lay public who take an interest in the issues underlying Slovakia's domestic and foreign policies.

1. What is Slovakia's "National Interest" and Where is it Created? In Lieu of an Introduction

Juraj Marušiak

In their attempt to influence public opinion both in domestic and foreign policy matters, politicians and journalists tend to bandy about the term "national interest." However, it is profusely used not only by the traditionalist and nationally-oriented camp but also by those in favor of an enhanced integration process.

The following excerpts illustrate it well: *"Slovakia needs to think and act more in accordance with its interests"* (Brožík 2012). Or: *"What kind of a president would prioritize equipping an army over tackling the problem of his nation being brainwashed, its lack of education, or inadequate health care... Is he more concerned about foreign interests than Slovak ones?"* This was the question Maroš Smolec, the editor of the weekly newspaper Matica slovenská, fired at the Slovak president Andrej Kiska (Smolec 2013). In contrast, Kiska believes that *"the ones who threaten national interests are those who clamor for the need to protect the sovereignty of the country while spreading hoaxes and propaganda"* (Teraz.sk 2018). Meanwhile, Andrej Danko, the Speaker of the National Council of the Slovak Republic, claims that *"Slovak politicians and those working in the civil service must hold the country's national and state interests sacred"* (Sme 2018).

With regard to the European Union's anti-Russian sanctions, Robert Fico, then Slovak prime minister, said: *"As an EU member, Slovakia supports taking a uniform approach to the Ukrainian situation. However, as a sovereign state we reserve the right to defend our national interests, without disrupting the unity of the EU and its uniform position"* (Noviny.sk 2015). He repeatedly described his Russia policy as one in accordance with the national interests of Slovakia: *"Where Slovakia's national interests are concerned, no one can stop me. We had to turn to Russia because the volume of economic and business relations has been diminishing"* (Sme 2015).

However, his critics and political rivals also argue for "national interests." For instance, conservative journalist Jaroslav Daniška opined that *"with his foreign policy, Prime Minister Fico is also harming Slovakia's national interests. His first year of premiership offers us several examples, the three most serious being obsequiousness toward the EU, hypocrisy toward the traditional Balkan ally, and underrating Poland's strategic significance and the Visegrad concept of Central Europe"* (Daniška 2007). Veronika Remišová, a member of the National Council for OĽaNO ("Ordinary People and Independent Personalities") claims that *"with its inability to manage EU funds in an honest and fair way, the government has been damaging the national interests of Slovakia for a long time"* (Králik 2018). However, even those members of the intellectual elite who question the idea of a state being built on the values of ethnic nationalism talk about "national interests". They believe that what they see as the National Council's nationalistic manifestation in regard to the Act of Hungarians Living Abroad of February 2002 threatens such interests (Changenet.sk 2002).

In public discourse, Slovakia's presence in the EU is also seen through the prism of "national interests" which, according to Slovak politicians, do not necessarily have to overlap with "European interests." The supporters of European integration talk about the alignment of national interests with European ones. This idea appeared in the rhetoric of Robert Fico, the leader of Smer-SD ("Direction—Social Democracy") and the former prime minister, when addressing the issue of Ukraine's natural gas supplies (Aktuality.sk 2015) as well as in the discourse of Ivan Štefanec, MEP for the opposition party Kresťanskodemokratické hnutie ("Christian Democratic Movement," KDH), who described the EU as a "union of nation-states." He believes that in this context, the most important interest is "aligning [Slovakia's] national interests with the common European interest," defining a common goal for the future, and being able to operate in the common European system (Glob.Zosnam.sk 2018). Euroskeptic political parties have a much clearer idea of the contradiction between "Slovak" and "European" interests. Richard Sulík, the leader of the right-wing Sloboda a Solidarita ("Freedom and Solidarity," SaS), makes practically no mention of "European" interests in his agenda, stating that *"in Brussels, I am representing Slovak interests and I will continue to do so"* (Sulík 2016). The extreme right-wing party Ľudová strana Naše Slovensko ("People's Party Our Slovakia") referred to supporting a pan-European solution to the refugee crisis by establishing mandatory quotas for refugee reallocation as passed by the European Parliament (EP) in the 2015 BC-R8-0367/2015 resolution as "a betrayal of the national interests of the Slovak Republic." urging Slovak MEPs who voted for it to give up their mandate (Ľ'sNS 2015).

The theoretical and methodological framework

The above-cited excerpts clearly indicate that political discourse sees "national interest" as one of the country's key priorities — if not the most important. Because of the high emotional value and relevance certain politicians attach to "national interests," it is evident that they still consider the nation-state to be the most important and dominant participant in international relations. This is also how they see the European Union and its common foreign and security policy in spite of the transnational elements that characterize its economy and some other areas of society (Weiss 2008, 113). Referring to certain topics as the "national interest" has a strong mobilizing effect on voters. In naming a particular priority a "national interest," politicians try to emphasize its relevance. The attribute "national" indicates that it is a society-wide priority. On the other hand, saying that an idea, priority, or policy goes against the national interest results in discrediting and delegitimizing it as well as its supporters. Therefore, politicians tend to delegitimize their rivals by misusing the term "national interest."

As Oldřich Krpec points out, politicians try to define the "national interest" in "objectivist" categories. This is especially true for the realist tradition of political thinking where politicians define the "national interest" normatively as an objectively existing category that primarily concerns issues that affect the basic survival of a state. It is thus considered a category of power. A "subjectivist," or so-called structural functionalist, definition does not try to objectively define the national interest but attempts to identify the process of its formation by means of the social sciences (Krpec 2009, 16-17). The present publication is based on the assumption that a state's behavior in an international environment is defined not only by its interactions with other states but also by the activity of its domestic political actors. As Krpec points out, citing Alexander Wendt, a state's identity and interests are to some extent dependent on a social environment, and the international system constitutes such an environment. Within such a system, the state is perceived as a corporate agent through which individuals enter an international process. Thus, the above-mentioned authors maintain that common interests are formed as a result of social interaction around shared values and ideas (Krpec 2009, 45-48). According to Krpec, this interpretation of "national interests" is characterized by a contradiction between the fact that externally "the state speaks in a unified voice" while internally it is significantly divided (45-48). Similarly, supporters of liberalism recognize a plurality of actors and interests, taking into account the internal subjects as well as cultural values and institutional traditions (62-63).

The formulation of national interests is critically influenced both by the interests of particular political actors and the values and concepts shared by a society (or at least the majority of its members). So, if we agree that the national interest is the result of social interactions, we cannot interpret it as a static and objectively definable category but only as a phenomenon that is subject to changes dependent on the actors who participate in its creation. A state's foreign policy as a set of external activities in an international environment is also subject to changes. According to Šárka Waisová, if in the pre-WWII period a considerable part of a state's policy was autonomous and independent from internal political affairs, in the second half of the twentieth century it started to become increasingly domesticized, meaning that the influence of domestic actors grew and civil society started to take a keener interest in foreign policy matters. It also had to reflect the growing influence of transnational actors, which resulted in the expansion of the economic factor (Waisová 2011, 9-10). Thus, we can observe an increased interconnectedness between a nation-state's internal and foreign policies.

State sovereignty as we currently understand it is also subject to change. In the past, its interpretation was based on definitions like those of Jean Bodin, who believed it to be "the absolute and permanent, legally guaranteed" (1955, 25) power of a state, independent from external actors. It is therefore considered to be an indisputable and essential aspect of a conditioned life (Königová 2001, 41). On the other hand, authors nowadays emphasize that it is a socially and historically conditioned entity which can be obtained or lost gradually, while the *"Westphalian idea of states as cue balls with an impenetrable surface"* (Königová 2001, 41, 47) is now being contested. Richard Bellamy opines that the transnational interpretation of human rights is above all challenged by the traditional concept of state sovereignty.He talks instead about a post-sovereign or late-sovereign international order (Hloušek 2004, 94; Walker 2003, 3-32). He believes that state sovereignty, which is defined by the "demos" and its ability to rule, together with "popular sovereignty," which defines the scope and nature of the law, can endanger human rights, since state sovereignty might impede humanitarian intervention against repressive regimes while popular sovereignty can lead to the tyranny of the majority (Bellamy 2003, 168). Human rights violations and the compromised safety of individuals are legitimately recognized reasons for external intervention (Königová 2001). Where the EU's multi-level governance is concerned, Bellamy talks about an organisation betwixt and between a sovereign and a post-sovereign system, which is built both on a federal and an intergovernmental principle, while also being characterized by a regulatory regime based on the rule of law (Bellamy 2003, 186-187). In this situation, as Brian Hocking and David Spence note, the role of foreign affairs ministries as gate-keepers, responsible for controlling a state's borders and all communication that occurs through them, is replaced by the role of the boundary-spanner, who is aware of the mixed character of the international system, the increased permeability of state borders, and the multi-layered nature of foreign policy, leading to an increased demand for interactivity and complexity (Carlsnaes, Sjursen, White 2004, 11).

From this point of view, an "objectivistic" interpretation of national interest seems insufficient. According to Oldřich Krpec, an "objectivistic" approach means that a national interest enters politics from an international environment at the moment of its articulation, which occurs at the domestic political level and is based both on collective and individual interests and shared values. It is then incorporated into foreign policy (Krpec 2009, 68), having progressed from social groups and individuals through interest groups all the way to political representation (71).

Even nowadays, there are authors like Oskar Krejčí who base their definition of the national interest on realist or neorealist interpretations such as those of Hans Morgenthau, for instance. Krejčí opines that the national interest is marked by a struggle to survive and represents a policy geared towards "survival" and *"the protection of physical, political and cultural identity against encroachments by other nation-states"* (Morgenthau 1951). Based on these definitions, Krejčí sees national (or state) interest as an "objectively determined set of goals of a state, defined by its material characteristics and external environment" (Krejčí 2014, 265). Jiří Valenta also largely agrees with Morgenthau's definition, especially where the relevance of interests and the stability of their vital importance are concerned. However, he also shares Arnold Wolfers' opinion that *"the decisions of policy-makers based on national interests cannot be separated from moral and ethical interests"* (Valenta 1992, 16-17).

The state is not a homogenous actor. Therefore, an "objectivistic" definition of national interest only reflects the subjective beliefs of the entity who offers such a definition, whether it is a politician, or an expert, or the state and its administration. Especially in democratic conditions, a state cannot be perceived as monolithic, since public authorities are not separate from society. Society is differentiated and its individual segments or political actors have different priorities, which are then pursued at the state level through political competition.

On the other hand, liberal (e.g., Robert Keohane, Andrew Moravcsik, David Mitrany, and Robert Putnam [cf. Drulák 2010, 13]) and constructivist authors (Jutta Weldes and Martha Finnemore [Drulák 2010]) reject the "top-down" perspective. The liberal thinkers base their theories on the idea that the state is not a homogenous actor and that the national interest as the guiding principle for a state's foreign policy is the result of the aggregated interests of individuals and groups in the domestic political scene. Meanwhile, constructivists rely on discourses, norms, and identities (Drulák 2010).

To analyze the processes which govern the creation of Slovakia's foreign policy, identify the factors that influence it, and examine to what extent these issues become a national interest, we used Petr Drulák's and Petr Kratochvíl's criteria (Drulák 2010; Kratochvíl 2010a, 21-34). This approach allows us to separate scientific analysis from the political elite's attempts to have their particular goals accepted as the "national interest" and converted into the normative principles applied to foreign policy. On the contrary, Drulák's and Kratochvil's approach allows us to discern the legitimacy of goals — defined as national interests — as a socially construed phenomenon and not as an empirical necessity (Kratochvil 2010a, 24). It also takes into consideration plurality and the existence of several parallel and often competing state interests (Bátora 2004a, 40).

The first criterion is the criterion of relevance; that is, whether certain issues are of importance to Slovak society and the political elites, and to what extent they constitute a long-term interest. The criterion of consensuality allows us to identify how acceptable — and therefore legitimate — a particular policy seems to the majority of society, which is also the precondition for an interest's long-term relevance, regardless of changes in government brought about by elections (cf. Drulák 2010, 14).

Finally, if we accept that the "national interest" is not an objectively definable category but is rather the result of interactions between domestic actors and the external environment of the state, then its development is dynamic. It can be defined in relation to a specific issue, but it can also be redefined, challenged, and re-established. The goal of this publication is to identify the topics that are becoming a part of Slovakia's national interests in its foreign policy, together with the actors who participate in their formation and the platforms where they are negotiated or where attempts to challenge and renegotiate them take place.

The conceptual definition of foreign policy depends on a state's identity — that is, the way it defines its own position in the system of international relations, the type of relations it establishes with the external environment, and the partners it chooses. But at the same time, a state's identity is also defined by the way it is perceived by other states. For this reason, when analyzing national interests, we also need to identify how acceptable a particular policy is to other states. Last but not least, a state's identity at the international level also depends on its internal policies. Choosing a domestic policy direction has a crucial impact on a state's foreign policy orientation, since to identify its potential partners, a state has to take into account its economic or security interests as well as the extent to which cooperation with those partners allows it to fulfill its domestic political goals. According to political scientist Erik Ringmar, a state's actions are not necessarily driven by rational motives, but also by irrational or non-rational ones. As he further notes, citing philosopher Georg W. Hegel and the sociologists George Herbert Mead and Alessandro Pizzorno, *"an individual cannot decide on their own who or what they are, as every such decision is made collectively. We need approval to become the person we want to be, and only when approved can we finally create the identity"* (Ringmar 2008, 13). On the other hand, direct and long-term state interests can also affect the process of identity-building. Thus, even a measure (or a set of measures) with the aim of forming a postulated identity can become an interest.

After the fall of communism, Slovakia as a newly established nation-state faced several challenges in reformulating its identity, which meant renouncing its previous identity and embracing new metaphors, meanings, and narratives. Erik Ringmar calls these crucial moments in the creation of a new identity "formative" (Ringmar 2008, 81, 86). Because of its multiple internal and external conflicts, we can identify several formative moments in the history of Slovakia when the country had to decide about its future.

Attempts at institutionalizing Slovakia's "national interests" by means of a "State Doctrine"

In post-1989 Slovakia, a discussion about national interests as a set of consensually defined priorities to designate the further development of the country's internal and foreign policy had been long absent or at least marginalized. With the exception of the fall of communism in 1989 and the accession to the European Union in 2004, all major changes—including the formation of an independent Slovak Republic, the choice of a socioeconomic transformation model, accession to NATO, and the rise and fall of the somewhat authoritarian "Mečiarist" regime—happened amidst much internal political dispute. Politicians failed to reach an agreement on what direction Slovakia should take. They started to exploit foreign policy matters in domestic political discourse and ignored any alternative scenarios, converting the issue into a question of their prestige

Another such divisive moment was the problem of defining the term "nation," which, especially during the 1990s rule of Hnutie za demokratické Slovensko ("Movement for a Democratic Slovakia," HZDS), Slovenská národná strana ("Slovak National Party," SNS), and Združenie robotníkov Slovenska ("Union of the Workers of Slovakia," ZRS), was often interpreted solely in ethnic terms. This was the time when the expression "nation-state interests" came into use, also being advocated by prime minister Vladimír Mečiar (HZDS), even though the academic literature, including Slovak and Czech authors (cf. Valenta 1992; Krejčí 2014; Weiss 2010; Kratochvíl 2010b), did not use this term. On the other hand, it was Mečiar's party that often called itself "the defender of Slovak interests," while accusing its opponents of being anti-Slovak (cf. Sme 1996). Similarly, HZDS and its leader Mečiar also blamed the Hungarian minority for sabotaging Slovakia's nation-state interests (cf. Haughton 2001, 112). The discussion about the "national interest" as an integrating factor of Slovak politics was therefore limited only to a fragment of the political spectrum. It was systemically advocated by František Šebej, a member of Demokratická strana ("Democratic Party") as well as Peter Weiss, the leader of Strana demokratickej ľavice ("Party of the Democratic Left") (Weiss 2009). In fact, Šebej refuses to use the term "nation-state interest," as he considers the state an institution that should be neutral in terms of interests and opinions. He sees the nation as a whole as consisting of equal citizens, which is why he finds the term "national interest" more democratic (Šebej 2000).

An attempt to consensually define the priorities across the whole political spectrum appeared only later, after the establishment of a broad coalition of centre-right and centre-left parties following the parliamentary elections of 1998. The coalition government led by Mikuláš Dzurinda was in favor of accelerating the process of accession to the EU and NATO; however, the political scene continued to be strongly polarized. This is why in November 1999, when President Rudolf Schuster (1999–2004) made an appeal in the National Council to create Slovakia's state doctrine, which he hoped to be "*the result of an agreement between relevant political powers [...] jointly defined by the coalition and the opposition*" with the aim of defining "*the reasons behind the creation of our state and its real goals for the future*" (Kancelária prezidenta 1999) he did not meet with much success.

Instead of reaching an agreement regarding the country's priorities, several competing state doctrine proposals appeared. These looked more like party manifestos, or projects approved by only one ideologically defined circle of intellectuals and public figures. That was the case with the national-conservative state doctrine proposal put forward by the members of Matica slovenská, Nezávislé združenie ekonómov Slovenska ("Independent Association of Slovak Economists," NEZES), and Ábel Kráľ, the leader of the executive committee of Spoločenstvo Kresťanské Slovensko ("Christian Slovakia Society"), who drafted the proposal (Kultúra 2001, 14-15). This circle was close to the HZDS. The doctrine's foreign policy plan for Slovakia was to "join the family of European states" as "a sovereign subject, in accordance with its own needs." The document makes no mention of Slovakia's membership in NATO, but it does not question the process of integration into the EU. However, it states that Slovakia's foreign policy should be "balanced" and its activities should be *"multilateral by gearing towards Western and Eastern Europe and the rest of the world."* Slovakia should therefore perform a *"mediatory role in the strategic power interests of the world powers"* (Kultúra 2001, 14-15). The document shows that in 2001 Slovak society was still divided on the country's foreign policy and the consequences that the integration processes would have on its character.

The opposition party Smer also prepared a state doctrine proposal, drafted by the party's vice-chair Boris Zala (Smer 2001). The document was approved at an extraordinary party conference in May 2001 in Stupava. Unlike the document prepared by the HZDS-friendly grouping, Smer unequivocally advocated Slovakia's entry into the EU and NATO while also emphasizing the need to cultivate friendly bilateral relations with Russia and building European security in cooperation. The document also speaks of a readiness to support all Russian activities *"in accordance with the principles of European civilization and its values, especially those concerning fundamental human rights and democracy"* (Smer 2001).

The Slovak National Party also wanted to prepare its own version of the state doctrine (Sme 2001a). These examples show that these proposals were the projects of opposition powers who saw an opportunity to merge their particular ideas on Slovakia's future development with the interests of the whole society, perhaps even with the help of the president. On the other hand, the government coalition regarded the project with skepticism. The only exception was Vladimír Palko, the vice-chair of the Christian Democratic Movement, who agreed with Ábel Kráľ's theses but raised an objection to the political environment in which the document was conceived, as he believed that it was the HZDS who compromised the term "nation-state interest" (Palko 2000). Slovakia's ex-president Michal Kováč (1993–1998) also agreed with the proposal to create Slovakia's state doctrine, wanting it to be approved at the National Council by a constitutional majority (Sme 2001).

Arriving at a foreign policy consensus after Slovakia's independence in 1993 was a complicated process. The newly formed state carried on with the foreign policy priorities of its legal and political predecessor, the Czech and Slovak Federative Republic (ČSFR): namely, its efforts to join the European Union and NATO and establish good relations with neighboring countries. The desire to cooperate with Western, European, and Euro-Atlantic structures was seen as a civilizational choice, leading not only to the re-orientation of the ČSFR's foreign policy after 1989 but also to the creation of a model of parliamentary democracy and a market economy. One of the key formative moments in the development of Slovakia's external identity as an independent state was the third term of Vladimír Mečiar's government between 1994 and 1998. At that time, the authoritarian tendencies of the coalition, comprising the HZDS, the Slovak National Party, and the Union of the Workers of Slovakia, led to the elimination of Slovakia from the first phase of the NATO and EU enlargement process, when the country was not invited to the 1997 NATO summit in Madrid or to the subsequent EU summit in Luxembourg, where enlargement negotiations took place. Meanwhile, cooperation with Russia — which went beyond trade exchange and involved a political and military partnership — was seen as an alternative to the officially declared course of foreign policy (Duleba 1996; Samson 2000). Therefore, the acceleration of economic and political reforms with the aim of obtaining an invitation to EU and NATO accession negotiations proved how closely Slovakia's integration processes in the 1990s were tied to the transformation processes, constituting a highly relevant interest for the country.

Although there were several instances when the deciding political powers reached a consensus — as on Slovakia's EU membership, the enforcement of the concept of nation-states in Europe after 2004, and cooperation during the implementation of some of the European policies, the refusal to recognize Kosovo as an independent state in 2007 and 2008, the gas conflict between Russia and Ukraine in 2009, and the rejection of Crimea's annexation by Russia — Rudolf Schuster's proposal to create Slovakia's state doctrine in 1999 was the only attempt to formally reach a consensual definition of Slovakia's foreign policy through presidential mediation. Schuster's endeavor proved to be futile. In Slovakia, consensus regarding several important foreign policy matters has often been reached informally at a non-legislative or non-executive level. However, it also needs to be added that the state doctrine proposals did not concern just foreign policy matters but also priorities of internal development, which complicated any agreement regarding their content.

The role of the referendum in the formation of national interests in Slovakia's foreign policy

The Constitution of the Slovak Republic recognizes the referendum as an instrument of direct democracy, noting that joining a union with other states or seceding from it should be confirmed by a referendum (Article 93, Paragraph 1). The president can also declare a referendum upon a petition submitted by at least 350,000 citizens or upon a resolution of the National Council of the Slovak Republic (Article 95, Paragraph 1). No issues of fundamental rights, freedoms, taxes, duties, or the state budget may be decided by a referendum (Article 93, Paragraph 3). The results of a referendum are valid if at least 50 percent of all eligible voters have participated (Article 98, Paragraph 1) (Constitution 1992). Slovakia's only successful referendum after 1993 concerned a foreign policy matter: the country's accession to the European Union.

Besides disputes regarding the regime, the question of whether Slovakia should join the EU and NATO was one of the main sources of domestic political conflict between 1994 and 1998 (Hloušek, Kopeček 2005, 4). The interconnectedness of these two issues was highlighted by the fact that in 1997 Slovakia was not invited to the accession negotiations with NATO and the EU because of the country's inability to fulfill the political conditions for membership of these organizations. The opposition parties blamed the government coalition for this failure, especially the HZDS. Meanwhile, the two other coalition members, the Slovak National Party and the Union of the Workers of Slovakia, were opposed to Slovakia's membership in these organizations until 1998.

The acceleration of the integration processes became a priority for a broad coalition formed after the parliamentary elections of September 1998, led by Slovenská demokratická koalícia ("Slovak Democratic Coalition," SDK), a bloc of three right-wing parties (Kresťanskodemokratické hnutie – "Christian Democratic Movement," Demokratická únia – "Democratic Union," and Demokratická strana – "Democratic Party") and several smaller left-wing parties (Sociálnodemokratická strana Slovenska – "Social Democratic Party of Slovakia" and Strana zelených Slovenska – "Slovak Green Party") together with the post-communist Strana demokratickej ľavice ("Party of the Democratic Left"), Strana maďarskej koalície ("Party of the Hungarian Community," SMK), and Strana občianskeho porozumenia ("Party of Civic Understanding," SOP). An all-around consensus on the issue was only reached after 2000, when even the HZDS expressed support for Slovakia's accession to NATO and the EU (HN 2000). As a result, there were only two political parties in the National Council during the pre-accession period that opposed Slovakia's entry to NATO and partially to the EU as well: the Slovak National Party and Komunistická strana Slovenska ("Communist Party of Slovakia," KSS; 2002-2006). Although the majority of the opposition claimed to support Slovakia's joining the EU, the HZDS, the Slovak National Party, and the leader of Smer, Robert Fico (who was an independent member of parliament at the time), refused to back the constitutional amendment of 23 February 2001, which enabled the Slovak Republic to join a union with other states and transfer some of its competencies to EU bodies. The amendment established the superiority of the European legislation over Slovak laws (NRSR 2001).

The pre-accession referendum held on 16 and 17 May 2003, in which 92.46 percent of the participating voters decided in favor of Slovakia's entry to the EU, showed that the political parties reached a consensus regarding the matter and that Slovakia's EU membership was seen as one of the country's national interests. The referendum's turnout was 52.15 percent of all eligible voters

(Štatistický úrad 2003). The fact that two political rivals, ex-PM Vladimír Mečiar and ex-president Michal Kováč (1993-1998) both participated in the pre-accession campaign illustrates the importance the political elite attached to Slovakia's membership in the EU (Cuprik 2017). This allowed the referendum to be used for the formation of Slovakia's "national interests." It would not have been possible without the consensus of the majority of relevant political parties.

However, in Slovakia a referendum can also serve as an instrument to challenge or re-evaluate and modify the established national interests. This was the case of the attempted referendum on Slovakia's accession to NATO in 2003. Its advocates from the civil initiative Nech rozhodnú občania (Let the Citizens Decide), led by left-wing activist Eduard Chmelár and former prime minister Ján Čarnogurský of the Christian Democratic Party (1991-1992), tried to call a referendum by collecting citizens' signatures despite the fact that the matter counted with the support of the majority of the political parties in the National Council (Čarnogurský 2003). This initiative proved to be unsuccessful, similar to a 2016 attempt made by the far-right Ľudová strana Naše Slovensko ("People's Party Our Slovakia"). Inspired by the successful Brexit referendum, the latter began to collect signatures for a petition demanding the convocation of a referendum on Slovakia's withdrawal from the EU and NATO. However, they were not backed by the rest of the political parties, not even by the other Euroskeptic party, Sme rodina ("We Are Family") led by Boris Kollár (Kyseľ 2016).

The formation of Slovakia's national interest at the parliamentary level

Since Slovakia's political system is a parliamentary democracy, the activities of political parties between elections are focused on their work in the National Council. The National Council's responsibilities include accepting government policy statements, laws, and political documents regulating, among other things, Slovakia's foreign policy. Many of its competencies, as defined in Article 86 of the Constitution of the Slovak Republic, directly affect foreign policy, such as the approval of treaties on Slovakia's union with other states and the repudiation of such treaties (Article 86 (b)); the approval of international treaties on human rights and fundamental freedoms, international political treaties, international treaties of a military nature, international treaties from which the membership of the Slovak Republic in international organizations arises, international economic treaties of a general nature, international treaties for whose exercise a law is necessary, international treaties conferring rights and imposing duties on natural or legal persons, and deciding on whether they are international treaties according to Art. 7 para. 5 (Article 86 (d)); and debating on basic issues relating to domestic, international, economic, social, and other policies (Article 86 (h)). Competencies concerning state security include declaring war in the event of an act of aggression by parties hostile to the Slovak Republic, in the event that obligations under international joint defense treaties must be fulfilled, and after the end of war on concluding a peace (Article 86 (j)); deciding on dispatching military forces outside the territory of the Slovak Republic if it does not concern a case stated in Art. 119, letter (p) (Article 86 (k)); and approving the presence of foreign military forces on the territory of the Slovak Republic (Article 86 (l)).

Foreign policy issues of the Slovak Republic that are indirectly affected by the competencies of the National Council include deciding on a proposal for the declaration of a referendum (Article 86 (c)); debating on the Program Proclamation of the Government of the Slovak Republic, monitoring the activities of the Government, and debating on a vote of confidence regarding the Government or its individual members (Article 86 (f)); legally establishing ministries and other governmental bodies (Article 86 (e)); and the right to approve the state budget, supervise budgetary policy, and approve the final state budgetary account (Article 86 (g)). This shows that the National Council has the key instruments to influence the conceptual definition of foreign policy and its practical implementation. Although its political resolutions are not legally binding, the parliamentary powers of scrutiny and the ability to pass a vote of no-confidence on the Slovak government allows its members to shape the country's foreign policy priorities and to negotiate the key issues that might become a matter of national interest. On the other hand, given the fact that the Slovak political system is built on the principles of parliamentary democracy, even in areas that, according to the Constitution, are in the exclusive competence of the Slovak government, the government has to take into consideration the opinion of the parliamentary majority. This is the case regarding the approval of international treaties entered into by the Slovak Republic, whose negotiation the President of the Slovak Republic has delegated to the Government (Article 119 (f)); proposing the declaration of a state of war, the mobilization of military forces, and the declaration of an state of exception as well as a proposal for their termination or declaring and terminating a state of emergency (Article 119 (n)); dispatching the military forces outside of the territory of the Slovak Republic for the purpose of humanitarian aid, military exercises, and peacekeeping missions, consenting to the presence of foreign military forces on the territory of the Slovak Republic for the purpose of humanitarian aid, military exercises, and peacekeeping missions, and consenting to the passing of foreign military forces through the territory of the Slovak Republic (Article 119 (o)); and deciding on dispatching military forces outside of the territory of the Slovak Republic if it regards the performance of obligations resulting from international treaties on joint military action for a maximum period of 60 days; the Government shall announce this decision without undue delay to the National Council of the Slovak Republic (Article 119 (p)) (Constitution 1992). Parliamentary debates on foreign policy issues are also an instrument for dialogue between the government and opposition parties. At the beginning of every year, the Ministry of Foreign and European Affairs presents the National Council with informative material about the foreign policy direction of the current year, together with a report on the fulfillment of foreign and European policy tasks of the previous year. Since 2017, the Ministry of Foreign and European Affairs has presented both reports within a single document.

After its accession to the European Union, Slovakia adopted a key document regulating its foreign policy priorities, the Medium-

Term Strategy for Development Cooperation of the Slovak Republic, valid until 2015 and approved by the National Council of the Slovak Republic on 14 December 2004 (NRSR 2017). It was backed by the majority of parliamentary deputies. The document regulated Slovakia's activities in the EU, NATO, and the broadly defined region of Central and Eastern Europe. Constitutional Act No. 397/2004 Coll. on cooperation between the National Council of the Slovak Republic and the Government of the Slovak Republic in matters concerning the European Union became a new instrument to reach internal political consensus on European affairs (NRSR 2004). This act obliges the Slovak government to provide the National Council with proposals of legally binding acts and other acts of the European Communities and the European Union, which will be discussed by the representatives of the EU member states. It also obligates them to inform the National Council about other matters related to Slovakia's membership in the European Communities and the EU. It also binds the government—or rather, its authorized member—to submit a draft opinion on the proposed acts to the National Council in due time, together with an estimate of their impact on the Slovak Republic. The act only allows entrusting a competent committee with this activity, which means that parliamentary control is performed by a substantially smaller committee.

An example of the National Council declaring consensual foreign policy priorities that were accepted by both coalition parties and the opposition occurred when it adopted the Declaration of the National Council on the Integration of the Slovak Republic into the European Union on 1 December 1998, i.e., after the establishment of Mikuláš Dzurinda's broad coalition government. Their goals included the pursuit of "the core values of European integration on which the European Union is built"—namely, the values of democracy, the rule of law, human rights, and the protection of minorities—so that Slovakia can obtain membership in the European Union (NRSR 1998). The declaration was supported not only by the coalition but also by the majority of the HZDS group, while most members of the Slovak National Party did not participate in the vote. One hundred and eighteen deputies voted in favor, and only Eva Slavkovská, a member of the Slovak National Party, voted against it.

Another priority on which most of the Slovak political powers agree is the preservation of the territorial integrity of the Slovak state and the rejection of the building of institutional ties between Hungary and members of Hungarian minorities in neighboring states. For instance, at the beginning of 2002, the National Council adopted a declaration on the unacceptability of the principle of extraterritoriality by means of the Act on Hungarians Living Abroad (NRSR D). The result of voting is relevant for the formation of the national interests. One hundred and ten deputies voted in favor of the declaration, whereas only fifteen voted against it, all of whom were members of the Party of the Hungarian Community (SMK) (NRSR D). This vote created an ethnic divide in the National Council, as deputies representing the Hungarian minority voted against the declaration even though they remained in the governing coalition. However, this ethnic conflict was not necessarily present in their discussions on Slovak–Hungarian relations. For instance, in 2008, members of the opposition parties (SDKÚ-DS and KDH) did not support the government majority's resolution expressing concerns about the establishment of the Forum of Hungarian Representatives of the Carpathian Basin as an advisory body to the legislature of Hungary, in whose formation the members of the Party of the Hungarian Community also participated, and they abstained from voting (NRSR A). A similar situation occurred during the vote on the response to the statement of the leader of the Hungarian party Fidesz. In a campaign before the European Parliament elections in 2009, Fidesz questioned the territorial integrity of its neighboring states; again, they abstained from voting on the issue. However, in neither case did they support the members of the Hungarian Coalition Party who voted against both documents (NRSR B).

Nevertheless, ethnic conflict was notable in a vote where the National Council refused to recognize the unilateral declaration of independence of the Serbian province of Kosovo. The manifesto said that "the full and unrestricted independence of Kosovo is not in the interest of the stability of a region that has long been exposed to tragedies and crises," claiming that the future of Kosovo must be in accordance with Serbia's legitimate requirements, the UN Charter, and other international legal norms (NRSR 2007). It was supported by 123 deputies. Nineteen decided to abstain from voting, eighteen of whom were the members of the Party of the Hungarian Community (SMK), and one from the Christian Democratic Movement (KDH) (NRSR C). We can therefore observe a consensus between the government and the majority of the opposition.

The National Council also reached an agreement regarding the issue of amending the Act on the Citizenship of Hungary in the Hungarian National Assembly. All the deputies present agreed with the National Council's statement expressing concern about the forthcoming unilateral imposition of dual citizenship for members of Hungarian minorities who hold a citizenship in the neighboring states. The National Council found it unacceptable for a country to adopt legislation that would have extraterritorial consequences for Slovak citizens without a prior consultation with the representatives of Slovakia, as foreseen by the Treaty of Good Neighborliness and Friendly Cooperation between Slovakia and Hungary. They also worried that Hungary might challenge the 1920 Treaty of Trianon and Europe's post-war arrangement. The representatives of the parties Most-Híd ("Bridge"), SMK, Konzervatívni demokrati Slovenska ("Conservative Democrats of Slovakia"), and eight members of the Slovak Democratic and Christian Union (SDKÚ-DS) did not take part in the vote (NRSR 2010). On the other hand, members of the opposition Christian Democratic Movement supported the statement, while the party's vice-chairman, Daniel Lipšic, called it as a measure to protect Slovakia's nation-state interests (Domino Forum 2000a).

Respecting the inviolability of the borders of European countries without the consent of the affected party remained a relevant foreign policy priority for Slovakia even in the ensuing years, when the National Council refused to recognize Russia's annexation of the Ukrainian province of Crimea. Immediately after its annexation in 2014, the National Council accused Russia of violating international law (NRSR 2014). The National Council reached an agreement on this issue based on a majority vote. On the other hand, the anti-Russian sanctions proved to be much more divisive. Meanwhile, there continues to be a disagreement regarding the interpretation of the Ukrainian crisis that began in autumn 2013. For example, while Nova's leader Daniel Lipšic called it a values dispute (Piško 2014), ex-PM Robert Fico interpreted it as a geopolitical conflict between Russia and the United States (Pravda 2014b).

Regarding the refugee crisis that broke out in the European Union in 2015, the political parties shared a negative attitude to accepting refugees, particularly from Muslim states. At the Justice and Home Affairs Council on 21 September 2015, Slovakia, together with the Czech Republic, Hungary, and Romania, rejected the imposition of mandatory quotas to redistribute asylum seekers among EU member states. And even though in 2015 and 2016 the opposition criticized prime minister Fico for his hostile attitude on the issue, they also refused the taking in of refugees (Poláčková, Brhlíková 2017). Although this stance was primarily shared by political parties, the National Council also rejected the imposition of mandatory quotas, calling them "a non-systematic solution to the resettlement or relocation of migrants" in a statement of 24 June 2015 (NRSR 2015). This draft statement was supported by 125 out of the 128 deputies present from all the parliamentary groups (NRSR E). This joint anti-migration stance was further confirmed by the National Council's statement on the Global Compact for Migration of 29 November 2018 (NRSR 2018), which rejected this document. Besides the deputies of the governing coalition, a substantial part of the opposition (90 out of 142 present), including members of the Ordinary People and Independent Personalities (OĽaNo), Sme rodina ("We Are Family") and the People's Party Our Slovakia voted for the adoption of the statement (NRSR C). Apparently, Slovakia regards this issue as one of its national interests.

These instances show that in Slovakia, parliament plays an important role in reaching a consensus regarding foreign policy priorities, allowing constant communication between the government and the opposition. Their positions significantly influence the formation of national interests, whether in terms of defining them or suggesting a common procedure.

Other levels of the institutionalization of Slovakia's "national interests"

Besides parliament, the president's activities, and the referendum, national interests are also conceptualized at other levels. The government, or more precisely the relations between coalition parties, play an important role in the formulation of the state's foreign policy. They must reach an agreement in the form of a government policy statement that also defines the country's common foreign policy priorities. However, in Slovakia's case, different opinions on foreign policy have often led to conflicts within coalitions. Such was the case in the above-mentioned dispute regarding the Act on Hungarians Living Abroad in 2001 and 2002, when the government coalition parties and the opposition were both opposed to the coalition's Party of the Hungarian Community (SMK). A similar incident occurred during the vote on the National Council's statement on the Global Compact on Migration in 2018, when most of the members of the coalition party Most-Híd abstained from voting. Lastly, in October 2011, the party Freedom and Solidarity (SaS), which formed part of the government coalition between 2010 and 2012, rejected a proposal to increase the funds allocated to the European Financial Stability Facility to help the member states affected by the debt crisis, such as Greece. In consequence, a confidence vote in Iveta Radičová's government took place in the National Council on 11 October 2011. This resulted in Radičová's downfall and the convocation of early elections in March 2012. The rest of the coalition parties, together with Smer-SD, which was an opposition party at the time, approved the proposal. Slovakia's relations with Russia are also a subject of political disagreement.

In 2018, this was illustrated not only by the disputes between the highest constitutional officials but also within the government coalition, when at a session of the National Council the coalition member Slovak National Party prevented the discussion of key documents regulating Slovakia's security policy, the Defense Strategy of the Slovak Republic, and the Security Strategy of the Slovak Republic, even though in October 2017 both documents had been approved by the Slovak government. SNS members disagreed with the documents' claim that Russia was an enemy. In autumn 2018, both documents were submitted to the National Council by the opposition, namely, by Freedom and Solidarity (SaS) (Pravda 2018).

Because some opposition parties, mainly the People's Party (ĽSNS) but partly also Freedom and Solidarity (SaS), started to increasingly question Slovakia's membership in the EU and NATO, the three highest constitutional officials of the Slovak Republic at the time — President Andrej Kiska, Speaker of the National Council Andrej Danko, and Prime Minister Robert Fico — issued a joint statement on Slovakia's foreign policy orientation on 23 October 2017. This statement defined the country's "unambiguous continuation of its pro-European and pro-Atlantic orientation" as its "strategic interest" while also drafting Slovakia's priorities within the EU and NATO, such as Slovakia's incorporation into the core of European integration, equal treatment in the internal market and non-discrimination of citizens and consumers in all parts of the EU (including the dual quality of food), and the fulfillment of allied obligations in defense and security policy.[1] Seeing the ongoing internal political conflict between Kiska — who counts on the support of right-wing opposition parties — and Smer-SD's leader Fico, we can see that there might be another national interest at play.

At the level of European institutions, a national interest is being formed, for example, where Slovak–Hungarian relations are concerned. For instance, Slovak politicians all across the political spectrum were unified during the formation of the new European Commission following the European Parliament elections in January 2010. MEP József Szájer (Fidesz) questioned the

---

1 Declaration by the President, Speaker and Prime Minister on EU and NATO. *Andrej Kiska — President of the Slovak Republic — official website*, 23.10.2017. 23.6.2017. Available online: https://www.prezident.sk/en/article/vyhlasenie-prezidenta-predsedu-narodnej-rady-a-predsedu-vlady-k-eu-a-nato/.

nomination of the diplomat Maroš Šefčovič, who counted on the support of the European Socialist Party (PES), accusing him of anti-Roma racism. Szájer's objections were also shared by the European People's Party (EPP) (Domino Forum 2010). Members of the far-right party Jobbik ("Movement for a Better Hungary") were also opposed to Šefčovič's candidature because of the allegedly racist character of the Act on the State Language of the Slovak Republic of 2009 (Novotný 2010). However, some of the Slovak members of the EPP group backed Šefčovič's nomination; especially the Slovak Democratic and Christian Union (SDKÚ-DS) led by Mikuláš Dzurinda, who discussed the issue with the president of the European Parliament, Jerzy Buzek, and the president of the European Commission, José Manuel Barroso (Domino Forum 2000b). Ševčovič's nomination for the post of European Commissioner proved to be a common priority for most Slovak political parties, even though between 2006 and 2010 the SDKÚ had criticized the government's and the leading Smer-SD's attitude to the Hungarian minority and Hungary.

Finally, national interests are formed not only at the level of state institutions but also at a less formal one. In Slovakia, analytical centers such as the Euro-Atlantic Center, the Research Center of the Slovak Foreign Policy Society, the Globsec Policy Institute, and others play a significant role in the creation of foreign policy consensus. They organize important conferences discussing Slovakia's foreign policy and security issues which are attended by representatives of multiple political parties and experts of various opinions, like the Slovak Security Forum (Euro-Atlantic Center), the Foreign and European Policy Review Conference (RC SFPA) and the Globsec Bratislava Forum (Globsec Policy Institute). Nevertheless, it would not be possible to reach consensus in parliament and other state institutions if political parties were unable to reach some kind of an agreement beforehand, at least informally, or in their public discourses.

Conclusion

From an institutional point of view, the National Council and the political parties represented in it play a key role in the formulation of Slovakia's national interests in its foreign policy matters. Paradoxically, the consensus on foreign policy is not a key factor in the creation of government coalitions, as evidenced by the different approach coalition parties take toward matters such as the perception of some EU policies and Slovakia's relations with Russia. Presidential attempts to reach a foreign policy consensus by creating a "state doctrine" proved to be unsuccessful and resulted in rivalry between political parties. Slovak political representatives reached something of a consensus only on some issues, such as Slovakia's accession to the European Union. Slovakia's political scene is still strongly in favor of the country's EU and NATO membership, even though its interpretations of some of their processes differ.

Another consensual issue that can be seen as one of Slovakia's national interests is respecting the integrity of state borders on the European continent and the sovereignty of European states. This was illustrated by Slovakia's attitude to Kosovo's unilateral declaration of independence in 2008 and to Russia's unilateral recognition of the independence of the Georgian separatist provinces Abkhazia and South Ossetia in the same year. The political representation of the Slovak Republic adopted the same attitude when Russia recognized Crimea's annexation in 2014. Slovak politicians also joined together in their rejection of the Hungarian legislature's questioning of the Peace Treaty of Trianon of 1920 and the territorial arrangement of Europe after World War II, even though politicians representing the Hungarian minority were opposed to it. The majority of Slovak politicians find the adoption of minority legislation with extraterritorial validity and the establishment of institutional links between Hungary and members of the Hungarian minority in neighboring states unacceptable. After the outbreak of the refugee crisis, the National Council reached a consensus on refusing to accommodate the influx of migrants from third-world countries and insisted on the fact that

EU member states should be able to decide about their migration policies themselves.

Meanwhile, in a joint statement of October 2018, the three highest constitutional officials of the Slovak Republic defined Slovakia's main priorities in European and Euro-Atlantic structures. Even though the ethnic divide used to play a dominant role in the formation of Slovak foreign policy in the past, the main question nowadays is the perception of Russia, even though some members of the government coalition, namely the Slovak National Party, refuse to see Russia as a potential source of danger.

As a result of the Slovak parliamentary elections of March 2016, the Euroskeptic People's Party Our Slovakia (ĽSNS) entered Parliament and demanded the convocation of a referendum on Slovakia's membership in the European Union and NATO. Although this party remained isolated in its efforts, and in spite of their declarations being similar to the statement of the highest constitutional officials of October 2017, the consensus on the country's foreign policy affairs at the governmental level seems somewhat fragile. Because of the Slovak National Party's initiative, the documents regulating the key priorities of Slovakia's security policy – the Defense Strategy of the Slovak Republic and the Security Strategy of the Slovak Republic – still have not been discussed at a National Council session. The fact that Slovak political forces reached no consensus on the country's "national interests" is also illustrated by the absence of a key strategic document that would regulate the priorities of Slovakia's foreign policy. Since the Medium-Term Strategy of the Slovak Foreign Policy expired in 2015, no similar document has been adopted as of the end of 2018. Therefore, since 2015, we can observe the erosion of foreign policy consensus.

2. The Temptation of Underdevelopment

László Öllös

In its current form, we would be hard-pressed to call the European Union a strong institution. Its common legislation works slowly, and where foreign policy is concerned some member states have decided to forge their own path. They tend to act in an uncoordinated way, sometimes even against themselves. However, the European Union still offers possibilities and opportunities for its citizens that were previously unavailable to them or their ancestors. Although being presented with opportunities means a lot, one has a choice to either seize them or waste them. A united Europe stands for the unity of diversity and forms a cooperative whole of different values, opinions, cultures and, naturally, languages. In addition, it fosters the tradition of development, even of the most advanced region in the world.

However, Central Europe has always been oscillating between a state of backwardness and endeavors to catch up.[2] The West saw this region as part of the underdeveloped East, even though on several occasions, Central Europe almost managed to become part of the West. However, these attempts eventually failed, and Central Europe always provided a different justification for its relative backwardness (Hurka 1997, 140-141). It put the blame on the selfish West and its expressed contempt for the underdeveloped but strong East. While trying to catch up with the more developed regions, Central Europe decided to see its backwardness as an asset.

On a global scale, Western Europe could eventually find itself in the same scenario. Central Europe might not catch up with the developed West, but the West might end up in a similar underdog position as Central Europe used to be in relation to it. This means that even though Western Europe will not be hopelessly

---

2   According to István Bibó, the uncertainty of their national existence also slowed down their development. See Bibó I.: *A kelet-európai kis államok nyomorúsága* (Bibó 1986, 197).

underdeveloped, its own internal problems and constant need to provide justification for its backwardness will thwart the region's occasional attempts at advancement. The spirit of Central Europe will dwell in the West, but Westerners will be unaware of it, blinded by their disdain for Central Europe that stems from their unfamiliarity with the region.

The historic causes behind the backwardness of Central Europe are country-specific and therefore unique in many aspects; however, we can point out a few that apply to several countries. We could mention an inclination to disintegration along with the stubborn insistence on persevering in it despite its unfortunate consequences.[3] After all, it can always be transformed and given an appearance that seems novel and different every time.

Another explanation for Central Europe's backwardness lies in its tendency to only change what is absolutely necessary. These reforms are only introduced to eliminate the biggest threats, such as having their government toppled or social hierarchy disrupted by more developed countries or internal reformers. Changes are thus not introduced to acquire a leading position or strengthen the country's status and maximize its efficiency, but to keep a better eye on more developed countries. Everybody knew that besides controlled and limited education, there was a need for innovations as well. In times of stability, such innovations can only be implemented if they do not threaten the structure or value system of the ruling hierarchy. In spite of this, there are extraordinary times that stir up the desire for big social changes; however, these often go awry because of the society's lack of solidarity and greed for power. Again, this results in an in-between society with too many people longing for progress while also insisting on preserving many of the elements that contributed to the country's backwardness in the first place. Meanwhile, a progress-preaching propaganda emerges, concealing the real state of affairs.

Such propaganda would have—and indeed has—a much stronger effect in Western Europe than in the central part of the continent, since the West has long enjoyed being a highly

---

3   Oszkár Jászi described one such important occurrence (Jászi 1918, 21-25, 31).

developed region, setting political and cultural trends. The propaganda thus has to conceal the factors contributing to the region's backwardness, which also need to be accepted by society. Therefore, ideologies based on the principles of modernization could seriously endanger a society's value system, since what they propagate is, in fact, a state of gradual lagging behind.

Therefore, it is high time for the West to replace its current attitude of disinterest and occasional disdain for Central Europe and start observing it with interest, especially the tireless endeavors to catch up that tend to end in failure.

One of the obvious reasons behind this is the lack of proper discussion about this issue. To change the current state of affairs, a carefully elaborated social and political program should be drafted, offering one or more new alternatives; taking into consideration the nature of European pluralism, maybe several such programs should be proposed. However, this topic has always been kept on the back burner, unable to enter into mainstream political and cultural discourse. Even though the human rights of liberal democracies allow such discussions to emerge, their ideas could not yet be transformed into a political program supported by the majority of states (Coudenhove-Kalergi 1988, 9-12).

Europe argues for its stability by claiming that it does not interfere with the way its member states see and present their national identity where ideology or armed conflicts are concerned (Kedurie 2000, 13). This is why, in the second half of the twentieth century, the Anglo-French Wars that followed the French Revolution were interpreted by both the British and the French in a different manner. Similarly, the Austrians, Hungarians, and Czechs might each have a different take on Habsburg rule in Central Europe. We could go on; such examples abound. This difference in interpretations still persists. A more recent example includes the different attitude Germany and France took regarding Croatia and Serbia after the breakup of Yugoslavia.

Because of the relativity of national interests in the past, the presumed interests of one country can lead other EU member states astray (Dunn 1993, 62-64). This is well exemplified by the particular stance Central European governments have adopted toward

Putin's Russia, the attitude France took toward Saddam Hussein before the First Gulf War,[4] and Britain's approach to the Second Gulf War. In short, many EU states try to cope with a controversial situation by claiming to safeguard their national interests and implementing a foreign policy that runs counter to the basic principles declared by the EU.

However, it should also be noted that EU membership does not prohibit such practices. On one hand, the declared value system of the EU contains some loopholes, while on the other hand it tacitly allows geopolitical maneuvers based on the alleged national interests of a particular member state. The primary limit of these maneuvers is not determined by their content but by the fact that they should not cause conflict among members that would threaten the EU's unity in its current form. For such a rhetoric to succeed, it needs the support of the majority of a country's citizens, which can be gained when political argumentation is based on the current form of its people's identity—even when it obviously differs from declared EU principles. National arguments seeking support are almost always efficient, since their interpretation of the nation's past is relative. While European nation states are currently weak, they want to be internally strong (Rougemont 2004, 121-122).

Besides inflicting economic damage on Europe, the two world wars also rattled countries' political roles and confidence.[5] Before then, a true patriot would strive to elevate his homeland and render it superior to its rivals—that is, the other nation states. However, the two world wars pointed out the internal contradiction of such a vocation.

In this globalized world, lagging behind its competitors would jeopardize Europe's belief in development and success (Kershaw 2016, 13-21). This crisis would also affect European values and the

---

4   They change their attitude when it proves to be inefficient or if it would force them out of the country.
5   The experience of the First World War and its impact on the creation of the modern idea of European unification is aptly described by Christopher Booker and Richard North in *Skryté dějiny evropské integrace od roku 1918 do současnosti* (The Great Deception: The Secret History of the European Union). Barrister & Principal, Společnost pro odbornou literaturu, 2006, 23-25.

institutional system that was built on them (cf. Balibar 2004, 203-206). Western Europe would eventually have to face up to the fact that after all this time, other regions would take the lead and exert their influence (Coudenhove-Kalergi 1988, 9-12). The West would lose its grip not only on others but also on itself.

If this scenario came true, it would probably provoke a deep distrust in the institutions whose very purpose is to represent the people's will. After all, what is their point if they fail to do so? If they hampered societal progress, it would clearly signify that decision-making is not in the hands of the citizens. If the control of certain social classes and groups, high levels of manipulation, and a wide network of interdependent relationships would allow the influencing of voters to such a degree that a big proportion of citizens would not see the freshly formed governments as representing their goals, values, and interests, but as serving some other interest groups, it could even undermine the authority of elections as such, not to mention the basic principles of constitutional construction, human rights, and the principle of the separation of powers. In their current form and interpretation, these principles are hindering the region's progress instead of granting it a leading position, and they are creating dependence instead of independence. One possible alternative for Europe would be a popularly-based dictatorship (Barnard 1988), whose theoretical and organizational aspects have already made an appearance in the majority of EU member states.

The West can gradually, almost imperceptibly, adopt that in-between political and cultural behavior that used to characterize Central Europe when the West was the most developed region in the world. Western Europe is not yet aware of—or cannot quite recognize—the temptation such an in-between identity holds. This includes the occasionally resurgent hope of catching up with the developed world, rekindling memories of one's former glory, availing oneself of opportunities that being underdeveloped presents, and learning the art of doing away with responsibility. Parties opposed to progress will emerge. However, this incipient state of *inbetweenness* that appeared in the West would not be fully identical to the Central European situation (though it should be noted that its manifestations differ even within Central Europe). Western countries would probably use this *inbetweenness* to justify their inability to seize the opportunities that arose after the Second World War. Political discourses would then revolve around this topic, either trying to confirm or deny it. Other frequent topics would probably include the justification of passed-up opportunities, the social impact of modernization and the contradiction that characterizes it, the ideological basis of these contradictions, and the people bearing political responsibility for their consequences. The discourse would be primarily aimed at their current representatives and supporters.

If this gradual falling behind that started after the First World War were to carry on, the perception of Europe as one of the most developed regions with a political system functioning as a lever for progress would gradually start to dwindle. Political conflicts would thus also revolve around questions concerning constitutional construction (Thibault 2006). Seeing the present ongoing disputes, we can predict some of the arguments that are sure to come up in future discussions. For instance, some would want to introduce into their countries certain characteristics of the regions that have surpassed Europe. They would probably try to adopt their customs and religious beliefs, and imitate their social structure and political system(s) — all of which would markedly differ from European ones.

Central Europe's take on the migration and refugee crisis is, to some extent, prompted by the fact that these nations could almost never make decisions about their own fate. Their borders were determined by world powers who took advantage of their conflicts and battles; their insurrections were put down; and their political systems and social structures were laid out by their conquerors (Jászi 1918). The strong Western countries were either such conquerors, or, based on their presumed national interests, they recognized and accepted the situation as a geopolitical reality. What is now seen as a destabilizing factor could be considered a stabilizing element in a different geopolitical situation (and vice versa), since this sort of assessment disregards basic values such as national freedom and equality, considered the birthright of every human being. These principles are not lacking in just any historical period but are lacking in the era of nation states.

One of the fundamental features Central European nations share is the belief that when a large group of people from a different culture appears and by the sheer number of its members acquires political power, an authoritarian ruler should take over and decide the country's future. In their experience, such a leader will already prioritize interests that are not yet recognized but are expected to develop in the future. Therefore, the current state of affairs is uncertain and dangerous, as the West cannot be trusted; not even Great Britain has any friends, only interests.[6]

The power games Western European countries engaged in after the breakup of Yugoslavia only reinforced this belief among Central Europeans, whose mistrust was further intensified by their own tirelessly fuelled and carefully maintained national aggression toward other nations. The flexibility that characterizes their endeavors to catch up with the West would be considerably weakened by one or more new and populous national minorities.

The uncertainty shared by Central Europeans was further strengthened by factors such as Germany's strategy, the changing attitudes of other EU members, the inflow of hundreds of thousands of migrants whose number was expected to rise to the millions or even tens of millions, and the unchecked process of countries modifying their legislation to appease the ruling political elite. In consequence, Central Europeans regard Western powers and the European Union with much wariness and distrust.

Central Europe fears that encouraging the development of national minorities might have a considerable impact on the internal policies of these countries and could even lead to their disintegration. This interpretation of national identity seems to suggest that by its mere existence, a large minority might endanger the sovereignty of a country or even its territorial integrity.

---

6   Henry John Temple Palmerston: "We have no eternal allies, and we have no perpetual enemies. Our interests are eternal and perpetual, and those interests it is our duty to follow" (1 March 1848).

However, the desire to conquer a neighboring territory does not only appear when a nation state wants to annex parts of another country where a considerable ethnic minority lives; it also appears when they wish to conquer a non-related nation or acquire a strategically important territory. Such behavior is a source of total uncertainty. After all, one cannot be sure of anything, as neighboring countries could at any time present us with their intention to conquer our territory, provided that there is an adequate historical context to back up their claim and they can count on the support of major powers (Giddens 1985, 116-121). Therefore, the political cooperation that can currently be seen in Central Europe is purely interest-oriented. These countries are united by their intention to protect their interests within the EU and their similar take on the refugee crisis; however, their mutual conflicts remain unresolved.

Those advocating for a close cooperation between Central European countries usually try to argue by pointing out the similarities in the cultural values of these nations, claiming that Central European writers, artists, and thinkers were also profoundly inspired by neighboring nations, which means that these cultures are interconnected. Central European identities share so many features that there is absolutely no natural reason for political conflicts to arise, and therefore they should come to an end.[7]

This mentality strongly defined the way Central Europeans handled their mutual conflicts. In the era of nation-building, these nations were ready to form an alliance with any conquering power just to ensure themselves a better position or even the possibility of partially or completely conquering their neighbours. Instead of forming a Central European alliance, they chose to support a world power whose only aim was to gain complete control of the region (or even to subdue it), while they also took over their political

---

7   According to István Bibó, the two main sources of political hysteria in Central and Eastern Europe are the national existence of the small Central European nations that stems from their territorial disputes and the greater uncertainty about their territorial status than exists in the Western European countries. See Bibó 1986, 197.

system and ideology. These small nations thus endorsed the conquering ambitions and inhuman acts of the big players, for which they later apologised (mainly to their own national public). They shared a common argument: our nation is (was) threatened by its neighbour(s), and averting the threat ultimately justifies everything.[8]

However, they had to conceal one evident fact: these nations can only experience progress based on the principles of freedom and equality if they support one another, not just in general but also individually. This means that the contemporary version of Central Europeanism does not only consist of an effort to catch up with the developed world and celebrate world-class performances on a local level; it also signifies that there is a constant lagging behind. One of its major causes is the servile submission of these nations to stronger powers in the hope they will outplay their neighbours.

The Central European identity is therefore simultaneously defined by the region's effort to catch up and its constant backwardness. This *inbetweenness* forms the very essence of being Central European: *inbetweenness* as the reality of living conditions, then as a value that should be protected, then as a goal that should be pursued, then as a succession of events that should be justified.[9] With this kind of identity, small nations try to adopt the most important elements of *inbetweenness* while concealing the price at which they acquired this knowledge; if given the opportunity, they will try to defeat their neighbors, subjugate them, or even destroy them. To achieve this, they are ready to form an alliance with practically anyone. However, these alliances are only occasional,

---

[8] A conference in Bratislava in 2002 revealed their current problems with solidarity. See Stredoeurópska identita—Central European Identity, Stredoeurópska nadácia, Bratislava, 2002.

[9] In his essay *A Kidnapped West or Culture Bows Out*, Milan Kundera describes Central Europe as "a reduced model of Europe made up of nations conceived according to one rule: the greatest variety within the smallest space." He sees it as an "uncertain zone of small nations between Russia and Germany". He believes this region is a cultural part of the West which only belongs to the East geographically as a result of historical circumstances. He tries to identify the region's cultural identity, which I do not believe to be that straightforward. See Kundera 1984.

formed in pursuit of a particular interest, and if the circumstances change, the allies are replaced as well. Even after joining forces, these partners are extremely unreliable, as they cannot count on each other. They are able to cooperate in one matter and hurt each other in another.

If we assessed in a similar way the present understanding, whose fundamental aspect is the individual's freedom of national development—that is, the elevation of national freedom and equality to a universal value—it would clearly show the periods of power expansion and national oppression as well as a desire for them. Since nationalism is a group identity, such an evaluation would also demonstrate how the national subjugation of others was converted into a mass demand and how national inequality within a state has become acceptable and even desired by the national majority. It would also reveal the role the national intelligentsia played in this process,[10] and finally how individual states were one by one deformed by the transformation of national interest into a mobilizing ideology in the interpretation and subsequent application of human freedom and equality.

This contradiction is well illustrated by the way Germans struggle with the dominance of the French language, even as German dominates over the Central European languages which in turn struggle with its dominance while trying to assert the dominance of their own language over neighboring ones. However, the lesson of this language struggle is not the national freedom of all people but only the national freedom of those sharing a language.

Because of their inability to join the Austro-Hungarian Empire as an ally, nations of small Central European states lost their positions of power, having to put up with being subjugated over and over again, with their political and social systems changed every time. However, the tradition of their national struggles continues to be maintained by their leaders, and even a large proportion of their exiled opposition remains on this path. Oszkár

---

10 To learn more about the role of the intelligentsia, see Coudenhove-Kalergi 2004, 106.

Jászi, István Bibó, Milan Hodža, and Karl Renner did not become central models; instead, what did were attempts to justify the consequences of subjecting neighboring nations to oppression, ethnic cleansing, and various atrocities while keeping silent about these heinous crimes both on a national and an international level.

These nations have become slaves to their own struggles, dependencies, and the crimes against humanity that they committed against one another. Their ruling elite, together with a significant proportion of their society, was involved in the destruction (or at least debilitation) of neighboring cultures to such an extent that being openly confronted with this reality is perceived as a threat to their very existence. However, without such a critical confrontation the old world lives on; and from its point of view, even the present situation must be seen as a tactical state rather than a selection of values. This perspective has an impact on the Western allies as well. Even though these nations have ties to the West, as soon as they gain other interests, they do not hesitate to change direction. Meanwhile, they keep systematically showing their public that the example is right in front of their eyes. People can see and experience with every example that the European Union is ruled by the interests of certain groups.

Central European leaders believe that the most telling sign of prioritizing certain interests is that when joining the EU (cf. Judt 2002, 87), association members like them were not required to critically re-evaluate the aggressive chapters of their national past. All Westerners needed was for them to pacify their past conflicts, thus allowing them to maintain their strategy of national separation in the most important aspects.

Of course, their domestic discourse backs all this up, claiming that Westerners do not really differ from them, the only real difference between them being that Westerners are richer. Therefore, the small Central European states should pursue their own interests and safeguard them by using whatever tools they have. However, the declared values are nothing more than propaganda, and those bandying them about merely use them to conceal their real interests, which are of a personal nature even though they try to pass them for national ones. This is why coercion and blackmail are considered acceptable and even useful.

Therefore, effectiveness is the primary criterion for asserting their interests. In other words, everything that is effective is also right. This is why Western rules need to be adopted; strong states based on this system are the most efficient in enforcing their interests. However, they should be applied only occasionally and only to a certain extent so long as they serve their particular interests. Violating these rules is acceptable, even potentially useful, as it might lead to a better blackmailing position within the EU.

The EU should have tried to balance the weakness of democratic heritage by subjecting it to thorough criticism and raising public awareness, but it did not do so for several reasons. One of them is that the states themselves separate their nations, so they also would have become targets of criticism. The second reason is that Western European states have their own and often conflicting opinions regarding the post-communist countries.[11]

The current crisis has found the new Central European EU members amidst an incomplete transformation process, with weak central governments, experiencing the crisis of the family, the terrifying vision of mass migration, and the prevailing legacy of national aggression, all of which hamper the transformation of their basic value system. Unlike the older member states of the EU, they are currently undergoing economic growth, reinforcing the feeling in governments and a significant part of the public that everything is fine; they are catching up, and there is no need for substantial changes. The main aspect of the monitoring strategy is not to turn the participants into leaders. Therefore, if observing the more developed countries does not force them to take some steps, they have no reason to risk it.

The dominant political strategy so far has tried to create an image of European togetherness by turning a blind eye to the internal contradictions of the present national identities in Europe.

---

11 The attitude of France and Germany at the beginning of Yugoslavia's breakup is one of the most recent examples.

This is especially true for Central European nationalism. However, if the aim is to create a solidary political community, these contradictions cannot be ignored. Europe should move on from its current state of gradual lagging behind. In this condition, Europe has reached its greatest achievements in the last two centuries; but it also experienced crises and stagnation. This condition is the European national state. However, in spite of the contradictions that presently characterize this institution, it should not be considered wholly undesirable, as it contains values that deserve to be preserved while its shortcomings could be remedied. To achieve this, a political decision is not enough. All of society must stand up for it. Such a strong-willed society has already helped Western Europe—and therefore the whole continent—a few times. But for this to happen, Europe must decide if it will conform to the current state of stagnation or want to become the most developed region in the world. However, this intention should not only manifest itself in the form of political declarations; it must be real, and one of the first steps would be acknowledging the true reason for its backwardness on a local, regional, and international level. This, however, requires great political and cultural courage.

There are two possible scenarios for Central Europe, and both of them look rather bleak. If these countries do not realize their need to stick together, they cannot grow stronger, only weaker. The old threat of being subjugated by stronger players will reappear. In addition, a new challenge will present itself; after a lengthy, fruitless period of stagnation in the era of globalization, the younger population will move abroad as the old form of national consciousness will provide them with no prospects.

The dominant political strategy so far has tried to define European togetherness by ignoring the internal contradictions of the European national identities instead of reconciling them.[12] But if we want EU citizens to form a political community, we cannot ignore the issues regarding their value systems which have turned

---

12 See, for example, The Future of the Union—The Laeken Declaration (Presidency Conclusions, European Council Meeting in Laeken, 14 and 15 December 2001); or the Declaration on European Identity (Copenhagen, 14 December 1973).

these nations against one another, leading to armed conflicts and mutual oppression. As these problems have not yet been subjected to relevant criticism, the mentality that contributed to Europe's decline as a world power still persists.

However, these topics have little priority in European social discourse. European citizens tend to discuss the problems of their own countries and the problems of their own nation, which is even more important to them.[13] Their knowledge of their neighbors and other countries is still limited; on top of that, they are taught to see them through the prism of their own nation. This means that the success of their own nation is still the most important element in their hierarchy of values; it comes before anything else and defines the way everything is evaluated.

There is no public forum where common opinions could be exchanged. However, without a common public discourse, individual countries, separated by their nations, mainly exchange ideas locally. Even though they usually know what is going on in other countries and are exposed to their opinions and attitudes, none of this provides a forum for a common public discussion.[14] Post-democratic tendencies may further strengthen the elite's control of public opinion in a country. In this light, the EU is an area of balance between national interests and their potential connection. The strongest and smartest players affect this game the most; however, unlike in the past, the weaker and less clever parties are not subjugated by others but are given opportunities to advance and achieve their goals if some conflict of interests arises.

In their current state of dwindling, European nations should think about the potential sources of their future dynamism. The strongest negative argument is that without sufficient dynamism, traditional European countries will gradually lose even the limited relevance they currently hold in the world. One possible source of cultural dynamism could be putting an end to the separation of national cultures. With this program, Europeans could draw from

---

[13] Often believing in their unique antiquity (cf. Smith 2004, 201).
[14] Jürgen Habermas calls for opening up such forums for national public debates (cf. Habermas 2011, 77-78).

a much richer and deeper source of cultural heritage than before. Nations thus would not look at Europe's past, present, or future through the prism of their own national culture but also through that of others. It would not be the first time that the coexistence of various cultures invigorated European culture, as this is what encourages the birth of new ideas, views, emotions, and perspectives.

Compared with the world's dynamism, the current separation is becoming obsolete. National cultures are no longer the source of a sufficient pace of development.[15] In this case, we should accept the fact that in their current form, European national cultures are an impediment to progress.

One of the best-known historical examples is the coexistence of ancient heritage with the rules of barbarian societies during the Roman Empire and after its fall. Barbarians conquered various parts of the empire, and after an initial clash of values the new states adopted some of the Roman rules and combined them with their own. Europe's political and cultural diversity, combined with Christian universality, allowed the free flow of ideas, technologies, and artistic styles from one state to another; in addition, persecuted innovators were often granted asylum. One united empire surely could not have created such a space; but neither could a state of total political and cultural separation. The fact that in the Middle Ages another model of European unity appeared in the form of a voluntary association of states shows the creative force that characterizes the fusion of Christian universalism with the political diversity of the continent.

The post-communist countries hardly ever experience the problems that plague the more developed Western Europe. This is partially because they have never belonged to the most advanced countries, as they always lagged behind the West; under communism, this difference grew even greater. After 1989, they were given a chance to catch up with Western Europe. To this day, this experience of modernization still does not allow the public to

---

15 Richard Hill believes in getting acquainted with individual European cultures (cf. Hill 1997).

see the region's relative position. It is hard to explain that the sacrifices they made for progress have led to another period of backwardness—but this time it concerns all of Europe. The desire to become the best is not that strong in these countries, unlike the tendency to constantly justify their underdevelopment. Therefore, these countries are used to falling behind in areas such as politics, economy, technology, and culture, just like they are used to constantly trying to catch up. Unlike Western countries, they do not expect to be the greatest. Moreover, after the dissolution of the Austro-Hungarian Empire, these nations lost their prior leading position. Instead of arriving at a national agreement, their elites chose to quarrel with their neighbors, and their geopolitical strategy consisted of supporting the ambitions and interests of various world powers and counting on their support in their national conflicts with their neighbors. Support also meant that they helped world powers in their efforts to gain dominance over Central Europe. In order to be able to carry on with their national quarrels, these nations gave up their leading position and chose to collaborate with various world powers.

The countries could only justify their continuing backwardness and limited sovereignty by resorting to positional maneuvers in their national quarrels with their neighbos. Both in their national and international discourse, significant groups of their elites justified their national legitimacy with this line of argument; they did so to such an extent that a fundamental change would have jeopardized their national legitimacy. This is the main reason why the behavior of these countries has not changed much, despite having joined NATO and the EU. Even as members of these institutions, they keep scheming and maneuvering among the stronger member states. They also act similarly around the powerful and influential countries outside NATO and the EU. Even if they do not see eye to eye where democratic values and goals are concerned, they often end up representing the interests of these countries in these institutions instead of promoting the values and goals of the institution itself. They see this behavior as a necessary geopolitical maneuver to keep the intentions of their similarly behaving neighbors in check. This regional interconnectedness keeps all the players in a tight grip. They write their own histories according to their positional successes and failures. Changing their regimes, helping various aggressive powers, and supporting similarly aggressive actions against other states and minorities are just some of the essential characteristics of their national quarrels. So, if we want a change of identity to occur, based on the idea of pan-European togetherness and a respect for values such as the national equality of citizens, mutual recognition, and universal national rights, we must first subject the twentieth century to criticism. However, such scrutiny would publicly reveal how these countries tend to separate their national interests from democratic values, depending on the strategy they pursue at any given time.

In addition to such scrutiny, a new Central European future concept—a kind of new identity—should be developed for a change to take place, and the old one should be destroyed, since the damage that these nations inflicted on one another cannot be resolved by quietly continuing on the same path. Besides subjecting this period to criticism, it is also crucially important to develop a new sense of togetherness. However, none of this will convert the region back into being a strong player until the small nations start to cooperate and mutually support each other's national growth. The national struggle as understood so far should be replaced with a new concept. Instead of allowing themselves to be used for the purposes of national mobilization, they should return to the worldview that used to characterize them before and during the beginning of their national struggles.

Central Europeans share the tradition of underdevelopment together with endeavors to either overcome it or preserve it. In this case, we have to consider the positive as well as the negative aspects of this condition. Both the successful and futile attempts should be seen as part of a common heritage. Not only because they are similar to each other but also because they were often related. Another similarity consists in their efforts to preserve this tradition of backwardness and refusing modernization. The criticism of this region could also become a part of its common heritage, not only because of their similar behavior but also because even in this they are linked.

Central European countries are members of the EU and NATO. Their state security in the twentieth century was never as strong as it is now. Their mutual relationship could be based on national freedom and equality, regardless of the country one lives in. Furthermore, they share several positive values, such as their attempts to overcome underdevelopment and efforts to catch up with the most developed countries or to gain national freedom. All of them should recognize and publicly declare that their common negative traditions include their repeated attempts to oppress neighboring nationalities who also long for national liberty and growth. However, the values of civil and national liberty are interconnected. One can only exist without the other in a distorted form. Central European history illustrates this really rather well.

3. Security as a National Interest after EU Accession

Radoslava Brhlíková

Security—an abstract term denoting a rather emotional phenomenon—is defined in specialized literature as the fundamental value and ultimate goal of every state or security community. It is considered to be the ultimate and most fundamental nation-state interest or, to be more precise, state interest.[16] We can basically conclude that state or national interests are identical to security. While defining its main objectives and functions—which, figuratively speaking, are in fact state, national, or nation-state interests[17]—every state is essentially thinking of its own security. National interest defines the overall objectives and value systems of a state's foreign policy, being the last decisive factor in shaping its foreign policy with all its security-related consequences. It is therefore a set of requirements whose fulfillment

---

16 The term "national interest" will be used throughout this chapter. Careful research has shown that in the domestic political environment, talking about "state interests" could have negative connotations in cases when such a interests clash with the rights of the individual (e.g., the expropriation of private property to build infrastructure). As a rule, national interests tend to be linked to foreign policy and the external actions of a state on the international scene.

17 These terms are used interchangeably in both specialized literature and strategic policy documents. However, this is more of a linguistic issue than a definitional one. Anglophone literature tends to use the expression "national interest," where it is interpreted as the interest of a political nation state that concerns the whole state and all its ethnicities. The terminological inconsistency is caused by the lack of consensus on how to translate this particular expression from English into other languages, including Slovak; therefore, its translation is context-dependent. In Europe, especially in the central and eastern regions, the term "national" is often synonymous with "ethnic." Therefore, "national" is used to denote the interest of a certain nation or ethnic group, not a state. This is probably the reason why the adjective "národnoštátny" ("nation-state") was coined in Slovak, which implies that a nation and a state form a single entity; however, in the case of multinational states, the expression can sometimes refer exclusively to the national majority, excluding any national minorities.

determines a state's ability to maintain its sovereignty (cf. Krejčí 2001, 645).

In the following section, we will define what is meant by "security" and then move on to compare the interests of the European Union (EU) with those of Slovakia as a member of a wider community. All of this will be examined within the context of national interest and Slovakia's EU membership. We will assume that with the progression of the integration process, even in the field of foreign policy — which is still seen as an intergovernmental pillar within the EU[18] — the national interests of Slovakia are gradually nearer and more identical to the foreign policy interests of the EU, or rather to those who define these interests in the name of the EU in the first place: mainly the French and German foreign affairs officials and the multinational team of officials at the European External Action Service, led by the High Representative for the Common Foreign and Security Policy.

Where states are concerned, security[19] is generally seen as a systematic and multidimensional phenomenon that, in addition to including a military dimension, also emphasizes other areas that the state considers among its interests and that have a strategic importance. These are the areas where the state then strives to achieve stability, balance, and a level playing field to ensure its sustained development without any complications or conflicts. The ideal state for a country is not to be plagued by wars or other types of armed conflict.

For a state or an individual, achieving absolute security is something of a pipe dream, as there is an abundance of potential threats of a military, economic, environmental, or cybernetic nature. Because of this, a community's security "can disappear in many different ways: militarily, economically, by ideological

---

18 This is further proved by the fact that this policy exists mainly on paper and in the heads of European officials. The 28 EU countries form a highly heterogeneous community with different approaches to security and defense policy. Some of them are also members of NATO, whereas others are neutral, which causes the Union's overall incapacity.

19 When talking about individuals, security is a mental and legal condition in which a person feels secure and supported by others, while he or she also has confidence in the existing legal system.

domination or internal disintegration" (Woyke 1993, 291). A state's ability to accumulate and utilize military assets in order to prevent the military actions of an opponent is not its biggest asset; rather, in this globalized world with increasingly interdependent and interconnected regions and social phenomena, establishing amicable and peaceful relations is probably the main tool of building a secure environment.

In the context of states, security can be understood in two ways. Broadly speaking, we can see it as stability, order, certainty, reliability, balance, an existence devoid of threats, and a state and sense of security. Narrowly speaking, security is characterized as the absence of wars, threats, and armed violence (Škvrnda 2001, 16) ensured by security forces such as the army, police, and the information and intelligence services. In the context of international security, we can talk about three forms of security: a relative absence of threats; a state devoid of potential threats; and a state characterized by order, compliance with the rules, adjustments, and agreements (Kulašík 2002, 22). Where external security is concerned, the state is responsible for ensuring protection from being subjugated or threatened in its existence from the outside, in which the main role is played by military force and such tools as coercion, threats, blackmail, boycotting, and imposing embargoes. Objective security is thus understood as the absence of threats endangering the social system and its values, while subjective security is seen as not having to be concerned about the endangerment of the social system and its values. Therefore, national security is a state's ability to protect its own values from external threat, which can be either achieved by victoriously surviving an attack or by victoriously resisting pressure, threats, and blackmail (Kulašík 2002, 22).

The security policy of a state denotes the effort a state — or rather, its decision-making bodies — makes to create a sense of security in society. The state thus assumes responsibility for ensuring the safety of its citizens, assets, and information, while defining its own protected interests and specifying the principles of their protection. It represents a complex set of state objectives, principles, procedures, and measures whose aim is to ensure the security of the state and its citizens. Aside from defense, it also concerns external, internal, economic, social, and environmental aspects, among others (Security Strategy 2005). Its efficacy depends on the degree of cooperation between the public authorities, non-governmental organizations, and legal and natural people. To protect its sovereignty, a state adopts various measures: it fends off attacks by means of its army, builds up arms, ensures the supply of energy and food, builds zones of protection, spies on foreign governments, and establishes amicable foreign relations (Brockhaus Enzyklopädie 1993, 231). A country can never count on creating a state of absolute, constant security. *"Security is not a state that can be achieved once and for all. It is a constantly developing process that on one hand involves the interaction of security threats, risks and challenges, and on the other hand, our responses to them"* (Figel 2001). This means that if a state wants to ensure at least relative security for itself, it needs to consider various factors that threaten or change the security environment and then take adequate measures to resolve the situation in a systematic and complex way. The state has basically two approaches to choose from: it will either defend its security solely by its own means and possibilities, or it will combine its material and human resources with other sovereign states by forming a system of collective security which will then guarantee mutual help to its members if their safety is endangered, based on previously agreed principles.

After international relations ceased to be bipolar, countries attempted to overcome the past and use the newly opened space to establish friendly and peaceful relations which would then ensure a stable security. The Cold War, underpinned by the balanced military potential of the Soviet Union and the United States, represented a certain sense of security, as in a way it could prevent and provide certain security against a so-called "second strike"; however, this security was replaced first by the instability of a unipolar world and now of a multipolar one. The threat of a global war has decreased to zero, and the majority of EU member states have therefore reduced their defense expenditure. It was inevitable that such a change in the strategic environment would require different approaches and different ways to resolve conflicts. This change has resulted in positive expectations, as the fear of a nuclear disaster has abated and the armaments policy has been replaced by an effort to establish friendly and open relations with former rivals. However, this relative peace is now being threatened by the possibility of nuclear blackmail (North Korea), asymmetric attacks, or the use of weapons of mass destruction by terrorist organizations or unpredictable regimes (e.g., Islamic State, Al-Qaeda, and Boko Haram).

These are the challenges brought about by the globalization process and the appearance and deepening of tension-inducing global problems that could escalate into a crisis or even a war (Kulašík 2002, 19). Under their influence, states modify their security policy and set new goals. Such actions, however, carry certain risks;[20] since the likelihood of a world conflict has partially been reduced (Woyke 1993, 292), these risks concern the economic, scientific, technical, environmental, and social aspects of security, while their source is the national interest of the state. Security risks are then security situations (both internal and external) that can endanger the state (Kulašík 2002, 20). These phenomena and processes can have a direct or indirect impact on society, the functioning of the state, and its citizens (Krejčí 2000, 258). Slovakia's Security Strategy of 2001 identifies the country's potential risks in the following areas: the ambition of several unstable states to increase their arsenal of weapons of mass destruction, persisting long-term conflicts in unstable regions, uncontrolled migration (even though the Slovak Republic is not the main target of migration flow), international organized crime and terrorism, the activities of foreign special services, the violation or total failure of the information systems, the Slovak Republic's excessive dependence on unstable sources for some basic raw materials and energy, negative demographic development contributing to the decrease of the working population, the degradation of the environment with precisely unpredictable consequences, and the

---

20 Risk is the possibility of something happening where the result, based on an objective probability, will differ from the presumed goal; or rather, it is the possibility of something unwelcome happening (cf. Buzalka 2001, 35).

decrease in food security below a threshold level (Security Strategy 2005).

A risk can increase or materialize in the form of direct actions taken by other states or other agents of the international system. These activities could potentially hurt the interests of other states and grow into a threat that could escalate into a conflict or a crisis (Ivančík, Jurčák 2014). A threat can be characterized as a potential crisis whose solution requires extraordinary measures. This means that a threat is a situation preceding the outbreak of a crisis when events are either purposely influenced or naturally deteriorating (Kulašik, 2002, 137).[21]

When it comes to defining the challenges, threats, and risks that concern Europe, the EU, and the Slovak Republic, we can state that the beginning of the twenty-first century brought together strategically entirely different cultures[22] and principles in the form

---

21 However, Jan Eichler defines "threat" as a manifestation, gesture, measure, or act that reflects an ability or intention to harm. It is a phenomenon of an objective character which impacts the victim's interests independently; by taking certain measures, a victim can mitigate, aggregate, or even completely eliminate a threat. It is the sign of warning of an imminent event that raises the victim's concerns. Risks are social phenomena derived from threats that always have a subjective character and reflect the decisions and acts of those who evaluate a situation and make decisions. Such decision-makers are heads of states and leaders of international organizations who take responsibility for the riskiness of their actions, which may either end with success or failure. Decision-makers have to assume responsibility in two extremes. Eichler defines the first one as complacency — that is, the irresponsible neglect of a threat — and the second one as paranoia or the securitization of non-existent threats (see Eichler 2009, 43). On the other hand, Volner says that risks can be understood as the awareness of real threats. He believes risks are of an objective character and do not have a direct impact on mankind, nations, states, or individuals. Meanwhile, Volner insists that a threat is an objective phenomenon which, contrary to risk, is more current, real, open, and imminent. It is an immediately destructive event (see Volner 2007, 104). Škvrnda and Polonský second the view that a risk is a potential danger that can occur in a certain time and place, while a threat is an ongoing state of danger with an imminent effect (see Škvrnda & Polonský 2003, 30).

22 Strategic culture is defined as a set of proven intellectual processes and specific measures when using armed force to achieve political goals. For example, the strategic culture of the US is characterized by an emphasis on total war that should be over as quickly as possible and that should end with the unconditional surrender of the enemy. Propaganda identifies the enemy as evil

of pre-emptive actions[23] on the margins of international law. Military dominance as such is not sufficient anymore and is becoming insignificant; what matters more now is the power of propaganda and beliefs, the surprise element and the swiftness of the attack, and, naturally, the technological sophistication of the deployed armed forces. A quick victory does not always guarantee the total elimination of the enemy. The remaining enemy could go underground and engage in guerrilla warfare, and in consequence the number of troops must be increased at the place of conflict and their stay prolonged. This subsequently complicates the process of stabilization and reconstruction, which is badly received by the local inhabitants. If the enemy units avoid direct confrontation and focus on indirect forms of fighting such as infiltration, laying traps, bombing, raiding, kidnapping, and using civilians as a shield, then having air and ground supremacy or using better information technologies is not enough to break the resistance. Conventional armed forces are not trained and prepared for these types of fights. Although military operation can solve one part of the problem, it might also open a Pandora's Box, containing new and even more serious issues (Ivančík, Jurčák 2014). Even if a military intervention aims to promote democracy and bring stability to a region, it does not always succeed in establishing stability and peace; the consequences of the so-called Arab Spring illustrate that well.

The 1990s may be seen as a period of seeking a new European security architecture based on collective security. However, the beginning of the twenty-first century witnessed the terrorist attacks

---

to achieve broad public support. The American strategic culture does not use indirect strategy or try to wear the enemy down in a long-lasting war. Its opposite is a culture that relies on guerrilla and terrorist organizations. These avoid direct battles, use traps, psychologically affect morale, and focus on killing unarmed civilians. This strategic culture is becoming the basis of the security environment of the twenty-first century.

23 This new security approach by the US first appeared in the National Security Strategy of 2002. This approach is based on attacking the enemy before he attacks. Pre-emption should be used when deterrence would not work. Its targets are either non-state actors or states that do not respond to deterrence. Pre-emption is also to be used when the deployment of weapons of mass destruction is expected. Pre-emption relies on air strikes followed by the rapid advance of ground troops numbering one or several brigades.

in New York on 11 September 2001, in Madrid on 11 March 2004, and in London on 7 July 2005, all of which drew attention to the fact that states are not ready for hostile activities by non-state actors. The quick reaction scenario, in which the time and place of the conflict are unknown, replaced the classic linear strategy known from the Cold War. It is practically impossible to predict the time and place of a military conflict, and consequently only a technologically advanced and highly flexible professional army can effectively intervene and defend an entrusted territory. Countries do not know how to handle cases when attackers do not come from the outside but from within the country and are not organized in the traditional sense; it is often an individual or an isolated cell that does not use traditional weapons but vehicles or explosives instead. This kind of threat requires a different approach — one that relies more on police work and secret services than on conventional military activity, which is more suitable for external threats. The United States responded to the changed circumstances by intervening in countries such as Iraq, Afghanistan, Libya, Yemen, and Syria, while Europe sees military solution as a last resort. Stanley Hoffman notes that the US administration has replaced its policy of deterrence with military operations and interventions in order to overthrow the regimes US planners considered hostile, along with a preference for unilateralism and planning military operations without NATO (Hoffman 2003, 13). On the other hand, Europeans — and especially the EU — emphasize the complexity of the world and focus more on cooperation and globalization. In general, the EU does not believe that big states with great military strength should have the right to decide when and where an armed intervention is needed, and it initially did not share the American theory of rogue states and axes of evil. Until recently, it put more emphasis on prevention, economic activities, and a political resolution of conflicts (Brhlíková 2014). It is now evident that both of these strategies are ineffective. While the US approach provokes disgust and resistance,[24] the European one is considered soft and slow.

The Russian approach also must be mentioned; it started to form with the beginning of the new millennium following the economic consolidation of the country.[25] Russia has been seeking a position on the international scene ever since the collapse of the Soviet Union, after which it withdrew from its traditional geopolitical position and even allowed NATO to approach its borders, thus narrowing the buffer zone between the Russian western border and NATO to only Belarus and Ukraine. Russia is currently striving to recover its former position on the international scene by means of dynamic leadership and a vigorous enforcement of national interests at all levels. Until the outbreak of the Syrian conflict, Russia had only dealt with threats coming from its immediate neighborhood; however, it gradually started to meet the goals of its National Security Strategy, which anticipates that Russia will acquire even greater international influence and will become one of the world leaders with a global influence (Strategia Nacionalnoj 2009). The strategy is to control resources, enforce interests by means of "soft power," and resolve potential conflicts using military force. It also emphasizes respecting the principles of international law and the equal security of states, and considers the United Nations with its Security Council as the most significant element for ensuring stable international relations (Strategia Nacionalnoj 2009, Article 13). Russia is also using other platforms, such as the G8, G20, and in particular RIC (Russia, India, and China) and BRIC (Brazil, Russia, India, and China). Where foreign policy is concerned, it focuses on establishing cooperation within the Commonwealth of Independent States and the Collective Security Treaty Organization. On a regional level, Russia is a

---

24 Despite sixteen years of military presence in Afghanistan, the US and its allies have not been able to eliminate the Taliban and consolidate the country, which has been damaged by the US's intervention and the ensuing war. Some European countries are similarly engaged in Africa (Libya, Cote d'Ivoire, and Togo) and face a similar lack of results.
25 This approach is gaining attention in relation to the conflict in Syria and the problems with the Islamic State.

member of the Eurasian Economic Community and the Shanghai Cooperation Organization (Strategia Nacionalnoj 2009, Articles 14 and 15).

On a global scale, the recent development of the security environment and security relations (2008 to 2017) has been characterized by poverty, an increasing income gap, mass migration, and the related migrant crisis that affected the EU in particular, the scarcity and uneven distribution of energy resources, a widespread economic and financial crisis and its related economic instability, and the indebtedness of the US and the EU, which the US sought to overcome by means of geopolitical agreements such as the Trans-Pacific Partnership (TPP) and the Trans-Atlantic Trade and Investment Partnership (TTIP), which Hillary Clinton once called the economic NATO. Both of these partnerships are geopolitically planned. The TPP's aim was to cut off its members from China and restore the economic dominance of the US in Southeast Asia, while the TTIP's goal is to cut the EU off from Russia economically and subject it to a stronger US influence than at any time before, according to Zbigniew Brzezinski's feudatory scenario. Moreover, both these partnerships benefit US corporations while being symmetrical toward both sides of the ocean. They can be understood as an effort to preserve a zone that will be forced to accept the US dollar as a reference currency, which will allow the US to accumulate debt and maintain control over its capital. Economists and analysts have already voiced serious doubts about the benefits of these trade agreements and their possible implications for the EU's geopolitical position.[26] It also provoked a wide range of responses: the creation of the Eurasian Union, the long-awaited reopening of the Silk Road, and the speeding up of the convergence of the BRICS countries (Brazil,

---

26 For example, Joseph Stiglitz, Ilona Švihlíková, Paul Krugman, Noam Chomsky, and Pascal Lamy. Chomsky claims the TTIP and TPP agreements are a continuation of the neoliberal project, while Joseph Stiglitz maintains that they only serve the interests of the richest population, as they could increase the competence of corporations to control intellectual property rights and establish a legal monopoly in this area. Even US senators are opposed to these agreements.

Russia, India, China, and South Africa) by setting up a joint banking institution and creating an original form of the SWIFT system to ensure the independence of their banking operations.

However, since the last presidential elections, US politics has been characterized by a sense of protectionism based on the America First policy. Fearing job losses, President Trump has so far refused to sign the Trans-Pacific Partnership Agreement; recent reports indicate that some of the other partners are also reluctant to sign the agreement. President Trump has also brought about changes in international relations and security policy. His unclear and erratic behavior has also contributed to the deterioration of the security environment and the reappearance of a nuclear threat.

New phenomena affecting the current security environment, safety, and the formulation of national interests include the violations of international law, double standards, fake news and media manipulation, trolling, post-factuality, post-truth, populism, multipolar order, shared interests, mass migration, moderate opposition and moderate terrorism, Brexit, increasing military budgets, increased perception of otherness (who belongs to us and who does not), the relativization of values and authority, the establishment and the mainstream versus the periphery, cyber war, and hybrid war. International security relations are socially constructed, which means that the outcome of security policy depends on how it is being interpreted by the related parties.[27] This creates a security culture that acts as a stabilizing structure based on the mutual influence of security discourses. If we want to change the nature of international security, first we must change the way we approach it and the way we look at it.

The EU's primary concern—as well as its main objective—is described in Article 21 of the Treaty on European Union, which states that the Union's main objectives include preserving international peace and security through conflict prevention, supporting developing countries with the aim of eradicating

---

27 This also poses a certain danger to the security environment and the decision-making process, as the erroneous interpretations and shifted perceptions of security signals could lead to bad decisions that could escalate into a global conflict.

poverty, assisting countries confronting natural disasters, and promoting stronger multilateral cooperation (Treaty EU 2012, Article 21(2)). While also respecting and maintaining principles such as democracy, human rights and fundamental freedoms, equality, and solidarity, and respect for the principles of the United Nations Charter and international law (Article 21(1)). We should not forget that those responsible for the formulation and fulfillment of these EU goals and interests are specific EU authorities and the state apparatus of the member states, even though the EU – despite being a notable player in the field of international relations – is made up of 28 (so far sovereign) member states that pursue their own national interests by means of their own foreign and security policies.

First of all, it should be stressed that the EU's security policy forms an integral part of the EU's common foreign and security policy and is only a sub-category of its broader external action. This external action is based on the EU's external relations that used to belong to the so-called Communities pillar prior to the ratification of the Treaty of Lisbon. These include development policy, humanitarian aid, the European Neighborhood Policy, enlargement policy, trade policy, and a common foreign and security policy. A separate EU foreign policy started to emerge as an informal gentlemen's agreement between the top representatives of the member states in the 1970s. It was guided by an unwritten set of rules, while the security dimension was added to it after the ratification of the Maastricht Treaty. Gradually, this policy evolved into a system of formal obligations and an organization with its own budget, staff, and headquarters, where decision-making evolved from negotiation to problem solving. It fuses intergovernmental, transgovernmental, and transnational decision-making methods by involving the European Council and the Council of the European Union. The European Commission plays only a marginal role, while the European Parliament and the European Court of Justice are entirely excluded from the decision-making and evaluating process. Other forms of the EU's external action are based on the traditional Community method, which signifies the transfer of the member states' competencies to the

European Commission in the fields of policy development and management, instruments, and agreements. Where foreign and security policies are concerned, it is entirely obvious that national governments maintain a considerable degree of autonomy, meaning that the EU institutions only reflect the strengths, interests, views, and concepts of the member states, along with the level of compliance regarding the extent, possibilities, and nature of the way the EU resolves conflicts (Brhlíková 2014, 58-61).

When analyzing the development of this policy, we can notice several attempts to strengthen the EU's institutions and unify national positions into a common EU position, along with efforts to convert the EU into a political entity and transform it from a political dwarf into a relevant global actor that should contribute to tackling the issues of terrorism and the arms trade, be actively involved in resolving the conflicts and problems that concern the Balkans and the Middle East, and participate in development aid for Africa. Despite these efforts, member states are still successfully maintaining their sovereignty in this area, firmly controlling their individual foreign and security policies. However, they still support the creation of a chaotic web containing political and bureaucratic actors with various competencies and resources at an EU level (Brhlíková 2014, 58-61).

Until the ratification of the Lisbon Treaty, there were at least three types of representation: the European Commission, the Council represented by both the High Representative for the CFSP and the Presidency of the Council (that is, the country that holds the Presidency), and the member states. The Commission used to be responsible for international representation and external relations in the field of economic relations, while the member states, the High Representative, and the Council of Ministers acted within the context of political affairs. This often led to problems with the duplication of both geographic and thematic departments within the Commission and the Secretariat of the Council of the EU; the duplication or scatteredness of resources; the regularly changing High Representative, who was replaced every six months; and the inability of a certain party to act because the resources were in the competence of another party or even of another pillar.[28] Naturally, this compromised the EU's authority as a leader, together with its continuity and credibility. It was up to the Treaty of Lisbon to eliminate these shortcomings by abolishing the pillar structure introduced by the Maastricht Treaty in 1993[29] and unifying the EU's external activities and representation so that the High Representative for the Common Foreign and Security Policy is both the Vice-President of the European Commission and the President of the EU Foreign Affairs Council, while also leading the newly-established European External Action Service, created by the merger of the relevant Directorates-General in the EU Council and the Commission (Figure 1).

Figure 1. The organizational structure of the European External Action Service

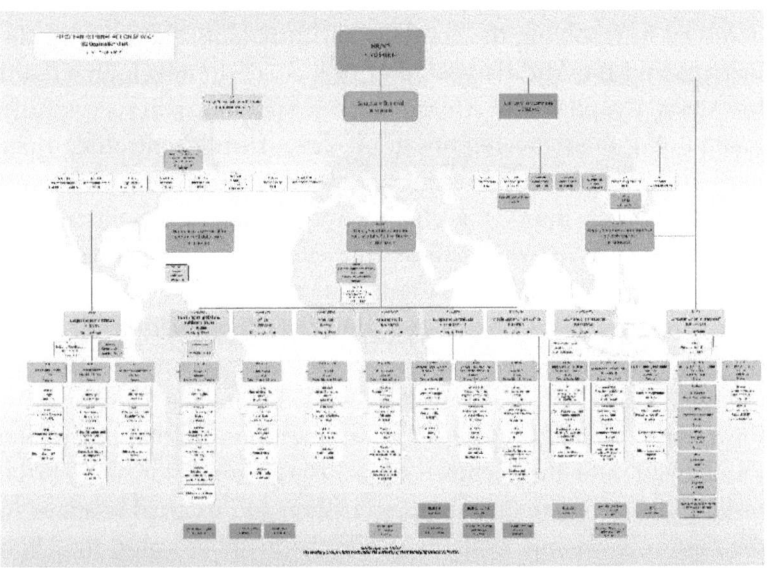

Source: https://eeas.europa.eu/sites/eeas/files/2019-01-10_-_eeas_2.0_org chart.pdf

---

28 This confusion in representation and competence is well illustrated by Henry Kissinger's famous remark: "Who do I call if I want to call Europe?"
29 Nevertheless, this notional pillar is still present in foreign policy, as foreign and security policy has remained an intergovernmental policy, which excludes the European Parliament and the European Court of Justice.

The treaty also introduced the post of the President of the European Council, who is considered to be the President of the European Union. Despite this quasi-simplification of the Union's external representation, the problem with authority and leadership persists, as in some areas the EU is represented either by the President of the Commission, the President of the European Council, or the High Representative.

Foreign and security policy is a highly sensitive and specific matter that, together with an attempt to at least partially preserve the pillar division, can be seen in their inclusion in the first part of the Treaty on European Union and not in the section describing the functioning of the EU that characterizes all its exclusive, shared, and complementary competencies. The Treaty on European Union deals with foreign and security policy in Articles 21 to 46, with Article 42 defining the Common Security and Defense Policy as *"an integral part of the common foreign and security policy"* (Article 42(1)). This placement was justified by the distinctiveness of the EU's foreign and security policy. However, decisions continued to be taken by unanimous vote, and thus the intergovernmental approach with the strong position of nation states to the detriment of EU institutions remained unchanged. Maintaining unanimity and defining foreign policy as a specific EU policy demonstrate the preservation of the duality and ambiguity of integration in this area, while confirming the intergovernmental approach to foreign policy at the EU level, which means that it remains a policy with an integrationist ambition, albeit still controlled by intergovernmentalism, particularly by strong member states (Brhlíková 2009).

The EU's foreign and security policy is framed broadly. The EU's priorities can be divided into three levels: vertical, horizontal, and multilateral. These levels are basically identical to the interests the Union strives to follow and address on the international scene.[30]

---

30 It is problematic to talk about national or state interest in the case of the EU. Although the EU has a legal personality and is therefore both an object and a subject of international law, and as such can enter into relations with other subjects of international law, it cannot be considered a state, a superstate, a

On the vertical level, the following may be considered the EU's interests:

- the enlargement of the Union
- the European Neighborhood Policy and its related activities: The Eastern Partnership, the Southern Neighborhood, the Euro-Mediterranean Partnership, and the Middle East Peace Process[31]
- relations with strategic partners, i.e., the United States, Canada, Australia, Japan and the BRICS states (Brazil, Russia, India, China, and South Africa)

At a horizontal level, the EU focuses on:

- security, which includes a common foreign policy and a common security policy
- development and humanitarian aid and crisis management
- the economy, trade, and finances
- terrorism
- human rights
- climate change and energy
- migration

On the multilateral level, the EU is establishing cooperation with a number of existing global and regional organizations:

- security organizations, i.e., the North Atlantic Alliance (NATO) and the Organization for Security and Cooperation in Europe (OSCE)

---

federation, or an international organization because it has long ceased to be one. Therefore, it is problematic to talk about the EU's interests; even its treaties tend to talk about priorities or objectives. However, this does not mean that the EU has no interests. The national interests of the member states are also the EU's interests.

31 According to Article 8 of the Treaty on European Union, the Union is to develop special relations with its neighboring countries in order to create an area of prosperity and a good neighborhood that is based on the values of the EU and characterized by close and peaceful cooperative relations. The European Neighborhood Policy focuses primarily on the EU's 16 closest neighbors: Algeria, Armenia, Azerbaijan, Belarus, Egypt, Georgia, Israel, Jordan, Lebanon, Libya, Moldova, Morocco, Palestine, Syria, Tunisia, and Ukraine.

- global international organizations such as the United Nations (UN) and the World Trade Organization (WTO)
- regional organizations such as ASEAN, Mercosur, and the Council of Europe
- interest groupings whose common denominators are mainly economic parameters, i.e., G20, G8, and so on (Ružička, Karvašová 2012, 130)

The basic strategic security objectives of the EU, according to the European Security Strategy as outlined by Javier Solana, the first High Representative for Foreign Affairs and Security Policy and the former Secretary General of NATO, were adopted on 12 December 2003 at the EU summit in Brussels under the title *A Secure Europe in a Better World*, and include:

- extending the zone of security around Europe so that the countries on the eastern and southern borders of Europe[32] are governed and controlled correctly
- resolving the Palestinian-Israeli conflict
- strengthening the international order in a globalized world (Solana 2003)

According to the strategy, the most current and dangerous threats include international terrorism, linked to violent religious fundamentalism and the development of technology; the proliferation of weapons of mass destruction, including the spread of missile technology; regional conflicts; weak states threatened by the failure of their state systems, social structures, and territory; organized crime that presents both an internal and an external threat; piracy; energetic and cyber threats; and climate change (Solana 2003). The EU should actively confront these threats by strengthening its defense and striving to address the underlying causes by using a mixture of instruments such as spreading good governance, establishing the rule of law, and protecting human rights, while not ruling out the use of military means despite

---

32 Meaning the former Soviet republics and countries in the Mediterranean region.

recognizing their insufficiency in tackling some of the security threats (Solana 2003).

In addition, the document identifies two fundamental pillars of security:

- strengthening security in the neighboring countries that are geographically and strategically linked to the EU. Even though the integration of Eastern European states increases the EU's security, it also brings Europe closer to troubled areas
- creating a strong international order based on effective multilateralism, which, according to the traditional European approach, consists of enhancing the effectiveness of international law; increasing the UN Security Council's responsibility for world peace and international security; and strengthening the role of international organizations like the World Trade Organization and other financial institutions, OSCE, NATO, and the African Union (Solana 2003)

The document also defines the means by which the EU can build a safer, fairer, and more unified world, which include:

- the more active use of national and common instruments to achieve strategic objectives and a more coherent combination of means for crisis management and conflict prevention concerning the EU's political, diplomatic, military, civilian, commercial, and development activities
- an expanded capacity to act based on deeper military integration and the increased flexibility of armed forces; active diplomatic cooperation and common threat assessment as the basis for common measures; a wider spectrum of missions, including disarmament operations; support for third countries in combating terrorism; and security sector reform
- more coherent actions relating to security and defense policy, and bringing together the instruments and capabilities of the individual member states in the area of assistance programs, development funds, military and

- civilian activities, and development, trade, and environmental policy
- multilateral cooperation in international organizations and partnership with key actors, based on an effective and balanced partnership with the US, close cooperation with Russia, and a strategic partnership with Japan, China, Canada, and India (Solana 2003)

This strategy was created at a time when the EU was in two minds about attacking Iraq, creating considerable tension between the member states. The document's objective was to identify the looming threats and set up a framework for future joint action. It was also intended to build a greater European consensus regarding the member states' response to these threats and mobilize the EU to be a more active, capable, and coherent player on the international scene. In fact, the EU is still in pursuit of this goal, as described in the Treaty of Lisbon. The key goal was to achieve a Europe that would assume its share of responsibility in bringing about world security, whose main promoter was the US. Since its adoption fourteen years ago, this strategy has served as an internal guideline for establishing cooperation and it forms the basis of the strategic security dialogue that the EU conducts with the US, Russia, China, and India. Although the objectives and priorities it describes have not changed much, only a little progress has been made in their execution. The conflict in Libya, the creation of the Islamic State, the proxy war in Syria, and the migration flow into Europe in 2015 have all jeopardized the security situation of the member states, clearly showing the EU's lack of preparedness and its indecisiveness and sluggishness when it comes to tackling problems even on its own territory.

By joining the EU and signing the treaty, member states have committed to enhancing and developing their mutual political solidarity and respecting and supporting all steps taken by the Union (Treaty EU 2012, Article 42(7)). They have also committed to coordinate their actions according to the common position of the EU, while declaring on the basis of the solidarity principle that "*[i]f a Member State is the victim of armed aggression on its territory, the other*

Member States shall have towards it an obligation of aid and assistance by all the means in their power," adding somewhat slyly that *"[c]ommitments and cooperation in this area shall be consistent with commitments under the North Atlantic Treaty Organisation, which, for those States which are members of it, remains the foundation of their collective defence and the forum for its implementation."*[33]

In Slovakia, the Ministry of Foreign and European Affairs is responsible for drawing up strategic documents defining the basic interests of the country. However, these documents are prepared by the bureaucratic apparatus of the corresponding line ministries (either the Ministry of Foreign Affairs or the Ministry of Defense), or even — as in the case of Slovakia's new Security Strategy of 2017 — affiliated non-governmental organizations with a very clear orientation.[34] Such documents are usually drafted with the exclusion of the academic and expert community. Even though they go through a consultation process conducted by individual ministries, they remain largely unnoticed by the public. Finally, the outcome document gets approved firstly by the government and then by the Slovak National Council. Even though changes can be introduced in these documents to improve them while they are being reviewed, their essence remains mostly unchanged, meaning that these documents tend to be rather general in their character,

---

33 Treaty EU 2012, Article 42(7). The Treaty of Lisbon strengthens the solidarity between EU countries in dealing with external threats by introducing a mutual defense clause (Article 42(7) of the Treaty on European Union). This clause provides that if an EU country is the victim of armed aggression on its territory, the other EU countries have an obligation to aid and assist it by all the means in their power, in accordance with Article 51 of the United Nations Charter. This obligation of mutual defense is binding on all EU countries. However, it does not affect the neutrality of certain EU countries and is consistent with the commitments of EU countries which are NATO members. This provision is supplemented by the solidarity clause (Article 222 of the Treaty on the Functioning of the EU) which provides that EU countries are obliged to act jointly where an EU country is the victim of a terrorist attack or a natural or man-made disaster.
34 More precisely, a pro-NATO and pro-Atlantic orientation which rhetorically and ideologically goes beyond limits not even exceeded by NATO; it is therefore symptomatic that the proclaimed national interests benefit the US more than the EU or Slovakia itself.

neither specifying any interests, objectives, or priorities, nor defining the tools that should be used to achieve them. They seem more like documents defining and safeguarding the interests of some other entity instead of Slovakia. When compared with similar documents adopted in the EU or NATO, we can see the same diction and the same orientation towards foreign policy, without taking into account the geographical, political, or power position of Slovakia. We then find ourselves in a situation where even though we disagree with the solutions or policies proposed by the EU, believing them to be marginal to Slovakia's security interests,[35] we support them. After all, we do not want to come across as troublemakers.

Specifically, the Slovak government's policy statement for 2016 to 2020 states that *"[t]he national and state interest of the country is to ensure the clear continuity of Slovakia's pro-European and pro-Atlantic orientation based on a broad political consensus"* (Programové vyhlásenie, 3). Then it says: *"The foreign and European policy of the Slovak Republic is subordinated to the interests of the state and serves the interests of its citizens"* (4). The document then describes a security environment which is seen as complicated, unstable, and violent,[36] due to which the Slovak government guarantees that it will *"pursue [a] predictable, credible, and transparent foreign policy in line with Slovakia's membership of the European Union and NATO,"* and *"[o]n assuming the Presidency of the Council of the EU,"* the country will *"seek to strengthen the position of the EU"* (4) since the EU *"constitutes the primary milieu/main framework for the pursuit of Slovakia's key interests. The Government will strengthen the position of the country as a credible, respected, and transparent partner in the EU. Through its active approach, with an emphasis on common solutions and respect for*

---

35 For example, Slovakia disagrees with the sanctions imposed on Russia while also naming the country as its main enemy in the new Security Strategy of 2017.
36 According to the Policy Statement, these external challenges are the most acute: a belt of persisting instability along the EU border, armed conflicts in the EU neighborhood which give rise to mass migration and international terrorism, the violation of and departure from the basic standards of international law and the principles of the post-war European architecture, and traditional and new hybrid forms of threats and efforts to weaken the national and state identity of countries (Programové vyhlásenie, 4).

the rules, Slovakia will contribute toward solving the biggest challenges the Union is facing nowadays" (4). The document clearly shows an orientation toward the EU, as the government expresses a hope to strengthen the EU's position in the world even if it means accepting common positions and solutions and complying with the rules. However, this might create a dilemma for Slovakia when it will have to choose whose interests to pursue—its own national interests, or those defined by the EU's common position, since the Slovak government *"attaches a key importance to supporting (...) measures which improve the management of [the EU's] external borders and ensure [the] proper functioning of the Schengen area as a positive achievement of European integration,"* while it is also *"prepared to support constructive solutions to the unprecedented migration crisis, respecting the specificities and capabilities of individual Member States,"* support the *"additional strengthening of the internal market, which is the main EU tool for stimulating economic growth and new jobs[,] (...) pay particular attention to (...) the Energy Union, Single Digital Market, and the Capital Markets Union[,] (...) actively promote the deepening of the Economic and Monetary Union[,] (...) take a constructive approach to negotiations aimed at ensuring the sustainability and stability of the Eurozone and the European Union[,] (...) [and] support the enlargement of the European Union,"* while the *"Cohesion Policy and the European Structural and Investment Funds"* will *"also remain high on the agenda"* (5). Just listing these priorities implies certain contradictions and reservations regarding the pursuit of Slovakia's national interests.

Where security is concerned, even though the Manifesto claims that *"the main mission of the security policy of the state is to actively influence the security environment in order to protect, defend, and put through the security interests of Slovakia,"* adding that *"the security of its citizens [is seen as the] precondition for stability and the dynamic economic and social development of the country"* and that *"NATO's system of collective defense and the EU's Common Security and Defense Policy constitute the main determinants of security for the Slovak Republic"* (7), these security interests are not specified anywhere. However, the Security Strategy of the Slovak Republic of 2005 defines them, stating that *"[t]he key objective of the Slovak Republic's security policy is to guarantee the security of the state and its citizens in a stable and predictable security environment"* (Security Strategy 2005, 3). Slovakia's security interests include:

- guaranteeing the security of [the country's] citizens and protecting their human rights and fundamental freedoms
- guaranteeing [the country's] territorial integrity, sovereignty, inviolability of borders, political independence, and identity
- developing democracy, the rule of law, and the market economy
- creating prerequisites for the sustainable economic, social, environmental, and cultural development of society
- strengthening the strategic trans-Atlantic partnership and co-guaranteeing the security of its allies
- improving the effectiveness of the international organizations which the Slovak Republic is a member of and supporting NATO expansion and EU enlargement
- developing good partnership relationships and all forms of mutually beneficial cooperation with the countries with which the Slovak Republic has common interests
- contributing to strengthening and expanding freedom and democracy, respect for human rights, the rule of law, international law, peace, and stability in the world (Security Strategy 2005, 3)

When comparing the Security Strategy of the European Union and the Security Strategy of the Slovak Republic, it immediately strikes the eye that the EU document is shorter, logically better structured, and devoid of flowery but empty words; it directly names the threats and outlines possible solutions to tackle them. In contrast, both of the above-mentioned Slovak documents are verbose, and they never specify the country's interests, objectives, or the means that should be used to achieve them. As its main national and state interest, the Slovak government identifies the fostering of a pro-European and pro-Atlantic orientation—and that seems to be all. Its objectives are formed within the context of EU membership, which seems to imply that partnerships and coalitions are not established according to what the citizens want but are rather based on what can be achieved within the prescribed rules. If the country proceeded against them, it would have to face sanctions and isolation.

Seeing the situation as it is, can we still claim that it was the state that formulated its own basic interests? Does a state — a rather small one, considering its strength, capabilities, and skill — that has joined a wider community of states with a common policy still have its own national interest? We can see that its interests are usually presented through threats and risks. They are defined in an *ad hoc* manner as a reaction to already existing problems. Apparently, by being a part of a wider community, the state seems to have given up on its own interests, seeking protection — and therefore the fulfillment of its priorities and objectives — under the wings of a joint organization.

4. National Interest and Politicians

Norbert Kmeť

Every state has a set of interests that can be termed "national" or "state" interests, expressed by its political representatives. Defining them is rather problematic and it has been a much researched and discussed issue among political scientists. (See, for example: Bátora 2004a, 39-53; Clinton 1994; Drulák 2010, 7-16; Juza 2016, 142-162; Kratochvíl 2010, 17-30; Kratochvíl 2010b; Krejčí 2001, 257-266; Krejčí 2009; Łoś-Nowak 2000, 196-200; Rusiňák 2005, 35-38; Valenta 1992; Weiss 2010, 42-83; Weiss 2009.) During the hearing of the policy statement of Vladimír Mečiar's second government in the Slovak National Council on 14 July 1992, Peter Weiss, the vice-chairman of the National Council (1992-1994), spoke about the unwillingness of the post-1989 governments "to clearly define [the country's] long-term national interests." He thought this was the main weakness of Slovak politics and believed that political parties were largely responsible for it. He urged the representatives of the relevant political parties to define the country's interests together (NRSR 1992). However, even a year and a half after Weiss's statement the situation remained the same. Ivan Laluha, chairman of the Foreign Affairs Committee of the Slovak National Council between 1992 and 1994,[37] called attention to this fact during the hearing of the report on the performance of foreign policy tasks and objectives on 2 February 1994. He emphasized the need to define the country's state interests more clearly (NRSR 1994). In 1993, Slovakia's national interests were defined in a document called Fundamental Objectives and Principles of the Slovak Republic's National Security (*Základné ciele a zásady národnej bezpečnosti Slovenskej republiky*), ratified by Mečiar's third government on 23 April 1996. The document, discussed by the Parliament on 20 June 1996,

---

37 According to the Constitution of the Slovak Republic, adopted on 1 September 1992, the new name of Slovakia´s parliament is the National Council of the Slovak Republic.

guarantees sovereignty, territorial integrity, the inviolability of borders, security, economic prosperity, social stability, and international recognition (NRSR F). These are the political, military, economic, and cultural interests of the state (Had 1992, 25). In their 1994 program, the Slovenská národná strana ("Slovak National Party," SNS) identified *"the question of [Slovakia's] sovereignty, integrity and security"* and *"the establishment of friendly relationships with all the countries in the world, with special attention to its immediate neighbors"* as Slovakia's national state interests (SNS 1994, 34). The expressions "national interests," "state interests," and "national state interests" are mainly used by political nation-states, although the Anglo-American literature tends to work with them as well (cf. Valenta 1992a, 12). On 20 June 1996, Ján Sitek, the Minister of Defense, tried to justify the use of the expression "national interest" to the members of the National Council when drafting the above-mentioned Fundamental Objectives. He said that it cannot be interpreted in an ethnic sense because *"the entire document is based on a balance between ethnic and civil principles, which is why an Anglo-Saxon diction was applied which does not differentiate between the terms "nation" and "state," and therefore the expression "national" is always related to the Slovak Republic [as a whole]"* (NRSR 1996).

In some countries, national interests are the same as state interests while in others it is preferable to distinguish between these two concepts. Artificially creating a political nation in a multiethnic country is seldom successful. Most of the time, various nationalistic views tend to predominate, pushing the principle of civil society into the background. By emphasizing national themes, politicians and political parties instill in voters the belief—or rather, the feeling—that they are the ones protecting their interests from others who are usually presented as hostile. Using "national interests" and "state interests" interchangeably tends to create unnecessary tension in multinational states, not only internally but also by negatively affecting the country's bilateral relations, especially with its neighbors. Since November 1989, the terms "state interests," "national interests" and "national state interests" have been frequently used in Slovak politics, and in the early 1990s they were discussed at length by experts and politicians alike (Škvarna, Mojžita 1992, 29).

However, the Slovak political scene was clearly divided in the 1990s. The main conflict was between the Hnutie za demokratické Slovensko ("Movement for a Democratic Slovakia," HZDS) and their coalition partners and other parliamentary bodies represented by Strana demokratickej ľavice ("Party of the Democratic Left," SDĽ), together with right-wing parties with links to European political groupings. The latter pointed out that without these links, political integration was impossible.[38] Peter Weiss thought it important that the political parties should clearly define their ideological profile, as their political success depended not only on the population's support but also on their transnational affiliations. A state pursues its foreign policy and safeguards its interests not only via its official international relations but also with the help of transnational political groupings and powerful figures (Weiss 2009, 273-274).

Using the term "national interest," "state interest," or "national state interest" depends, among other things, on whether we identify the nation with the state or if we insist on their strict distinction. Petr Kratochvíl regards these concepts as synonymous, but he believes that when we refer to historical events, we should strictly differentiate between them (Kratochvíl 2010b, 8-18). He adds that as far as Slovakia is concerned, talking about "state interests" would be more appropriate, but the term "national interests" tends to be used more frequently, especially by conservative politicians. However, there is no strict distinction between "national" and "state" interests nowadays because the state is perceived nationally (Kratochvíl 2010b, 7-10, 152). Regardless of whether a state is seen as multiethnic or not, it is important to differentiate between the interests of the state and the interests of the nation, since they do not always correspond to each other, as Zbigniew Rykiel points out (Kałążna, Rosicki 2013, 124).

---

38 When discussing the report on Slovakia's fulfillment of foreign policy tasks and objectives in the plenary of the National Council on 2 February 1994, this was pointed out, among others, by Ľubomír Fogaš, Peter Lauko, and Peter Weiss. See also Weiss 2009, 16.

In Slovakia's case, it also depends on which particular years we focus on, or on whether we follow its overall development from 1993 up to the present. During Mečiar's (and the HZDS's) second (1992-1994) and third government (1994-1998), the relationship between the ruling majority and the opposition was extremely tense, and the government's minority policies were the target of much domestic and international criticism. We can see this as the promotion of the traditional national principle. The policy statement of Mečiar's second government of 1992 talks about state interests and establishing a constructive dialogue *"with everyone interested in the welfare of Slovakia"* (Vláda SR 1992, 33, 35). In its section on foreign affairs, the policy statement of Mečiar's third government talks about national, state, foreign, and domestic interests. Between Mečiar's second and third government, the cabinet led by Jozef Moravčík in 1994 expressed an ambition to alleviate the country's sociopolitical tension. Their policy statement talks about the country's "foreign" and "domestic" interests.

To describe the period between 1998 and 2006, when the Strana maďarskej koalície ("Party of the Hungarian Coalition," SMK) was part of the government coalition, we can undoubtedly use the term "state interests." In the policy statement of Mikuláš Dzurinda's first government, we can find expressions such as "the national interests of the Slovak Republic" and "the interests of the state." The policy statement of the next Slovak government mentions both "state interests" and "national interests," as well as "the interests of the homeland" and "the interests of the Slovak Republic." Robert Fico's first government between 2006 and 2010 faced international pressure due to the SNS's participation in the government, and since the end of August 2006 the case of Hedviga Malinová remains unclosed. During this period, the relationship with the Hungarian minority was tense but not as confrontational as during Mečiar's third term. It is debatable whether the promotion of national or state interests prevailed. The policy statement issued by Fico's first government talked about "national interest," "state interest," and "national state interests." Following the parliamentary elections in 2010, Iveta Radičová's coalition government of right-wing parties assumed power; however, their internal squabbles put an end to their rule in 2012. The policy statement of this government mentioned both "the interests of the Slovak Republic" and "Slovak interests." So, in this case we can talk about state or national state interests. The same applies to the majority government of SMER-SD ("Direction−Social Democracy") between 2012 and 2016 and Fico's third government that formed on 1 September 2016, together with Most-Híd ("Bridge") and the SNS, as a result of the disintegration of the Sieť ("Network") party.[39] These government statements mostly talked about national interests, state interests, and national state interests.

Clearly identifying what is a national interest, a state interest, and a national state interest is also complicated because these terms cannot be defined more precisely. However, what is more important is to reach an agreement on what is essential and desirable for a particular state (Drulák 2010, 9). The above-mentioned terms are ambiguous and this lack of a precise definition is a well-known problem in the social sciences. We could also work with the term "the people's interests," which would promote the principle of civil society. There are also some other expressions that are equivalent to the previously mentioned ones, such as task, strategy, priority, the consolidation of position, goal, giving attention, and accentuation. A similar situation arises when trying to define public interests (cf. Kratochvíl 2010b, 121-155; Krpec 2009, 86; Eichler, Hynek 2010, 121).

Most often, a country's national interest, state interest, and national state interest is what the executive and legislative powers, together with the president and other representatives of political power−that is, the people and institutions that actively participate in politics, including political parties−agree on. At present, other players in public life, such as third-sector organizations or the mass media, are also involved in shaping a country's interests or priorities.[40] There is an undeniable link between the declared

---

39 The four-party coalition lasted from 22 March 2016 to 1 September 2016.
40 Šárka Waisová divides foreign policy makers into two categories: official and unofficial. The first group includes "the president, the members of the government, the highest ministerial officials, the members of the parliament,

interests of a state and its identity (Bátora 2004a, 40-46). Indeed, they confirm the legitimacy of the state not only externally but also internally (Kratochvíl 2010b, 193). The Ministry of Foreign Affairs remains the most important element in the formation of state interests, reflecting the level of consensus among the relevant political forces. This is the ideal-typical form of state interests (Krpec 2009, 76, 89-95). In this case, there is an agreement between the government and the opposition regarding the state's true interests (Eichler, Hynek 2010, 121).

Since the foundation of the Slovak Republic in 1993, a consensus on foreign policy issues has been successfully maintained between political parties and parliamentary movements, which helped to integrate Slovakia "into the international community." It proved the fact that there was a common state interest (MZR A, 6). Milan Kňažko, the Minister of Foreign Affairs in January 1993, contributed to it; he "called for a meeting of parliamentary political parties and movements" in order to discuss Slovakia's foreign policy concept. No categorical objection was raised to the document, and Ján Čarnogurský greatly appreciated the meeting. He saw it as *"the first step of the Slovak government toward the opposition which feels equally responsible for the fate of our state as members of the ruling coalition"* (Mojžita 2004, 92-93).

When reporting on the performance of Slovakia's foreign policy tasks and objectives on 2 February 1994, Jozef Moravčík, the Minister of Foreign Affairs, emphasized the necessity of "constantly seeking and finding a high degree of consensus of all the political parties, or at least their vast majority" in foreign policy matters. He refused to favor party and personal interests in foreign policy, not only because of their harmfulness, but also because he thought they suggested "the immaturity of political structures." He stressed that without a stable internal policy, the Slovak Republic will not be able to pursue a foreign policy that would allow it to

---

and the highest representatives of the self-governing units." The second group includes "political parties, NGOs, companies, the media, universities, advisers and advisory groups, and trade unions" (Waisová 2011, 54; Weiss 2009, 335-337).

integrate into European democratic structures (NRSR 1994, 448, 457-459). Ivan Laluha of the HZDS and Peter Lauko of the Kresťanskodemokratické hnutie ("Christian Democratic Movement," KDH) also believed that the consensus of political parties was imperative (NRSR 1994, 463-464, 490).

Political parties, the public, and various interest groups can have different approaches to the state's interests, which therefore become part of the political struggle between individual political players. Society's consensus on state interests also demonstrates that individual goals can be subordinated to a greater, society-wide cause (Kratochvíl 2010b, 8). Despite declaring unity and accord in Slovakia's basic international matters, the country's foreign policy was uncoordinated, as there was a lack of cooperation between the individual political parties as well as between the government and the Ministry of Foreign Affairs, as outlined in the program of the Maďarská občianska strana ("Hungarian Civic Party," MOS) in October 1996 (MOS, 6). This problem persisted, as evidenced by the pre-election program of the Slovenská demokratická koalícia ("Slovak Democratic Coalition," SDK), which noted that the country's foreign policy was not properly coordinated between the Ministry of Foreign Affairs, the President, and the National Council (SDK, 106).

State interests were becoming increasingly concerned with economic issues that sometimes took precedence over a policy line based on respect for fundamental human rights and freedoms. When Mikuláš Dzurinda acted as the Minister of Foreign and European Affairs of the Slovak Republic, he thought that safeguarding Slovak citizens' interests should also be a part of a foreign policy based on human and civic values (MZV SR 2010). The KDH's pre-election program of 1992 clearly indicated in the section dedicated to foreign affairs that they will *"protect the interests of Slovak corporate entities and create the best conditions for their development and prosperity"* (KDH 1992, 10). Basically, every document or discussion regarding foreign policy emphasised the importance of economic diplomacy. Their interconnectedness was a much-debated topic in August 1992, when Milan Kňažko submitted to the Slovak government a proposal for creating a

Ministry of Foreign Affairs and External Economic Relations in Slovakia (Mojžita 2004, 60-61). When the Parliament discussed Slovakia's Foreign Policy Report on 2 February 1994, Prime Minister Jozef Moravčík did not find it necessary to divide diplomacy into a political and an economic part (NRSR 1994, 525).

In their 1994 program, the SNS pointed out the need to depoliticize the country's external economic relations, referring to Slovakia's historical experience and arguing that *"without economic prosperity, it is impossible to establish lasting political stability"* (SNS 1994, 36). In their pre-election leaflets of 1994, the Demokratická únia Slovenska ("Democratic Union of Slovakia," DÚ) promised citizens to *"safeguard Slovakia's economic interests"* (DÚ A). In their program of February 1996, the party stated that they will try to achieve having the Ministry of Foreign Affairs and the Ministry of Economy assess the functionality of the economic departments at the representative offices (DÚ B, 50). Promises to strengthen the economic dimension of diplomacy also appeared in the SDK's pre-election program (SDK, 109), just like they did in the HZDS's pre-election program of 1998 (HZDS B). In 2010, the SNS promised to ensure that the economic interests of Slovakia would become a part of its diplomacy. During this period, SMER-SD also called for strengthening the economic dimension of diplomacy (SMER-SD, 4). In the annual Assessment of Foreign and European Policy Tasks (*Zameranie zahraničnej a európskej politiky*), the Slovak Ministry of Foreign and European Affairs tends to list economic diplomacy among its priorities (as it did in 2014 or 2016, for instance) (MZVaEZ SR 2014 ;MZVaEZ SR 2016).

In Slovakia, the term "national" is mostly associated with nationalism and is associated with the fact that the political bodies proclaiming such interests did not entirely accept Western European political standards. In Slovakia, such political subjects were the HZDS, the SNS, and the Združenie robotníkov Slovenska ("Union of the Workers of Slovakia"). In the 1990s, Slovak society and politics were characterized by isolationism as a result of the policies the HZDS pursued, especially between 1994 and 1998. According to Peter Weiss, this ideology was underpinned not only by politics and the privatizers' support, but also by the rejection of

Western European political standards (Weiss 2009, 307-310). The representatives of the SNS were aware of the fact that their policies were incompatible with European political principles. In their 1994 program, they clearly stated that *"because of their principles, the SNS often come into conflict with transnational pan-Europeanism and global cosmopolitanism. In these confrontations, the SNS always argues in favor of [Slovakia's] national state interests"* (SNS 1994, 2). However, the party's program of 1998 states that *"economic, political, and cultural problems can only be resolved by accepting the values of Europe – that is, its politics, customs, and European public opinion – and by integrating into Europe's cultural, economic, political, and spiritual context"* (SNS 1998, 33-34).

Presenting the national principle and identifying with it in any form not only aroused an interest in the principle but also an immediate mistrust in it and its rejection. However, the civil principle as emphasized by the political opposition of the HZDS and their partners did not gain enough public support due to the inconsistency of the opposition parties. The conflict between the "national" and the "civil" principle persisted. This situation started to change following the failed attempts to integrate the country into the Euro-Atlantic structures during Mečiar's third government, because even though the HZDS supported such efforts, Western countries did not find the political activities and statements of the party's leaders credible.[41] During the hearing of the report on the performance of foreign policy tasks and objectives on 2 February 1994, Anton Hrnko, a member of the National Council, talked about the need to *"realize that the Slovak Republic will only be able to pursue its interests once its internal structure fits into [the country's] geopolitical*

---

41 The HZDS's support for NATO accession was not as unanimous as in the case of membership in the European Union. According to Miroslav Mojžita's information from the end of 1992 and the beginning of 1993, when the HZDS committee was debating Slovakia's foreign policy, it discussed the appropriateness of Slovakia's neutrality and its position as a bridge between the West and the East. At Milan Kňažko's above-mentioned meeting with the opposition, even Ján Čarnogurský objected to Slovakia's orientation toward NATO. Cf. Mojžita 2004, 87-88, 91, 93. The same applies to the KDH, who outwardly showed unanimous support for Slovakia joining NATO (Čarnogurský 2013).

environment. If [Slovakia] searches for other ways and ignores the general trends that prevail in Central Europe, it can only lead to [the country's] isolation and potential loss of identity" (NRSR 1994, 470). Milan Kňažko, a member of the National Council, seconded this observation, adding that the members of the Klub nezávislých poslancov ("Club of Independent MPs") *"called attention to many internal political affairs and inappropriate statements made by some of the representatives that will significantly hamper our foreign policy and cast a long shadow on Slovakia's reputation"* (NRSR 1994, 496). Since Mečiar's government refused to address the shortcomings of the country's democratic system and did not allow the parliamentary opposition to control it, it stirred doubts about Slovakia's ability to meet the conditions for integration into Euro-Atlantic structures, even as many believed the regime was becoming increasingly authoritarian.

Since the 1990s, it has been a much-disputed topic in society as well as in politics, whether it was really necessary to split up Czechoslovakia when the situation in the Czech Republic seemed far more calm; unlike Slovakia, it was not riddled with internal political conflicts. At the same time, Slovak society was divided into so-called "good" Slovaks, "bad" Slovaks ("anti-Slovaks," "Czechoslovakists"), and even "Hungarianized" Slovaks. Politicians and public figures alike were given such pointless labels, as were diplomats, as pointed out by Jozef Moravčík in 1994 when debating the report on the performance of foreign policy tasks and objectives in the National Council of the Slovak Republic. He strongly disapproved of such a categorization, as he thought it was both artificial and *"absurd and very harmful"* (NRSR 1994, 453). Peter Weiss, the vice-chairman of the National Council of the Slovak Republic, mentioned it in a similarly disapproving way, claiming that such labelling does not benefit the country in any way. He added that this artificial division and overt idealization of the Slovak state was also being noticed abroad (NRSR 1994, 507; cf. Weiss 2009, 108). In a pre-election leaflet of 1994, František Mikloško wrote that accusing people of Czechoslovakism *"is an artificially created problem"* (KDH 1994). In their 1990 pre-election program, even the KDH mentioned how they find the substitution of "the Czechoslovak nation for the fiction of a sovereign nation" bothersome. They thought it insulted *"the Slovaks and the Czechs as much as it did the Hungarians, Rusyns, Ukrainians, Germans, Poles, and Roma"* (KDH 1994, 2). In their pre-election program of 2006, the Občianska konzervatívna strana ("Civic Conservative Party," OKS) argued against the existence of a "European people" or a European nation. They thought that artificially creating such entities was unrealistic, as they disregard *"the interests of the individual nations, along with their historical interpretations and different experiences"* (OKS 2006, 55-56). However, this division of society into friends and enemies still persists, as proved by the SNS's pre-election program of 2006. It says that the Slovak Republic is mostly represented abroad *"by people whose actions and beliefs confirm that they were always opposed to Slovakia's sovereignty and who damage the interests of Slovakia even thirteen years after it gained independence"* (SNS 2006, 37).

These inconsistent interpretations of "national" and "state" interests are mainly caused by the already-discussed ambiguity that characterizes these terms. At the time when the Slovak Republic became a subject of international law, the HZDS was not only the ruling party but also the strongest political subject. This allowed them to set the foreign policy of the newly formed sovereign state. The foundation of the Slovak Republic occurred at a time when Western Europe was characterized by an intense integration process. Meanwhile, in the eastern and central regions of the continent, the Soviet Union, Yugoslavia, and Czechoslovakia were falling apart due to the collapse of the Soviet Bloc. Therefore, Central and Southeast Europe witnessed the total transformation of their political, social, and economic circumstances. This created the need in Slovaks to redefine the country's national interests, this time strongly influenced by Western European integration and the change in values that occurred in society. This was evidenced by the foreign policy agenda the Slovak government approved on 26 January 1993, especially Resolution 56 (MZV SR A) and the explanatory memorandum to the Slovak government's resolution on the proposed Fundamental Objectives and Principles of the Slovak Republic's National Security (NRSR F).

That the traditional understanding of national interests has been replaced by a new one can be seen in the effort to at least nominally shift toward a civil perception of the state's interests by adopting a Western European understanding of concepts such as the state and nation, resulting in a new foreign policy that also takes ethical values into consideration. Such a foreign policy emphasizes the importance of international cooperation, rights, morality, and multilateralism while also not ruling out the use of force if it can ensure security and the protection of human rights and the people's needs. However, the majority of states pursue a pragmatic foreign policy, as pointed out by Šárka Waisová, among others (Waisová 2011, 10, 27-28, 31). In consequence, they defend and safeguard their state's interests even when they run counter to the objectives of the institutions of which they form a part, as is the case with Slovakia's or Hungary's migration policy and attitude toward migration, compared with that of the EU and Germany. In their 1998 program, the SNS called attention to the fact that national interests can be contrary to "*panhuman interests*" (SNS 1998, 31).

Small states can only pursue their interests by supporting soft power (Waisová 2011, 13). When defining its state interests, the historical experience of a country plays an important role as well. In the SNS's 1998 program, a section dedicated to Slovakia's national interests emphasized the need to "*respect the geographical position of the state [and its] historical national objectives*" (SNS 1998, 32), and to clarify their relations with the centers of power. By referring to historical facts, their arguments supported the promoted interests of the state and provided an explanation for its attitude to certain issues. In the 1990s, the position and rights of minorities was a much-discussed topic in European politics, the main question being whether to apply collective or individual rights.

Jozef Moravčík, the Slovak Minister of Foreign Affairs, justified the rejection of collective rights on 2 February 1994 to the members of the National Council of the Slovak Republic by saying that, for a unifying Europe, applying the principle of multiethnicity is preferable to "*creating ethnically compact units*" (NRSR 1994, 452). In his defense of individual rights, Josef Zieleniec, the Czech

Minister of Foreign Affairs, argued using historical experience. At the World Conference on Human Rights on 15 June 1993 in Vienna, he reminded the participants of the crimes that had been committed in the name of collective rights and which violated the *"fundamental rights of individuals and groups"* (MZV ČR 1993, 475). In their program of 26 October 1996, the MOS advocated for the application of collective rights in the case of national minorities, arguing, among other reasons, that the two world wars "proved that nation states do not create a suitable framework for the further development of mankind," which is why they support the creation of *"bigger units"* (MOS, 1).

In the plenary session of the National Council of the Slovak Republic on 2 February 1994, Ján Čarnogurský used a historical argument in favor of establishing closer cooperation between the Central European states, as the conditions had been ripe for it since 1990 (NRSR 1994, 474). We can also regard a country's traditions as part of its historical experience, since these also influence its foreign policy and interests (Waisová 2011, 14-16). Taking into consideration historical facts also affects the approval and the subsequent pursuit of a state's objectives (Eichler 2010, 58). This is rather problematic in Slovakia's case as the country tends to reject any form of continuity, and, besides selectively choosing its historical figures related to its foreign policy, there is always the temptation of ever-popular "new beginnings."

Political parties form an important part of a pluralistic political system. They should actively participate in the formulation and promotion of the state's active foreign policy and defend its interests according to their capacities. In the majority of cases, political parties pay very little attention to foreign policy, except when they can use it in an internal political battle. Relevant political parties can affect foreign policy mostly through their MPs in the state legislature and nowadays also through their MEPs in the European Parliament. Nevertheless, the state remains the most important subject in international politics. The interconnectedness of states is becoming increasingly strong, and consequently states' position on the international scene is changing as well. Rather than promoting their interests individually, countries have started to advance them collectively, for example within the V4 or the EU. Besides state interests, other group interests are also pursued, creating transnational relations between various actors which weaken the state's dominant role in international politics and shatter the basic theoretical framework of realism and neorealism (Císař, Fiala 2004, 11-13; Pšeja 2005). The integration of states and the huge number of international treaties are also changing the foreign policy priorities and interests of states, the latter being promoted less and less to the detriment of other states' interests. Countries currently cannot pursue traditional *realpolitik*, since they try to attain their objectives by other means than traditional power: namely, the application of the principles of soft power (Waisová 2011, 26). This means, among other things, that Slovakia provides assistance abroad, which projects a positive image of the state while allowing the country to reinforce or modify its interests (Profant 2015, 27).

Until 1998 the majority of Slovak political parties attached more importance to defeating Vladimír Mečiar and his HZDS than to clearly defining Slovakia's interests. There was a strong fear of nationalism in the country, which is probably one of the reasons why political parties avoided using the terms "national interests" and/or "state interest" and preferred the expression "support for Slovakia's integration interests." The SNS's pre-election program of 1992 says that they *"steadfastly and indiscriminately pursue the nationwide objectives and interests of every Slovak citizen"* (SNS 1992, 1). In their 1994 program, they were trying to persuade citizens that they will promote Slovakia's national state interests "by means of serious active diplomacy" (SNS 1994, 34). The HZDS pre-election promises in 1994 talked about the country's national and state interests, which should be defended by means of diplomatic service and the promotion of Slovak culture abroad (HZDS A, 124, 81). The KDH promised voters to use their international contacts to benefit Slovakia (KDH 1994). In their 1994 pre-election program, the political movement Spolužitie/Együttélés ("Coexistence") stressed the importance of *"synchronizing the (foreign) political steps of the Hungarian national communities scattered across different Central European states"* (Együttélés 1994, 37).

Before the parliamentary elections of 1998, the SDĽ declared to their members, supporters, and voters at their fifth congress that they would actively promote the country's national state interests by using all their foreign contacts (SDĽ, 22). The Demokratická strana ("Democratic Party," DS) drew attention to the necessity to clearly define Slovakia's state interests (DS 1998). According to the SDK's program, state interests should be based on freedom, security, and prosperity (SDK, 107). The Strana občianskeho porozumenia ("Party of Civic Understanding," SOP) thought that Slovakia's main state political interest was its integration into Euro-Atlantic structures (SOP 1998). The SNS's 1998 program also emphasized the importance of promoting the country's national interests while adding that the priorities of other states need to be taken into consideration as well (SNS 1998, 31). In their pre-election program, the HZDS also talked about completing Slovakia's Euro-Atlantic integration in order to defend the country's "*geopolitical state interests*" (HZDS B, 57).

The 2002 pre-election programs of parties such as the HZDS, KDH, and SMER-SD all talked about "national state interests." SMER-SD also used terms like "state political interests" and "strategic national interests." The SDKÚ, SNS, and OKS mentioned "Slovak national interests," or just plain "national interests." These expressions gradually entered into the vocabulary of political parties, as evidenced by their pre-election material of 2006. The SNS used several terms, such as "state political interests," "national state interests" and "national interests." The Slobodné fórum ("Free Forum," SF) talked not only about "state interests" but also about "legitimate interests" and "our interests." The materials of the SNS, KDH, OKS, and the Aliancia nového občana ("Alliance of the New Citizen," ANO) all discussed "national interests." At the time, the expression "national state interests" was preferred by the HZDS, the Hnutie za demokraciu ("Movement for Democracy," HZD) and SMER-SD. The Slovenská kresťanská demokratická únia—Demokratická strana ("Slovak Democratic and Christian Union—Democratic Party," SDKÚ-DS) talked about safeguarding "the interests of the Slovak Republic."

The term "national state interest" was widely used by the HZDS in their pre-European Parliament election campaign in 2009, which also emphasized that the EU must be more active in safeguarding its interests. SMER-SD was trying to convince voters that they were the only party protecting "Slovakia's interests" in Europe. In their pre-election program, the KDH devoted an entire section to "national interests." Sloboda a solidarita ("Freedom and Solidarity," SaS) believed that Slovak politicians were not and are still not ready to defend the country's interests in the EU. They also expressed doubts regarding the competency of politicians in matters of the economy, claiming that their "attitudes are amateurish and superficial." During the next European elections in 2014, the SaS continued to criticize Slovakia's lack of conception regarding its long-term interests in the EU.

During the pre-election period of 2010, political parties used different terms to name the country's interests again. The SNS talked about "national interests," "national state interests," and even "state political interests." The OKS insisted on the promotion of the country's "national interests." SMER-SD promised to safeguard Slovakia's "national," "state," and "national state interests." SDKÚ-DS talked about "the interests of our homeland," while the KDH declared that it was promoting "the interests of the Slovak Republic" in the EU. Political parties mainly used the expression "interests," but what they usually meant was general welfare. However, they could not make use of this topic in their scramble for votes. Not only before the 2010 elections but already in 2006 parties such as the OKS, SDKÚ, and SNS tried to discuss what was meant by public interests. Before the elections of 2012, the KDH, SDKÚ-DS, and SaS all declared that they were protecting the "interests of Slovakia." SMER-SD used the terms "national interests" and "state interests," while the SNS presented themselves as the only political power capable of promoting "the interests of Slovakia and its citizens." In their pre-election campaign in 2016, the SNS paid the most attention to the "national," "state," "national state," and other interests of the Slovak Republic. In their program, the party promised to adopt "*a constitutional law for the national interests of the Slovak nation and the state interests of the Slovak*

Republic" (SNS 2015a, 7). The majority of the political candidates claimed to promote "the interests of the Slovak Republic," but not all of them talked about the "national interests," "state interests," or "national state interest" of "Slovakia" or "the Slovak Republic."

The main goal of most of the political parties in Slovakia was to secure the country's membership in the EU and NATO, which was also what the citizens expected. At the time, politicians and citizens interpreted state interests in the same way.[42] However, even though Slovakia managed to integrate into Euro-Atlantic structures, it did not lead to further discussions about the country's societal development or the position it should occupy in Europe and in the world. What is missing is a clearly defined common interest — not only public but of any kind — and therefore a policy of disinterest is being promoted; that is, the use of public resources for individual objectives, which results in the public's total lack of interest in politics (Drulák 2010, 7; Krpec 2009, 76-77; Novosád 2010, 30). Relevant political parties claimed to agree in matters of international politics even after Slovakia joined the EU. The successful integration created the illusion that the country was now in an ideal environment, while the security, economic, and political threats that Slovakia had to face more and more frequently were ignored. The Ukrainian crisis put an end to this consensus, something also mentioned in the Foreign and European Policy Tasks of the Slovak Republic for 2015 (*Zameranie zahraničnej a európskej politiky Slovenskej republiky na rok 2015*) document (MZVaEZ SR 2015). Slovakia's representatives demanded the preservation of Ukraine's territorial integrity. Slovakia has long expressed a foreign policy interest in the Western Balkans, which accords with the interests of the EU and NATO (Weiss 2009, 386-394). Besides the above-mentioned security issues, in recent years Slovakia has also declared the need for energy security, the promotion of economic diplomacy, and the enhancement of cultural and public diplomacy.

---

42 Príloha II. Konkretizácia hlavných zámerov Programového vyhlásenia vlády SR na rok 1998 v podmienkach rezortu MZV SR. In: Správa o plnení úloh zahraničnej politiky a zameranie úloh zahraničnej politiky Slovenskej republiky 1997–1998, 49.

A country's interests—regardless of whether we call them state, national, national state, or something else—are not constant despite the claims that they cannot be modified because they represent the citizens' interests (OKS 2002, 26). Their definition is strongly influenced by politicians and must be in some conformity with the interests of other states. Naturally, it also depends on the position of the particular political party; that is, whether it is a ruling party, an opposition party, or an extra-parliamentary one. However, the state agenda is not always that up-to-date, which is well exemplified by party materials which may refer to the state's interests by using different terms. Regardless of which political parties form the governing coalition, there has been no meaningful discussion about Slovakia's state interests since 1993 (Marušiak 2013). If politicians need to call attention to themselves, they tend to bandy about this topic, as calling your opponent an enemy of the state or the nation is the easiest thing to do. It is not likely to solve the situation, and it reinforces the country's negative image abroad, something the majority of politicians are constantly complaining about. In 1992 politicians were already trying to improve the negative image of Slovakia (Šebesta, Roth 2016, 153),[43] something they hoped to achieve by such things as administrative acts. In the HZDS's pre-election material of 1994, the party tried to convince voters that this can be achieved with an improved diplomacy whose priority should be "*to promote and safeguard Slovakia's national and state interests*" and "*to create a truthful and positive image of Slovakia abroad*" (HZDS A, 125). They did not manage to accomplish this objective, as prior to the following elections they again promised to "*pay special attention to significantly improve the reputation of the Slovak Republic abroad*" (HZDS B, 58). A concern with Slovakia's image appears not only in political materials but also in government policy statements. The policy statement of Vladimír Mečiar's second government talked about creating conditions that would project a "truthful, non-distorted image of Slovakia and its citizens"

---

43   Suverénne európske Slovensko. Nad dielom a činnosťou Svetoslava Bombíka. Bratislava: vydavateľstvo SAV -ÚPV SAV 2016, p. 153. Editors: Štefan Šebesta—Viliam Roth.

abroad (Vláda SR 1992, 33). The policy statement of Robert Fico's second government of May 2012 also mentioned the need to improve Slovakia's image abroad (Vláda SR 2012). According to Fico, journalists from *"the tabloids, the daily SME, the daily N, Slovak Television and Slovak Radio"* were the ones responsible for Slovakia's negative image; he even called them *"dirty anti-Slovak prostitutes."*[44] He believes that the above-mentioned media *"intentionally damage the interests of the Slovak Republic."*[45]

Regardless of whether we study Slovakia's pre-integration or the post-integration period, it is impossible to clearly determine whether the expressions "national interest" and "state interest" are more frequently used by right-wing or left-wing politicians. It is also problematic to decide which is preferred by conservative and which by progressive politicians. The SNS used the expressions "national interest" and "state interest" when they formed part of the government and were in the opposition. The same applies to SMER-SD, except for the Slovak government's manifesto for 2016 to 2020, which is rather brief. They tried to present themselves as the only governmental authority that truly defended Slovakia's state interests, especially regarding the migrant crisis. The majority of right-wing political parties used expressions such as "national" or "state interests" in order to persuade citizens that they were the real defenders of the state. Based on Petr Kratochvíl's previously mentioned observation, according to which the term "national interest" is more frequently used by conservative politicians, we can say that Slovakia's relevant political scene is predominantly conservative. Whether these different forms of conservatism — including the one represented by some of the politicians of SMER-SD — are really compatible with Western European ones would require to be further analyzed.

As far as the external and internal policies of a state are concerned, whether one uses the terms "state interest," "national interest," or "national state interest" is not the most important

---

44   http://domov.sme.sk/c/20394032/robert-fico-tvrdi-ze-nic-nebolo-predrazene-miroslav-lajcak-ma-jeho-doveru.html.
45   http://spravy.pravda.sk/domace/clanok/412101-fico-podozrenia-o-predsednictve-v-rade-eu-su-nezmyselne-a-vymyslene/.

issue. According to Ján Čarnogurský, state interests should represent a society-wide consensus concerning matters such as a balanced state economy, compliance with EU rules, the prevention of corruption, border protection, and state security (Áno 2015, 163). Slovakia's interests and strategic objectives should match those represented by the EU. In the pursuit of a common objective, individual interests must be pushed aside, while cooperation between the European and state institutions should be enhanced.

5. Migration Policy as National Interest

Radoslav Štefančík

Although the debate on international migration had been kept on hold for several years, with the refugee crisis that hit Europe in 2015 it resurfaced again even in countries such as Slovakia, which, unlike Western European states, was not faced with thousands of asylum-seeking migrants. In spite of this, international migration became one of the main topics of the pre-election discussion before the 2016 parliamentary elections in Slovakia. Instead of searching for constructive solutions to resolve this problem, representatives of the political elite made international migration out to be a threat to the country's national security and identity, with the quota system proposed by some of the EU member states then being seen as a threat to Slovakia's interests. All of this was despite the fact that Slovakia was far from being a sought-after destination for African or Middle Eastern refugees.

However, it was high time for Slovakia to finally address the question of international migration. In recent years, migration policy has become a priority for every economically strong and modern state, all of which now face the phenomenon of international migration (Liďák 2016). Since international migration entails entering or exiting the territory of a sovereign nation, migration policy should be one of the priority areas on every government's agenda. This topic has gained prominence especially in destination countries as international migration affects the constitutional framework of nations (Scholz 2011). Migration policy concerns a country's sovereignty—as modifying the laws on entering or exiting a nation or granting long-term residency to foreigners is only a part of the issue—and affects the question of forming a society in the territory of a sovereign state. Therefore, it is not simply about the formal adjustment of the conditions for entering and moving around the territory of a nation or the conditions for obtaining citizenship. When developing a migration policy, its societal impact must also be taken into consideration.

Slovakia's discussion of international migration was mainly characterized by a gradual semantic shift of the term "migrant." The originally neutral expression, denoting a person who moves from one place to another in order to settle down for a longer period, usually at least for a year, has gained a negative connotation in public debates. In the space of a few months, "migrant" started to designate a person who presented a threat to Slovakia's national interests, regardless of what motivated them to leave their country of origin. This is why it is important to emphasize that the terms used to discuss and analyze international migration should be interpreted correctly. We can assume—and Western Europe confirms this hypothesis—that international migration does not only have a negative impact on a nation's interests but also a positive one; one could even argue that immigration has helped to solve the problem of population decline, which has negatively affected the overall development of national economies.

It is more than obvious that the study of international migration has an interdisciplinary character, as it can be analyzed from the point of view of an economist, a demographer, a sociologist, a geographer, an ethnologist, and an expert on international and domestic law. In this chapter, we will mostly look at its political dimension; particularly the effect international migration has on the interests of a nation. According to James F. Hollifield, the study of international migration and its influence on nations as a separate field of social scientific research should focus on three main topics. The first concerns border control—that is, the nation's responsibility to set the requirements for entering and exiting its territory—and questions regarding the residence of foreigners. The second topic concerns international relations—that is, the influence of international migration on the sovereignty and security of nations, and the link between international migration and foreign policy. The third topic deals with the question of integrating migrants, especially the effect of migration on the rules of granting citizenship, political behavior, and public policy. This means studying the impact of migration on the political behavior of both the autochthonous and the allochthonous population, as the rising number of foreigners in the country could affect the voting behavior and value system of the domestic population, which might choose to support more radical political parties (Hollifield 2000, 137-185).

In this chapter, we will focus mainly on the first and the third topics, i.e., the circumstances defining a nation's approach to international migration. We will aim to reveal which factors play the biggest role in the creation of national immigration policies and which factors most determine the formation of integration policies. Throughout the text, we will take special care not to use the terms "immigration policy" and "integration policy" interchangeably with the vaguer "migration policy," as such an erroneous analysis could result in further misinterpretations. Even with a restrictive immigration policy, the number of foreigners in a country might grow; therefore, national governments should pay attention to their integration. If they neglect their integration policy, an increasing number of immigrants might lead in time to problems that would be very difficult to tackle.

Seeing the public debate on migration in Slovakia since the beginning of the refugee crisis in the spring of 2015, we could make the initial observation that many Slovak politicians interpret migration policy—at least publicly—chiefly as a policy regarding entry into the territory of a nation and maybe as border control to prevent illegal immigration (mainly of refugees from Africa and Asia). However, such an interpretation is extremely narrow, since the term "migration policy" has a far broader meaning. It also denotes the set of arrangements a state makes to manage migration matters: it regulates the admission of foreigners into its territory, determines the conditions of their stay, and arranges their integration into society. It is thus evident that migration policy is not only about crossing borders and residing in the territory of another state; it also concerns the integration of immigrants into the host society and ultimately deals with the reactions of the resident population. The events following the 2015 migration wave demonstrate that public opinion is of key importance not only when it comes to developing national migration policies, but also transnational ones.

The American political scientist Gary P. Freeman defines migration policy as *"state efforts to regulate and control entry into the national territory and to stipulate conditions of residence of persons seeking permanent settlement, temporary work or political asylum"* (Freeman 1992, 1145). However, this definition is itself insufficient, as it only takes into account the one-way movement of citizens; migration policy can also include return policy, i.e., incentives to motivate migrant workers to return to their country of origin. European states developed return policies after the onset of the global economic crisis in the autumn of 2008, when governments started to think about restricting labor migration and tried to motivate settled foreigners to return to their home country.

Essentially, migration policy is an important part of politics and affects the very sovereignty of nations (Štefančík 2011). Especially after the terrorist attacks committed by Islamic fundamentalists on civilian targets in the United States and Europe, a considerable part of the population has tended to see migrants as a danger to their country's internal and external security. This feeling of danger, often intentionally aroused by the domestic political elite (Lenč 2011), might intensify if some of the decision-making competencies of nations are transferred to transnational institutions, meaning that governments cannot independently regulate the migratory movements in their territories. This was very strongly felt by the V4 states during the discussions on refugee quotas in 2015 and 2016, which aimed to set a mandatory minimum number of African and Asian refugees for every EU member state to take in. These mandatory quotas, together with the issue of granting financial assistance to Greece, were some of the main points of criticism of those opposed to ongoing European integration, which contributed to the deterioration of Slovakia's long positive relationship with the EU. Because of the resistance of the Central European governments, the refugee quota scheme was eventually scrapped. However, this was not a Central European victory; after all, the quota system was meant to be introduced because Central European governments had refused to show solidarity with the states located at the Schengen border responsible for asylum procedures according to the Dublin Regulation. Since it was clear that neither Italy nor Hungary could cope with the huge influx of immigrants and process their asylum petitions in due time while maintaining humane conditions, some governments decided to solve these problems by establishing a quota system. Nevertheless, some of the countries were strongly against it, including, paradoxically, Hungary, which could have gained more by it than it would have lost.

As mentioned above, the term "migration policy" is used to describe three areas of international migration: immigration, asylum policy, and the integration of immigrants. However, some authors exclude asylum policy from this definition and regard it as a separate category. For example, the German author Jürgen Fijalkowski believes that migration policy is an umbrella term for "immigration policy and integration policy" and puts them both on the same level (Fijalkowski 1997). In terms of immigration policy, the governments of host countries consider questions such as who to let into the country, for what purpose, and for how long in the context of integration policy. They will ask themselves how to treat those who have decided to settle in their territory and how they will gradually integrate them into the domestic society in spite of their cultural differences.

Depending on whether the state creates conditions for welcoming more migrants or takes measures to decrease the number of long-term foreign residents in its sovereign territory, two ideal types of immigration policy can be distinguished: liberal and restrictive. According to the liberal concept, a state is accommodating to migrants as it recognizes their economic and demographic potential and organizes programs to recruit a foreign labor force. On the other hand, a state pursuing a restrictive immigration policy will curb the number of migrants entering its sovereign territory and will support their return to their homeland. In some cases, it might adopt a laxer attitude and grant some concessions. For instance, in its asylum policy it might facilitate the provision of protection for citizens from certain countries; in its immigration policy, it may authorize the issue of work permits for selected professional groups. Since migration policy is a highly complex system of multiple subpolicies (Wendekamm 2015), its division may not be this straightforward. A state might pursue a looser immigration policy by inviting foreigners to fill the labor shortage in certain sectors while also having a much stricter asylum policy that only approves a limited number of asylum applications.

The creation of a nation's migration policy might be affected by various economic, cultural, demographic, and political interests. It is evident that since the second half of the twentieth century states have tried to solve their economic and to some extent their demographic problems by means of international migration. With the rise of the median age, a person's median post-productive period also increases, meaning that the cost of maintaining the pension system in balance increases. If a large number of young people who acquired education in their home country decide to move to another country and settle there, the country of origin suffers economic losses, as it provided these young people with free pre-primary, primary, secondary, and possibly even tertiary education; having completed their highest level of education, young people still decide to move abroad. There are several ways to tackle these economic and demographic problems to ensure the sustainability of economic growth, and regulated immigration is one of them.

Let as assume that there are two sovereign countries with a similar economic and demographic situation: the first pursues a liberal migration policy, while the second is much more restrictive. Why is that? To answer this question, we need to look at several other factors that influence a country's migration policy.

The Czech authors Andrea Baršová and Pavel Barša say that factors affecting the migration policy of a particular nation can be found in the historical process of its formation and are based on two principles: nationalism and the universalism of human rights. While the first principle seeks the welfare of the collective entity, the second depends on respecting the rights of each individual (Baršová, Barša 2005). These principles are therefore contradictory. Nationalism strives to ensure the well-being of a particular nation, while universalism consists in respecting the rights of every human being, regardless of their nationality. A country based on nationalism is particularist, and its primary objective is to protect the nation; on the other hand, a liberal country based on universalism aims to protect the rights of every person, regardless of nationality. Baršová and Barša believe this contradiction between nationalism and universalism is one of the factors that contribute to the character of a particular migration policy. Depending on which perspective prevails, a country can adopt an open or a closed attitude toward immigrants. Western European states usually balance between the two principles.

Baršová and Barša further expanded this theory by differentiating between four types of migration policies, depending on which principle prevails and what they are based on: libertarianism, liberalism, communitarianism, and realism. In a libertarian state, freedom of movement is among the core values belonging to every individual, seen as part of their right to property. Libertarians believe that moving from one country to another should not be hindered by obstacles. At the same time, the arrival of more people is expected; therefore, citizens do not interfere with their right to freedom of movement. On the other hand, a liberal state adopts a different approach to individuals where their rights are concerned. It assumes that all have the same rights, but it gives priority to the members of its own community. Only after securing the rights of its own citizens will a liberal state become welcoming to foreigners as well (Štefančík 2011).

In his essay *The Politics of Recognition*, Charles Taylor also differentiates between two approaches to citizens' rights. His criticism is aimed at the interpretation of liberalism as a movement that treats all people equally and forgets about the distinctive features of individuals. Taylor believes that this respect for people's distinctiveness is the prerequisite for protecting the identity of members of other cultures in a multicultural society. According to Taylor, society can only be liberal "provided it is also capable of respecting diversity, especially when dealing with those who do not share its common goals, and provided it can offer adequate safeguards for fundamental rights" (Taylor 2001). An important prerequisite for accepting the diversity of another culture lies in getting to know its values, meaning that we should not see it through the prism of our usual value stereotypes but from the point of view of its own values. Therefore, in Charles Taylor's interpretation, a conflict occurs not only between those defending the protection of human rights on one hand and those advocating the universalistic principle of equality on the other; it also occurs when "correctly" defining the essence of liberal principles. Relying on Steven Lukes, Jürgen Mackert further examines this conflict by distinguishing between two principles: "the politics of equal dignity" and "the politics of recognition." Essentially, both these terms denote the egalitarian normative principles of political morality based on the assumption that the state regards all residents as equals. However, both principles interpret this hypothesis differently. The politics of equal dignity, as an abstract and unbiased principle that disregards differences, calls for treating all people as equals and respecting their individual notions of a good life equally. This principle has several consequences: (1) no one can be forced to pursue a particular form of life; (2) the neutrality of a state must be preserved, and its politics cannot be justified by saying that it prefers a particular form of good life; (3) individuals cannot be discriminated against because of their different lifestyle choices; (4) the impartial evaluation of public decisions must be preserved and be free from particular interests; and (5) this principle entails an individualistic principle, meaning that it converts the individual into an addressee of politics. On the other hand, the politics of recognition is a less abstract and more biased principle which pays attention to differences, focusing especially on the identity of an individual or a group. It does not matter what connects people together; what matters are their differences, which are of decisive importance. Similarly to the previous principle, this also has some consequences: (1) it is also characterized by a lack of coercion—not because coercion would curb one's autonomy but because it suppresses one's authenticity, i.e., the particularistic values of a group; (2) it refuses the principle of an impartial evaluation of actions and denies the possibility of evaluations and explanations based on differences; (3) the interests of disadvantaged minorities can only be safeguarded and promoted by positive discrimination; (4) the principle of bias must be preserved; and (5) this principle is not individualistic as long as individuals see themselves as members of a particular community which possesses collective traits (Mackert 2006).

Unlike the first two types of states that are based on liberalism, a community state prioritizes the common good of a nation over that of individuals (Štefančík 2011). The essence of communitarian thinking lies in seeing a particular community as a community of values that should guide people. A society consisting of individuals is only cohesive when they form an integral part of it. This is why in some cases the collective interests of a community are preferred to the interests of individuals (Neubert, Roth, Yildiz 2002). An individual can only develop through a voluntarily created society, but they must be part of the nation. A common culture, language, and common religious beliefs are some of the attributes that help a nation's future survival. Deviating from customary behavior could lead to a society's disorientation. The relationship between the members of a society should not only rest on a legal basis but more importantly on practicing common values (Neubert, Roth, Yildiz 2002, 11-12). According to communitarianist thinking, a society has no obligations to members of other nations. Aid is only provided when absolutely necessary. Where international migration is concerned, communitarianism means adopting an open attitude only to those immigrants who were forced to flee because of natural catastrophes, conflicts, or terrorism. Finally, similarly to communitarianism, realism also prioritizes the nation's interests over those of individuals. The difference is that the realistic approach does not aim to achieve the common good of a society, but to ensure order and security. Once they are established, only then can the society make sure that the general humanitarian principles are respected; however, the nation's interest is the main priority. Migrants are only given aid if it benefits the nation, such as in the case of a labor shortage (Baršová, Barša 2005).

Another factor influencing a country's attitude to immigration lies in its historical development (Štefančík 2011). We can assume that nations whose historical development was characterized by ceaseless immigration would be much more welcoming to migrants than nations whose history was not much defined by migration. While studying various migration policies, Baršová and Barša looked at a nation's self-image, which was formed during the creation of the nation, and alongside its national identity they juxtaposed its current government's attitudes regarding immigration policy and whether its approach was open or closed. However, this model does not have a universal character; it merely reflects the reality of a single historical period. Based on the different way nations were formed, they created a typology of national identities. Their model relies on two sets of opposites. The first is based on the opposition between a nation of "immigrant-settlers" and a nation of "native-settlers": i.e., between an *exogenous* and an *endogenous* nation. The second opposition is that between a *civil* nation and an *ethnic* one (Baršová, Barša 2005).

In the case of a nation of immigrant-settlers, the society's creation depended on migration and the conquering of new territories by members of other states; such societies are characterized by a more open attitude to immigrants, whom the residents already regard as future fellow citizens. In the second case, the nation consists of the descendants of the original settlers of the area who have been living on that particular territory for centuries without any or very little experience of migration.

According to Baršová and Barša, in addition to the way the native population formed, the character of belonging to the state-building nation also affects the development of a migration policy. Therefore, there are two opposing types of nations: ethnic nations and civil nations. In ethnic nations, belonging is determined by the criterion of consanguinity. In such states, citizenship is or was granted based on kinship; that is, being descended from a parent who is or was a citizen of the state (the principle of *jus sanguinis*). On the other hand, civil nations regard belonging as referring to the institutions of a particular state. Citizenship is granted according to the place of birth (the principle of *jus soli*). Based on these criteria, Baršová and Barša created four models of national identity, assigning seven states to them depending on their historical development (see Table 1).

Table 1: Four Models of National Identity

	Nation of immigrant-settlers	Nation of native-settlers
Civil nation	USA, Canada, Australia	France, Great Britain
Ethnic nation	Israel	Germany

Source: Baršová, Barša 2005, 31.

The table shows that the biggest contrast is between Germany (an ethnic nation of native-settlers with a closed immigration policy) and the USA, Canada, and Australia (civil nations of immigrant-settlers with an open multiculturalist policy). As a nation of native-settlers, the French are guided by the principle of universalism, whose roots reach back to the French Revolution. Their condition to openly admitting foreigners is that the latter accept the French national culture. Meanwhile, even though Great Britain is also a nation of native-settlers and despite its open attitude to foreigners, its immigration policy belongs to a different category.

International migration is a fairly complicated phenomenon, and if we focused solely on the two above-mentioned aspects, we would not be able to see its other facets. The model created by Ursula Birsl et al. presents the complexity of migration policy-making rather aptly (see Diagram 1). According to this model, at the core of migration policy is entry into the territory of a particular nation and its political sphere, which depends on the motives and interests of five sectors of public policy: labor market policy, economic policy, internal policy, foreign policy, and security policy. These interests are surrounded by several political and cultural factors, including the public debate on immigration and asylum policy, political discussions, and public attitudes. Finally, the outer square is put in the historically determined migration system of the target states (Birsl et al. 2003). In the past, European states were characterized by different migration systems based on their different relations with the countries of origin and destination which were determined, for example, by their colonial and post-colonial histories or their experiences with exile and immigration as a result of the war and Nazism. However, due to the development of economy and labor shortages, they had to recruit a cheap third-country labor force, leading to the previously diverse Western European migration systems starting to grow more and more similar in their character. This suggests that if international organizations pressure countries into closer cooperation, the nation will be the last authority to decide on the final form of its migration policy.

Diagram 1: The Migration Policy of Nationals

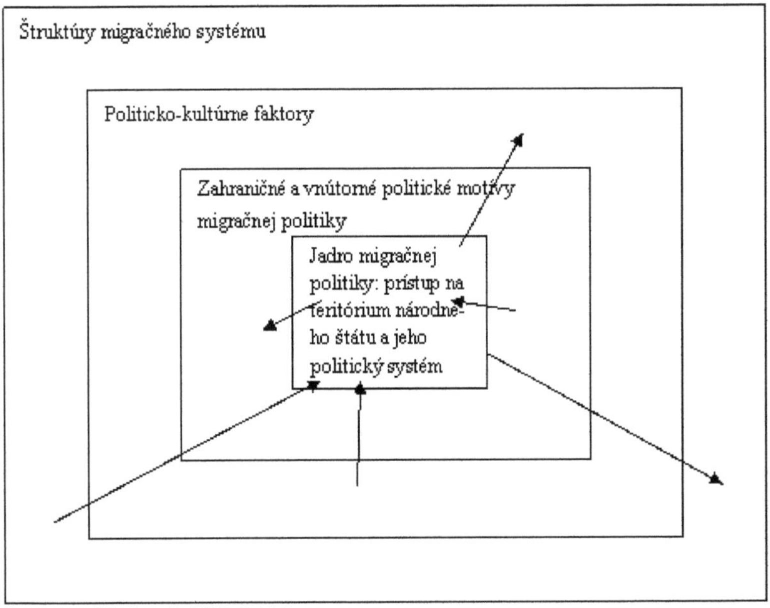

Štruktúry migračného systému

Politicko-kultúrne faktory

Zahraničné a vnútorné politické motívy migračnej politiky

Jadro migračnej politiky: prístup na teritórium národného štátu a jeho politický systém

Source: Birsl et al. 2003, 35-36.

The first sub-policy of migration policy is immigration policy, which concerns the arrival of foreigners in the territory of a nation. It includes all measures regulating the entry into the country, the length of stay, and the legal status of the foreigner in the host country (Vogel 1994). It can be assumed that for economic and demographic reasons, such a liberal immigration policy will be pursued mainly by traditional immigrant countries. States facing problematic demographic trends are not able to secure the natural growth of their population or sustainable economic development. Following a welcoming immigration policy allows them to address their own problems as well.

The second half of the twentieth century was characterized by two types of migration policy. By recruiting foreign workers, nations tried to tackle their own economic and demographic problems, resulting in their immigration policies being predominantly liberal until the beginning of the 1970s. Then the outbreak of the economic crisis compelled governments to take measures to prevent further immigration. This period was marked by a certain paradox, which political scientists called the "gap hypothesis" (Kolb 2003, 13-38). The expression denotes the gap between a liberal and expansive immigration policy and the mostly negative attitude of the local population toward immigrants.

Gary P. Freeman's theory might provide an explanation for this phenomenon and suggests we look at international migration from three perspectives: interests, rights, and institutions (Freeman 2004). Political economy focuses mainly on interests, whose pursuit leads to a liberal and expansive immigration policy. This is mostly enforced by lobby groups, while the nation only acts as the executive body of efficiently organized interests. Freeman's theory is based on the assumption that policy measures provoke certain responses and create certain expectations in a society, which will then affect the next stage of the decision-making process. The decisive factor is the objective or subjective apportionment of the costs and revenues of a public policy that produces various reactions in political actors. Freeman argues that there is an empirical distribution of "concentrated benefits" and "diffuse costs," which forms the basis of so-called client politics. According to this theory, those who receive benefits from immigration have greater incentives to organize their interests toward legislative and executive bodies than those who bear its costs. Freeman believes that such actors promoting a liberal and expansive immigration policy mainly include business entities in certain economic sectors and ethnic groups who wish to expand their population in the target country. On the contrary, those who stand to lose are the ones who see immigrants as their competition in the labor or real estate markets. A large part of the population has to bear the diffuse costs that arise in consequence of liberalizing immigration policy since it is mostly financed from the state budget, i.e., with taxpayers' money. However, unlike the groups that benefit from migration, their interests are not sufficiently articulated. Therefore, immigration policy is only seen as an instrument to promote the interests of well-organized groups. Political actors are involved in the process of migration policy-making only to the extent that their involvement would not thwart their chances in the next election. This is why they favor the relevant interest organizations. When it comes to the creation of immigration policy, the nation only acts as a body that implements the interests of certain groups in society. Meanwhile, those opposed to such a liberal immigration policy do not have enough means to enforce their interests (Freeman 1995, 881-902).[46]

The second perspective focuses on human rights. Freeman's theory is based on Hollifield's analysis of the relationship between rights policy and immigration policy. He believes that immigration policy has found a favorable environment in liberal democracies because of their efforts to promote and enhance human rights, which states commit to by signing international treaties. Any effort to enforce a restrictive immigration policy is seen as a violation of human rights (Freeman 2004, 111-128). States are thus forced to assume a rather passive role, and their endeavors to meet the public's demand for introducing a more restrictive policy are significantly curtailed (Kolb 2003, 13-38). This is well illustrated by the rising number of immigrants in Western Europe during the 1980s and 1990s. The arrival of family members of settled foreigners was mainly restricted by the European Social Charter, whose Article 19, paragraph 6 presupposes the facilitation of the reunification of families when the family members live in different countries.

---

[46] FREEMAN, G. P. Modes of Immigration Politics in Liberal Democratic States. 1995, pp. 881-902.

Freeman's third perspective concerns the institutional aspect. His first two perspectives looked at the state as an actor dependent on the actions of other subjects, be they social groups or international organizations. However, the study of international migration has paid very little attention to the causal relationship between the institutional arrangement of a state and its immigration policy, especially if we expect a state's structure to affect both its border control policy and its immigration and integration policies.

According to Dita Vogel, nations have certain political tools that allow them to influence the character and intensity of immigration. Two of them are related to the entry conditions and therefore directly concern immigration policy, while the other four affect the status of immigrants.

- The first tool consists of defining categories of foreigners whom the state regards as preferable. This allows the state to determine who can enter its territory and settle down based on criteria such as the country of origin and the situation in the domestic labor market. In the second half of the twentieth century, historical and cultural aspects played a significant role in deciding who could enter a country. For example, states with an imperial past preferred to employ the residents of their former dependent territories because of their language knowledge. Other immigration tools at a state's disposal include:
- determining the maximum number of incoming foreigners
- determining the maximum period for which their presence in the target country is welcome, including the conditions for extending it
- defining conditions for granting long-term residence; for example, for the purpose of study or employment or by means of marriage
- determining the conditions governing the rights and obligations of immigrants
- determining the conditions for granting an immigrant the same rights and obligations as a local citizen: the acquisition of citizenship (Vogel 1994, 132-155)

Immigration policy is also affected by the obligations a state has because of its membership in various international organizations (e.g., belonging to the Schengen area), due to binding international treaties (e.g., family reunification of foreigners) (Seifert 2000), or the ability of companies to meet labor demands by employing local citizens.

Integration policy denotes a set of measures a state takes to successfully integrate and assimilate immigrants into the new environment. It consists of the creation of suitable conditions where housing, employment, career growth, further education, and retraining opportunities are concerned and allowing access to healthcare, social care, and other services provided by the state. After leaving their home country, immigrants are faced with new living conditions which put them at a disadvantage compared to the domestic population. Bargerová and Divinský define integration policy as "a long-term, multidimensional, and dynamic two-way process based on the mutual respect for the rights and obligations of immigrants as well as of the majority society" (Bargerová, Divinský 2008, 14). Integration policy should strive to integrate foreigners into society in such a way that after a certain time they will no longer depend on state support and will respect the host country's legal and political system, culture, customs, and traditions, and will be able to speak the official language spoken by the majority of the autochthonous population. That means that the successful integration of migrants requires the active participation of both sides. The state must create suitable conditions for accommodating the foreign population, but immigrants must strive to advance their integration by adopting or at least respecting the legal and cultural traditions of the host society.

One of the objectives of integration policy is the political integration of immigrants. According to Marco Martiniello, this consists of four dimensions. The first one concerns the rights the target country grants to immigrants. Therefore, the more rights they have, the more they are integrated into the new society. The second level has to do with the immigrants' identification with the receiving country: the more they identify with it, the more they are integrated. The third level consists of adopting the norms and values of the autochthonous society, and the fourth dimension involves political participation, mobilization, and representation. Martiniello interprets political participation as an active dimension of citizenship and as different ways of actively participating in the management of public affairs. Meanwhile, political mobilization is the process of creating a collective actor and a collective identity. Lastly, he sees political representation as the exercise of power through a group of people who were legitimized to rule as a consequence of free elections (Martiniello 2005).

Dieter Oberndörfer believes that the prime political objective of integrating immigrants into a democratic state is to achieve their identification *"with [the state's] political values, from the constitution through the legal order to the political institutions"* (Oberndörfer 2001, 11). However, he regards identification as an ideal objective since it can never be fully achieved—not only because of the immigrants but also because of the resident population. Its main prerequisite is that an autochthonous society legally guarantee civil, social, and cultural equality to immigrants. The attitudes of the citizens of the receiving country are thus a precondition for successful integration. Without it, we cannot expect immigrants to fully identify with the values and the legal and political order of the constitutional state. According to Oberndörfer, equal social and civil rights could be ensured by granting immigrants the same rights as those enjoyed by the resident population, whereas cultural equality could be achieved by allowing immigrants to preserve their cultural behavioral patterns in the target country in accordance with the principles of the rule of law (Oberndörfer 2011, 11).

In academic literature, we come across different classifications of Western European integration policies at the end of the twentieth century (Baršová, Barša 2005). Most of them are based on two or three basic models: the French assimilation model, the British (or Dutch) multiculturalism model, and the German model of social exclusion.

The assimilation model sees immigrants as equals to the members of the domestic society, provided that they adopt the cultural patterns of the host country. Assimilation is not an immediate process but consists of several stages. The ethnic exclusivist model relies on minimizing the migrants' contact with the members of the autochthonous society and regards migration as temporary. The minimal integration of migrants into the host society signifies that there is a higher probability of them returning to their home country. According to Baršová and Barša, Germany is a typical example of this model (Baršová, Barša 2005), even though the German political scientist Dietrich Thränhardt does not put Germany's integration policy in any of the generally recognized categories. Nevertheless, Thränhardt's description of the German attitude to migrants shows similarities with the Czech authors' analysis. Therefore, Germany is at the intersection between the assimilation and the multiculturalism models, something that, according to Thränhardt, reaches back to Herder's idea of preserving one's identity. A nation that applies this model does not seek the means to integrate foreigners into its domestic society as it assumes that migrants will eventually return to their country of origin. However, the second half of the twentieth century showed that this assumption rarely holds true (Thränhardt 2005).

The third model of integration is the multiculturalism one (this term is used in various contexts, often as a synonym for the harmonious coexistence of different cultures). It does not pressure immigrants into adopting the cultural behavioral patterns of the domestic society; on the contrary, it recognizes the legitimacy of different cultures and the equality of ethnic minorities. The state takes on the duties related to the integration of inhabitants while reflecting their different cultural and social backgrounds (Stýskalíková 2005). A nation that pursues a multiculturalism model strives to preserve original customs and traditions.

Since the 1990s, Baršová and Barša (2005) have been observing the convergence of these three integration models. However, this process does not only take place in countries that follow the European integration models (Germany, Great Britain, and France); it also characterizes the USA's multiculturalism model, especially in the wake of the 9/11 attacks. Though originally a nation of immigrants, US citizens are gradually turning into a nation of old residents from the seventeeth and eighteenth centuries whose culture must be accepted by immigrants. Hispanic immigration brought about the emergence of the so-called neonativist theory, which sees American identity as the exclusive national identity of the original English-speaking settlers. French assimilationism, British pluralism, and German ethnic exclusivism are progressively converging into a new model: a new concept of "assimilation" or civic integration, which leads to the creation of a new model of individual civic integration. According to Baršová and Barša, this concept requires immigrants to accept the policy framework of liberal society and is characterized by the state's non-interference with the immigrants' cultural identity (Baršová, Barša 2005). Baršová believes that this shift from multiculturalism to individual civic integration in Europe was not provoked by the far-right populists' anti-immigration propaganda. Rather, it is the result of *"the European societies' search for a civilizational and national identity, justice and security in a global era"* (Baršová, Barša 2005, 1). At the core of this new immigration policy lies the requirement of speaking the language of the domestic society and respecting its fundamental values and legal and cultural norms. This change was mainly occurred as a result of the activities of Islamic fundamentalists. Baršová therefore emphasizes that the reason why even such traditionally multicultural countries as the Netherlands, Great Britain and Sweden reassessed their migration policy was not Islam as such, but rather a particular group of religious fanatics who direct their activities against the West and its lifestyle as well as its political and economic dominance.

The Slovak Republic's migration policy is fundamentally different from the ones pursued by states with a long experience of international migration. The country's immigration policy leaves much to be desired, and its asylum policy has long been defined by its restrictive character, which also became apparent during the public debates about the adoption of the quota system that would have obliged Slovakia to take in a certain percentage of refugees.

It is important to note, however, that the topic of international migration was of little importance to the political elite (Billý 2012), and that the first discussions arose during the election campaign before the parliamentary election in March 2016 (Štefančík 2016). It is thus understandable that with the lack of interest on the part of the political elite as well as the public authorities, the integration of immigrants into Slovak society has received scant discussion. This is further proved by the fact that until May 2009 an obsolete integration policy created in 1996 had been in use and was not flexible enough to react to the rapidly changing situation. Since the Migration Office of the Slovak Republic ignored the question of integration, for a long time Slovakia did not have an institution to coordinate the actions of government authorities. Despite plans to create a common office with exclusive competence to deal with migration matters and the integration of immigrants in 2010, it still has not come to fruition; even though the number of migrants living in Slovakia is gradually increasing, it probably will not be created in the foreseeable future.

The steps taken by the Slovak public authorities are very different from the British multiculturalism model or the French republican policy of integration. Despite an initially proclaimed willingness on the part of government authorities to look at the integration of foreigners from a multicultural perspective, the actual measures the Slovak government has taken do not correspond to the principles of a multicultural society. However, this was only the results of an unsystematically processed concept of foreigner integration, as in 2009 the multicultural integration model was already considered outdated. Even if integration policy-makers were interested in implementing the multiculturalism concept, it could not succeed under current conditions in Slovakia. Government bodies did not take adequate steps to support the preservation and protection of the cultural diversity of the allochthonous communities, and Slovak citizens and the majority of the opinion leaders in the political elite are reluctant to accept the otherness of autochthonous minorities. It is somewhat positive that because of the negative demographic changes and workforce shortage in certain sectors of the national economy, there has been some talk about taking in immigrants; however, since 2015 this suggestion has been put forward much less frequently than before. This might be the result of the cautiousness of politicians, who do not want to stir up the hornet's nest of extremely negative public opinion regarding migrants.

Despite the current difficulties, we can assume that in the years to come the discussion around immigrants coming into Slovakia will gain momentum, and both the political elite and the general public could take greater interest in matters concerning international migration. The latter may present the public authorities responsible for the preparation and implementation of a Slovak integration policy with a considerable challenge. Slovakia's foreign-born population is much smaller than those in typical destination countries such as Switzerland, Germany, or France; even the Czech Republic has considerably larger immigrant numbers. Because of the country's small migrant community, the government is not forced to think much about their integration, unlike the authorities of these other states. By recognizing this problem in time and taking proper measures, the government would be able to anticipate the problems that go hand in hand with immigration and the integration of foreigners into a new political, social, and cultural environment.

The political, economic, and social integration of foreigners is one of the main tasks the governments of nation will have to deal with in the years to come. It is imperative that the political elite and the general public realize that international migration is a highly important phenomenon which cannot be ignored. What remains to be seen is how society will react to the further development of international migration. Only then can the public see migrants in a positive light: not as a threat to their sovereignty but rather as a realistic means to solve economic and demographic problems. Last but not least, we should not forget that immigrants also enrich the autochthonous culture provided that their traditions are not diametrically opposed to those of the host society. The successful integration of migrants requires the elimination of the sometimes latent and sometimes very open sentiments that one part of society displays toward certain ethnic groups. Both the Czech Republic and Slovakia need to address racist attitudes toward the Roma. Moreover, anti-Hungarian xenophobia must also be addressed in Slovakia. The concept of individual civic integration seems to be the most fitting choice for the successful integration of foreigners. However, its implementation should be preceded by a bilateral public discussion about which values should be recognized by both foreigners and the resident population in order to achieve the harmonious coexistence of people of different origins.

Although many EU countries tried to limit the influx of illegal migrants, the question remains whether the European community can reduce the numbers of migrants flowing into the western and now even the central regions of Europe given the economic and political attractiveness of the European Union as compared with the conflict-ridden, economically less developed areas of the world. The actions taken by the European Union reveal an intention to control cross-border migratory movements by joint decisions, although when it comes to their implementation, certain member states have different interpretations. Cooperation between the European states could be increased if, in addition to tackling illegal migration, they also demonstrated a willingness to participate in further European integration, put a stop to the abuse of their national social systems, enjoyed the advantages of common border protection, and mutually guaranteed assistance to one another by relieving the burden on the regions that are the main landing points for migrants.

The reluctance of nations to transfer their entire gamut of competencies concerning migration policy to international organizations is one of the obstacles to taking joint action. This unwillingness to cooperate is based on the belief that the cross-border movements of citizens do not directly affect them, along with the conviction that they have this area under control. The main impediment to cooperation lies in the traditional concept of the sovereign nation, which is built on the belief that despite the increasing processes of globalization and European integration the state remains the most important subject in the creation of public policy and that the primary objective of nations is to preserve their sovereignty. After all, migration is a phenomenon that equally affects the external and internal security of a country, its border control policy, and the composition and size of the population living in its territory (Heckmann, Tomei 1997).

Where the development of a joint EU asylum and immigration policy is concerned, we can observe two opposing tendencies: on one hand, communities show a certain willingness to create such a policy, while on the other nations keep hindering it because of their reluctance to give up their decision-making competencies in an area which they consider to be of vital interest. Europe needs migrants both as a workforce and as a means to address demographic problems. An unresolved issue regards who should decide about the total numbers of immigrants to be taken in and how they should be distributed across individual states. Immigration policy therefore continues to be in the hands of national cabinet members.

Nations are reluctant to give up their exclusive competencies and delegate them to supranational organizations, something that is also true of their immigration and integration policies, since immigrants strongly impact the design of domestic policies. Baršová also sees certain discrepancies in the current European migration policy. She believes that the community has the right to influence the character of immigration policy; it is, however, unclear to what extent it should define the conditions linked to access to the labor market, something that falls within the competence of nations (Baršová 2005, 1). Nations are able to agree on a common migration policy where illegal migration control, border control, and the prevention of asylum abuse are concerned; what remains problematic is determining how many rights foreigners should be given and how and to what extent they should be integrated into the autochthonous society. If the European Union decides to enhance its integration policy, it will most likely be based on the individual civic model.

The coordination of labor migration poses another obstacle to a common strategy. Such situations are typical in the European Union, which is now caught between matters of common interest and the interests of its sovereign member states. Last but not least, it will have to address the sentiments and opinions of the public as well. If the influence of far-right parties inciting animosity toward immigrants continues to grow in the member states, migration policy in all its complexity will become an ever more serious common concern. The willingness of the European Union to solve the problems of negative demographic trends and labor shortage in certain industries by means of immigration suggests that we can expect a much more active public debate to come.

6. The Importance of Political Culture for the Slovak National Interest in the Context of the Migration Crisis

Dirk Dalberg

Politicians and society in Slovakia are almost completely opposed to the admission of refugees from the Near and Middle East. When the EU decided to release a binding number of refugees to relieve other member states in the autumn of 2015, the outrage in Slovakia was great. The government of Slovakia brought an action against the decision to the European Court of Justice. The reasons behind the rejection of refugee admission and the fear of majorization are to be sought in the political culture, which reflects the historical experience of the Slovaks in the Habsburg Empire, their exposure to Czech and Soviet domination as well as conflicts with the Muslims at the time of the greatest expansion of the Ottoman Empire into Central Europe in the sixteenth and seventeenth centuries.

In 2015, millions of refugees from war- and crisis-affected areas attempted to reach the territory of European countries. Where in Germany, the fate of refugees was at the forefront of political and social debate for months, public opinion in Central and Eastern Europe was dominated by the fear of penetration by elements of a foreign culture an a strong resistance to the reception of refugees (Łoś, Kobierecka 2017).

Critical commentators such as the Polish historian Jan T. Gross noted that societies in Poland, Slovakia, the Czech Republic and Hungary proved to be *"intolerant, narrow-minded and xenophobic."*. They were *"incapable of recalling the spirit of solidarity that had led them to freedom a quarter of a century ago."* Meanwhile, in the aftermath of the fall of Communism, Central and Eastern European states proudly declared that they wanted to return to Europe and to share the common values of the continent. To this aim, they received substantial financial aid from the European Structural and

Cohesion Funds. Now, however, they were not ready to *"contribute in some way to resolving the biggest refugee crisis on European soil since the end of World War II."* What Gross found particularly shameful was the fact that it was the Czechs, Poles, Hungarians and Slovaks, i.e., the very same nations whose ancestors had massively emigrated to Western European countries and North America in order to escape *"material suffering and political persecution."*[47]

Slovakia

Most opinion-shaping media in Slovakia have long spoken in favor of admitting refugees/migrants.[48] In this context, they have criticized the hardline attitude of Prime Minister Robert Fico (Smer-SD), who has opposed the admission of refugees for some time. Fico has also been criticized for his attitude by the right-wing parties (Sieť, KDH, OĽaNO, Most-Híd) (Obšitník 2016). At the same time, however, these parties have also refused to accept refugees, despite their being generally critical of Fico's policies in their role as opposition. A rapid increase in the number of refugees in 2015, as well as the March 2016 parliamentary elections, led to a change in the position of the aforementioned opposition parties. Smer-SD, a social-democratic party which ruled single-handedly from 2012 onwards, made the issue of refugees the dominant narrative of the election campaign. Within its framework, Smer-SD presented national-populist views disapproving of migration. These attitudes were shared by representatives of the other parties (Obšitník 2016; Vlčej 2016, 168; Androvičová 2016 39-64; Bolečeková 2017, 209-211, 215-224).

In May 2015, the European Union for the first time decided to introduce mandatory quotas for all member states, a binding system for the admission of refugees. Under Article 78.3 of the

---

[47] Gross 2015, 41. In the year 2016, 146 asylum applications were filed in Slovakia. A year earlier, there were 330 applications and, in 2004, the figure stood at 11,395. In 2016, 167 people were granted asylum in Slovakia, 159 of them for humanitarian reasons (IOM 2018).

[48] In 2012, most asylum seekers came from Somalia (222). In 2013 and 2014, the largest number came from Afghanistan (109 and 93 respectively); in 2015, from Iraq (172); and in 2016 from Ukraine (25) (MVSR 2017).

Treaty on the Functioning of the European Union, 40,000 people from makeshift refugee camps in Italy (24,000) and Greece (16,000) as well as 20,000 other people from non-EU refugee camps were allocated to EU member states (European Commission 2015; Treaty EU 2012). This proposal was rejected by the European Parliament in June 2015.

After the number of people migrating to Europe increased rapidly in August and September 2015, on 14 September 2015, the Commission issued a proposal to relocate 160,000 refugees from the camps in Greece, Italy and Hungary, or, more precisely, 106,000 refugees from Greece and Italy. This only applied to the refugees coming from Syria, Iraq and Eritrea—the countries of origin of asylum seekers, i.e., those countries where their residents' asylum applications were approved in 75 percent of the cases.[49] The Justice and Home Affairs Council approved the quotas by a majority of votes on 21 September 2015. The interior ministers of the Czech Republic, Slovakia, Hungary and Romania voted against the resolution while the Finnish deputy abstained.[50]

Prime Minister Robert Fico said in this regard that the Slovak Republic generally did not rule out receiving refugees. His government only rejected the admission of those of Muslim confession, but was open to accepting refugees from Ukraine as well as those of Christian faith (Sulik 2015).

Ľuboš Blaha, a member of Fico's Smer-SD (Direction—Social Democracy) parliamentary group and Chair of the Parliamentary Committee on European Affairs, said that most refugees were not

---

49 Trauner 2016, 102. The Slovak Republic was supposed to accept 903 refugees, the government promised to receive another 40, and by 3 March 2017, 16 refugees were admitted into the country. By that date, a total of 13,596 refugees had been relocated between member states across the entire EU (Medienservice 2017) relocation-programm-oesterreich-hat-noch-keine-fluechtlinge-aufgenommen.

50 (Sosnowska 2016, 15; Lang 2015). On the EU Council of Ministers, a qualified majority decides in the ordinary legislative process. As of November 2014, this means that at least 55 percent of the states representing at least 65 percent of the EU population must agree. A minority able to block a decision should be made up of four countries that together account for 35% of the EU population. The Czech Republic, Slovakia, Hungary, Romania and Poland represent 8.8% of the EU population.

interested in seeking asylum in the countries of Central and Eastern Europe. According to Blaha, refugees would eventually move to Western European countries. Blaha also said that quotas were a dictatorship against those refugees who would be relocated to countries where they did not wish to go at all (Blaha 2016, 168).

The result of the vote in the EU Council of Ministers showed, according to Blaha, the division of the European Union into two groups, wealthy countries such as Germany, which, as the target migration country, is interested in relocating migrants to other EU members, and poor countries such as Slovakia, which do not want to lose their sovereign right to control the process by which the burden is divided (Blaha 2015). Richard Sulik, chairman of the (neo)liberal and EU-critical Sloboda a solidarita ("Freedom and Solidarity," SaS) party, said that the debate on the reception of refugees does not distinguish between politically persecuted and war refugees on the one hand and labor migrants on the other, and most so-called refugees are, according to Richard Sulík, working migrants or "poverty migrants."[51]

On 23 September 2015, Robert Fico declared that the Slovak Republic would bring an action against the mandatory resettlement quotas at the European Court of Justice, and on 2 December 2015, the government did, indeed, file this action (Euractive 2015). Like the Hungarian government, which also filed a lawsuit, the Slovak Government shares the view that the Treaty on the Functioning of the European Union was violated in several respects when voting on quotas in the Council of Ministers. Last but not least, the Council, which, by its resolution, changed the Commission proposal, should, in the opinion of both countries, have voted unanimously.[52]

---

51 Sulik 2015. This view is shared by the Sme-Rodina—Boris Kollár party (Sme Rodina 2016).
52 A summary of the grounds for legal action can be found in Officin Journal 2016. According to the legal opinion, the Court must uphold the action because the Commission's proposals, which were amended by the Council, require unanimous approval (Schuberth 2016).. The complaint was dismissed in full early in September 2017.

Fico called quotas a "dictate" — hinting at the Munich dictate of 1938 on the ceding of the Czechoslovak territory of the Sudetenland and its annexation by the Third Reich (Fico 2015a). According to Fico, the sovereignty of the affected countries is violated *"when a third party simply prescribes how many refugees a country has to accept. This is a decision that requires serious political debate yet nobody has discussed it with us"* (Fico 2015b). As a result, Blaha likened the EU's policy to that of the USSR in the time of Leonid Brezhnev: *"Some Western politicians have apparently forgotten themselves and have stopped talking about the European Union using the jargon of ideology where Europe is described in terms of equality, debate, democracy. They have thrown away ideological rhetoric and have come straight to the point: if you do not obey, we will punish you. We are stronger, we are richer; we are more powerful [...] The cards are revealed: where the pathetic talk about human rights and democracy ends, comes dumb force... So, if we understand it correctly, the slogans about democratic Europe are just slogans while the reality is as follows: if one rebels, the great powers do not hesitate to use their economic and power dominance for the neo-colonial extortion of the smaller and weaker countries. Great! Doubtless, we all wished to live in exactly such a European family: for eternal times and never otherwise! Surely, even Uncle Brezhnev would have liked it"* (Blaha 2015).

Richard Sulík and his SaS held a similar view. In its program, the party had already spoken in favor of solidarity and joint funding of European border security. In addition, according to Slovak liberals, individual member states have the sovereign right to decide on who gets asylum. The party also called for the establishment of refugee camps outside the EU member states (in North Africa, the Balkans and in Turkey).[53] The conservative party Obyčaní Ľudia a nezávislé osobnosti ("Common People and Independent Personalities," OĽaNO) presented a similar view in its election program. It put forward a proposal to create internment camps outside the EU and demanded that more pressure be put on the Arab states to accept refugees currently in the EU (OĽaNO 2016, 26). The Catholic and economic-liberal party

---

53 DLF 2015; SaS 2016, 50. Sulík is also considered a critic of Islam (Sulík 2016).

Kresťanskodemokratické hnutie ("Christian Democratic Movement," KDH) called for controls on the Schengen borders both on land and at sea (KDH 2016, 76). The mandatory quotas were sharply criticized by Boris Kollár's Sme-Rodina ("We are Family — Boris Kollár") in his election program. In their view, this system did not work even among the federal states of Germany (Sme-Rodina 2016, 5). Right-wing radicals from Ľudová strana Naše Slovensko ("People's Party Our Slovakia," ĽSNS) stated in their election program that all immigrants enforced on Slovakia by the European Union should be expelled from Slovak territory (ĽSNS 2016, 2).

Such attitudes to mandatory quotas in general and to (Muslim) refugees in particular are accepted by the Slovak population at large, as evidenced by opinion polls (Pluska 2015a). In one survey, commissioned by the Call to Humanity initiative (Výzva k ľudskosti) in early September 2015, two thirds of the respondents rejected the introduction of mandatory quotas. Every fourth respondent categorically refused the refugees any assistance. Only 18 percent said that Slovakia should offer them a new home. On the other hand, one in two respondents agreed to provide refugees with asylum at least *temporarily*. A year later, research by the Institute of Sociology of the Slovak Academy of Sciences, revealed that 52.5 percent of the respondents said that Europeans should provide assistance to the refugees, but only in emergency situations.[54] These surveys can naturally be viewed against the background of current refugee movements. Several years ago, in May 2005, 72.6 percent of the respondents agreed that Slovakia should accept refugees and provide them with aid and protection; however, only if they had serious grounds for fleeing their country of origin.[55]

---

54 In the same poll, 36.6 percent of the surveyed expressed fears of a high crime rate and 28.8 percent fear of a high financial burden (Webnoviny 2016).
55 At the same time, however, 67.9 percent of the respondents agreed with the statement that refugees cost the country too much, while 65.8 percent of the respondents were of the opinion that refugees would bring in various diseases. In addition, 51.4 percent said that refugees would increase the crime rate in Slovakia (Vašečka 2009, 25). Similar results were reported by the surveys conducted in 1998 and 2001 (Divinský 2005, 92).

In the parliamentary elections of 5 March 5 2016, Smer-SD won the 28.28 percent vote against SaS (12.12 percent) and OĽaNO (11.02 percent). A further breakdown of election results by vote went as follows: SNS (8.64 percent), ĽSNS (8.04 percent), Sme rodina – Boris Kollár (6.62 percent), conservative Hungarian party Most-Híd ("Bridge") (6.50 percent), centre-right party Sieť ("Network") (5.60 percent). The KDH, represented in five governments between 1990 and 2012, failed to pass the mandatory five-percent quorum with 4.92 percent of the votes, and was left at the gates of the Parliament (Vlčej 2016, 179). After the election, the government was formed by four parties: Smer-SD, SNS Most-Híd and Sieť. Following the disintegration of Sieť, only the first three entities currently form the government with the tacit support of some of the former members of the fourth party.

The concept of political culture

The major reasons behind the attitude of Slovak political representatives and the population at large may be sought in the historical experience of the Slovak nation in the nineteenth and twentieth centuries, and also in part in events that are rooted deeper in history. These events constitute elements of a specific political culture and auto-stereotypes, and as such are still effective. Research into political culture makes a distinction between a quantitative and an interpretive, qualitative approach. Both approaches operate with different concepts; they capture different dimensions of political culture and use different methods (Dörner 2003, 593).

The quantitative approach, which was introduced under the influence of rational choice theory in the United States, is associated with the first and so far the best-known work on the subject, *The Civic Culture* by Gabriel A. Almond and Sidney Verba (Garsztecki 2001, 61; Almond, Verba 1963). In this approach, attitudes to specific political developments and institutions are identified through quantitative surveys. According to the aggregation rule of "one person, one vote," views of the entire society derive from individual attitudes and orientations (Dörner 2003, 596). Finding and exploring the attitudes and orientations toward certain (political) themes and institutions is a vital and interesting task for political science and political sociology. However, quantitative-based research is not sufficient for a proper understanding of the political culture of a state or group (Garsztecki 2001, 61). In this way, the researcher will only get to the border where questions about the nature of the models of perception and assessment criteria will arise; to a border where nothing can be said as yet about the role of culture and historical memory (Inglehart 1988, 1203).

Thus, the more important role is played by the interpretive, qualitative approaches to political culture research, based on the belief that history has a strong influence on the expression of individual as well as collective attitudes and orientations (Garsztecki 2001, 62-64). Political culture is not analyzed purely technically, i.e., with the tools of quantitative research, but hermeneutically through research into texts in newspapers and journals, political program documents, electoral posters, etc. (Dörner 2003, 598n).

An interesting qualitative perspective on the research into political culture was put forward by political scientist Karl Rohe, who drew on the approach of David Elkins and Richard Simeon. These Canadian political scientists suggested that *"rather than individual views on political objects, collectively shared views should be put into the basis of the conceptual core of political culture"* (Dörner 2003, 596). For Elkinson and Simeon, political culture represents a cognitive-normative "map" that mentally defines and structures the political world. Thus, at the center of attention are fundamental and relevant values of the social group, the essence of what politics actually is, can and should be (Rohe 1996, 1). This line of thought forms the basis of Karl Rohe's approach; in his view, political culture refers to the basic beliefs about the political world and related operative ideas (Rohe 1996, 1) These constitute the knowledge derived from the conventions of thought and action; the knowledge of how problems are dealt with; which answers proved correct in the past and which did not (Rohe 1996, 2). Political culture consists of two elements: political socio-culture and political culture of interpretation. Political socio-culture includes undisputed daily realities resulting from traditions and the certain collective memory of a political society. It stands above an individual and, like language, pre-exists. Individuals are born into it and are socialized in this setting. Political socio-culture is so fundamental that, as a rule, its bearers are not even aware of it. It is an implicit set of guidelines on how to act, highlighting the course of political and cultural normality through which one can discover and understand the actions of his or her fellow human beings (Dörner 2003, 604).

This allows one to decipher the codes of one's own community and adjust behavior accordingly. In short, political socio-culture is an unwritten constitution that guides the conduct of political actors within certain limits and at the same time rules out other modes of conduct (Rohe 1996, 4, 11).

If a society's socio-culture is to survive, it must be constantly updated and symbolically renewed. This is the responsibility of the political culture of interpretation, an area beyond the ordinary political world, with its own logic and norms. It is staged and managed by those who only partly participate in socio-culture part and perceive it consciously. The content of the political culture of interpretation is shaped by suggestions and/or proposals for how an existing society can be changed, how it can be further developed, or how it can be preserved in an unchanged form. The culture of interpretation includes theories, ideologies and images presented by politicians and intellectuals through which they attempt to change or stabilize an existing society. The political culture of interpretation is an expression of the cultural and political discourse of society. As such, it fulfills two tasks. Firstly, it thematizes the existing socio-culture and robs it of its spontaneity. Secondly, it creates a new cultural spontaneity. In other words, it opens socio-culture to new avenues of development. As a superstructure of political culture, the political culture of interpretation adequately consists of ideas and suggestions that are still in a state of flux and that can be obtained in the space between the cultural system and the political system. If the bearers of the culture of interpretation and their proposals for change and/or suggestions are successful, then the themes offered, or rather the proposals of the culture of interpretation, tend to shift into socio-culture, where they are (or can be) accepted for a certain period of time; there is no guarantee that they will remain there permanently (Rohe 1996, 9-10). If recipients do not identify with the possibilities of interpretation, the latter are soon abandoned (Dörner 2003, 605). The opportunities for exercising influence by the political offer of interpretation are thus limited by historical traditions. The very conduct of politicians is limited by the stable cultural patterns of political socio-culture.

This results in a tense exchange relationship between the two elements. New political systems must, if they want to be successful, bring about a change in the political culture of the population; they must offer a culture of interpretation that, over time, will manifest itself in socio-culture. To this end, they must be able to withstand the existing assessment criteria. On the contrary, the foundations of legitimacy of the established regime can be undermined if the political elite fail to adapt to the new political and cultural assessment criteria that have been asserted in society (Rohe 1996, 18).

Slovak fear of asymmetric relations

The system of compulsory quotas for refugee admission constitutes a political offer of interpretation from the European Union targeted at the population of Slovakia and its politicians. This offer of interpretation is perceived as "European solidarity,", as a "community of values," as "humanity." The quoted statements by Robert Fico, Ľuboš Blaha, and Richard Sulík also offer an interpretation to the Slovak population. These Slovak politicians, however, are themselves constrained by this offer. In this sense, their statements are an expression of Slovak political culture, which they consciously perceive from their own perspective. Politicians know which offers have a chance of being embraced by the Slovak population.

Robert Fico, Ľuboš Blaha and Richard Sulík see the quotas imposed by the European Union as an interference in national and state sovereignty and a dictate of Brussels, or, more precisely, of its large and powerful member states. Their statements may conceal an instrumentalized fear of EU centralism, of asymmetric relations with the EU, of Slovakia's subordinate position vis-à-vis the EU. These politicians also raise concerns that Slovakia might become a colony of the stronger EU member states. Such statements represent an offer of interpretation for the population of Slovakia. However, where the offer of interpretation presented by the European Union is concerned, they can fare better with the historically determined Slovak socio-culture mostly offered by Smer-SD, but also by Sloboda and Solidarita, the Slovak National Party (SNS 2013) and *We are family – Boris Kollár*. The reasons must be sought in history. The Slovaks had formed a standalone nation only in the latter half of the nineteenth century, and they lived in a multinational state up until the late twentieth century (Krekovičová 2007, 127; Zemko 2007, 189). Aside from the episode of the Slovak State (1939-1945), the ally of the Third Reich, an independent Slovak Republic has been in existence only since 1 January 1993 (Kipke, Vodička 2000, 13-16, 122-126).

The Slovak nation has often presented itself as a plebeian or an agrarian nation (Krekovičová 2013). This sense of smallness, reflected in its social awareness, is based on two frontier shifts, on the experience of the Austro-Hungarian monarchy, of Czechoslovakia, of the World War II period, and also of Communist Party rule between 1948 and 1989 (Lukáč 2003, 339) In the nineteenth century, the Slovak nation fought against Hungarian unitary centralization. After the fall of the monarchy and the establishment of Czechoslovakia in 1918, the image of the oppressor changed. In the eyes of the Slovak public, the Hungarian feudalist was replaced by "the godless Bohemian." In its national self-confidence, Slovakia now had to fight against Czech centralization (Chmel 1997, 9). In the 1920s, a metaphor circulated that Slovakia was a "Czech colony" (Krivý, Mannová 2013, 79). It arose from the fact that in the Czechoslovak Constitution of the 1920s, Slovakia was downgraded to a simple territorial-administrative unit (Bystrický 2007, 51). This argument reappeared during the Slovak State, which, in turn, was considered a German colony (Krivý, Mannová 2013, 79); while in the latter half of the twentieth century, Czechoslovakia became, in some respects, a colony of the Soviet Union. That period meant a double hegemony for the Slovaks: the subordinate position of Slovakia within Czechoslovakia on the one hand and its inferior status within the Eastern Bloc on the other, confirmed by the invasion of the Soviet troops and other states of the Warsaw Pact in August 1968. Generally speaking, the Slovak nation had, over the course of a few decades, repeated experience with the model of unilateral relations, with the dominance of one nation and the power ambitions of other states and nations. This experience, encoded in socio-culture, has been reflected in the Slovak auto-stereotype as an oppressed and threatened nation, which must defend itself against larger and more powerful nations (Škvarna 2007, 257-259). The struggle for survival of the Slovak nation and for the preservation of the nation's essence has existed since the nineteenth century as a leitmotif of its history.[56] Hence, Slovakia's experience is markedly distinct from that of countries such as France or England, which always existed as great colonial powers, and thus could put existential pressure on other nations. On the other hand, it is similar to the historical experience of the Czech Republic, Poland or the three Baltic States, Lithuania, Latvia and Estonia. In close connection with this experience is an auto-stereotype of a thousand years of slavery that dates back to the period of Ľudovít Štúr (Štúr 1998 [1848], 313). In other words, the Slovaks perceive themselves as a conquered nation (Kamenec 1998, 123). This self-perception has a very strong symbolic significance in Slovakia, being a verbalized expression of the Slovak nation's sense of being threatened by larger and stronger nations (Findor 2013, 72-73). It is on this auto-stereotype of a systematic threat to the Slovak nation, which, in turn, engenders fear (Kamenec 2007), that Robert Fico and Ľuboš Blaha base their policy derived from the same idea that other, more powerful, nations make decisions about "us without us" (Schöpflin 2003). How deep the roots of this sentiment lie is clearly demonstrated by the preamble to the Slovak Constitution: *"We, the*

---

56   Liptak 2013, 239-240. This idea is currently being promoted by the SNS (SNS 2013).

Slovak nation, heeding the political and cultural heritage of our ancestors and the centuries-old experience of the struggles for national existence and for our own statehood ... based on the natural right of nations to self-determination."[57]

Based on their experience with asymmetric relations, the Slovak population and its representatives are very sensitive to the curbing of their national sovereignty by the EU. The Union's effort to implement quotas despite Slovakia's resistance is yet another example of asymmetric relations. Thus, while the twenty-first century has seen Slovakia's subjection to the superiority of the European Union and its leaders, this fact is taboo in the social environment of Slovakia, a practice that is often criticized by Smer-SD or ĽSNS.[58]

The Slovak Dream of Equality and Equivalence

Although mandatory quotas are perceived by both political parties and the population as a manifestation of the EU's "paternalism," the long-term image of the European Union in Slovak public opinion is positive.[59] With the exception of ĽSNS, there is no party that would include withdrawal from the European Union on its agenda (Spáč 2016, 179). Most political parties see the European Union as the natural space for Slovakia's development (Novosad 1998, 140; Vláda SR 2016). Nevertheless, growing numbers of critical voices have been raised against some of the EU's far-reaching decisions and scope of power. In addition to the mandatory quotas, criticism has primarily been aimed at the financial assistance for Greece and the associated European financial stabilization mechanism, the so-called EU bailout fund, particularly rejected by the economic-liberal party Sloboda a Solidarita ("Freedom and Solidarity"), although without

---

57 Cf. Preambula. This position was also supported by the Poprad memorandum of the SNS (SNS 2013).
58 For the EU, the national and state sovereignty of member states does not imply any "nviolable quantity" (Handl 2007, 477).
59 Among the population, confidence in the EU continues to grow (Webnoviny 2017).

fundamental criticism of the European Union itself (Spáč 2016, 165, 172).

From 1993 onwards, i.e., from the establishment of the independent Slovak Republic, membership in the European Union had been a clear goal of Slovak foreign and domestic policy. To act against this goal meant to act against the vital interests of the state (Lešková 2006, 31, 33; Chmel 2007, 134). Slovakia's accession to the European Union was the wish of the majority of the Slovak public (Lešková 2006, 33; Schöpflin 2003). The country's integration into the European Union was one of the top priorities of the domestic government, especially when Vladimír Mečiar left the position of prime minister in 1998, for it was he who, due to his authoritarian policy, held back Slovakia's integration ambitions. Slovakia's accession to the EU in May 2004 had particularly strong support among the population. The official campaign run before the referendum on accession was supported by all political parties across the entire party spectrum (Spáč 2016, 164). Nevertheless, there were doubts as to whether, being a small state and a small nation, Slovakia would be of any benefit to the functioning of the (large) EU (Lukáč 2003, 345).

Despite all the criticism, diffuse EU support in Slovakia has been based on the country's historical experience in the eastern part of Central Europe. During the so-called "normalization" period (1968/70-1989), the European Community was perceived in Czechoslovakia as a symbol of freedom and economic welfare. The West, with its democratic political system and free market, acted as the positive opposite of the Communist ideology and planned economy of the Soviet bloc. Idealization of the EU continued especially after 1989. In Czechoslovakia as a whole, and in Slovakia in particular, the prevailing opinion of the EU among the general public and also among the political elite was one of euphoria, in which the desire for economic growth and material prosperity overshadowed the negative aspects of Western society (Handl 2007, 473; Lešková 2006, 33). However, material incentives were not the only reasons for supporting Slovakia's entry into the EU. EU membership was viewed as part of the national emancipation process, when Slovakia strove to liberate itself from both Czech and

Soviet hegemony (Schöpflin 2003). In terms of Slovakia's identity, EU accession thus represented completion of the process of building a modern state, i.e., recognition of the Slovak nation as an independent cultural-political entity, as a "mature" country on a par with the other members of the European Union (Novosad 2007, 141; Bátora 2004, 362).

This view became evident when Chairman of the Slovak National Party Jozef Prokeš made the following statement in 1991: *"An integrated Europe should be understood to mean a cooperative Europe, not one particular state termed Europe. An integrated Europe will survive only if all the cooperating nations have the same rights and obligations. If one nation were unhappy, this would be an instrument causing tension"* (Kirschbaum 1994, 127). Yet equality is not sufficient for Slovak identity, as long as it is guaranteed merely formally, by European conventions. According to the former Slovak Prime Minister Ján Čarnogurský, equivalence is also important: *"My idea is that we will be equivalent as well [...]. Since equivalence is also a matter of protocol, we can act as a subject in interstate relations"* (Kirschbaum 1994, 126). This desire was formulated by Vladimír Mečiar in 1996 as follows: *"We want to be fully integrated into Europe, but this does not mean that we will agree with the West on all issues"* (Samson 1999, 24). Today, this line of argument is of great importance; on the one hand, Slovakia wishes to belong to the Union, but, on the other, it also wants to pursue its own (asylum) policy. From the Slovak perspective, EU membership first and foremost constitutes recognition of the state as an equal and equivalent member and partner in a free and democratic Europe (Schöpflin 2003). This means that Slovakia wants to preserve a substantial part of its national and state sovereignty in the EU (Vláda SR 2016). The country accepts some elements of integration, but at the same time shows a certain reserve regarding the establishment of supranational elements (Handl 2007 473, 477; Novosad 2007, 142). In Slovakia's perception of its own identity, sovereignty does not only imply having its own state. Sovereignty means national autonomy, equal participation, and this particularly in larger political unit.[60]

The widespread belief, or rather wish of the population and politicians, to be an equal and equivalent EU member state, i.e., a member of a larger political unit, is part of the Slovak socio-culture, which has been shaped since the mid-nineteenth century. Already in the *Claims of the Slovak Nation (Žiadosti slovenského národa)*, put forward in Liptovský Mikuláš on 10 May 1848, a demand for emancipation was voiced while at the same time domination of one nation over another was rejected (Žiadosti 1848; Ďurovič 2007, 34). This demand was reiterated in the *Memorandum of the Slovak Nation* and approved by the National Assembly in Martin on 6-7 June 1868. The aim of the document, which included state, political, and cultural demands of the Slovaks, was to win cultural autonomy for the Slovaks in the Hungarian state formation (Ferenčuhová 1998, 175; Memorandum 1861, 336-343; Ďurovič 2007, 34). The New School representatives shared the same line of thinking. According to them, the Hungarian state was supposed to take this into account, to respect and to provide for the different needs and specific features of Hungarian national communities. The New School also rejected the political and cultural hegemony of the Hungarian nation as well as centralization of the Hungarian part of the monarchy. In the constitutional monarchy, the Slovaks were supposed to be culturally and politically equal citizens (Nová Škola 1868, 358-360; Martinkovič 2013, 122-128). During World War I, this reasoning played a prominent part in the plans to create a common state with the neighboring Czechs. The Cleveland Agreement of October 1915 presupposed the creation of a federation of the Czech and Slovak nations with full autonomy for the Slovaks. In the

---

60 Ferenčuhová 2007, 175; Novosad 2007, 140. There are two levels of meaning in the concept of sovereignty: sovereignty of the nation in the sense of independence and sovereignty of the state in the sense of autonomy in international law (Kirschbaum 1994, 124). The political thinking of Central Europe makes a clear distinction between the state and the nation, since in this region the frontiers between nations are often not identical with the borders between states. Either many nations lived in one country, as in the Habsburg monarchy, or nations were divided into several states, as with the Germans. As an example, the Polish nation has experienced both situations.

Slovak perception, this meant self-administration and equal status for both nations (Ďurovič 2007, 37; Clevelandská 1915, 445). When the Constitution of 1920 degraded the status of Slovakia to the level of a self-governing region, Andrej Hlinka, the leading figure of the Slovak autonomist movement, demanded that the Slovaks have their own legislative assembly and their own judiciary (Kirschbaum 1994, 114; Bystrický 1997, 51). Martin Rázus, Chairman of the Slovak National Party, voiced similar demands (Kusý 2016, 437).

The demand for the creation of Slovak autonomy within Czechoslovakia formed the basis of the process of federalization of socialist Czechoslovakia also in 1968 (Novomeský 1968a, 391-395; Novomeský 1968b, 396-399). On paper, Czechoslovakia was a federation composed of the Czech Republic and the Slovak Republic from 28 October 1968. In reality, however, it was a unitary centralized state. When the era of real socialism ended late in 1989, federation and confederation were *"an accepted spectrum for many Slovaks"* against the background of discourse on a new constitution. With regard to the third option, independence, no one knew *"whether it was feasible and whether it would actually win the public support"* (Kirschbaum 1994, 126-127). Slovakia was more preoccupied with pursuing the goal of being part of the EU as a sovereign constituent (Ferenčuhová 2007, 175). To summarize, it can be said that the offer of interpretation made by the EU to introduce mandatory quotas for refugees cannot be accepted by the Slovak socio-culture because it "disregards the dispositions, expectations and needs" of the Slovaks (Dörner 2003, 605). The Slovaks cannot identify with this offer because it only shows them the road to their own past. The Slovak nation, from its own standpoint, would once again find itself in a subordinate position. This offer is thus in stark contrast with the ideas and goals whose fulfillment the Slovaks expect from EU membership, specifically, that Slovakia will become an equal and equivalent partner. While Slovakia is ready to shift part of its sovereign rights to the EU level, as could already be seen in the case of mandatory quotas, it will do this only with reservations. It is on this issue that Slovakia strongly opposes the possibility of losing its sovereign right to protect its territory.

Slovak fear of Islam

Slovak rejection of quotas has been reinforced by the fact that, in the summer of 2015, most refugees came to Europe from predominantly Muslim societies. National and conservative-Christian-oriented political parties such as SNS, ĽSNS, KDH, OĽANO, but also Smer-SD, refused to accept Muslim refugees (Rogalska 2016, 47), basing their arguments on the belief that Christianity is the main pillar of Europe and also of Slovakia.[61] Robert Fico declared that the centuries-old "country character" rests on "Cyrillo-Methodian traditions" (Fico 2016). Here, it is necessary to refer once again to the importance of the preamble to the Constitution of Slovakia, which exactly describes what Robert Fico referred to, namely, "the spiritual heritage of Cyril and Methodius," i.e., the Christian heritage of Slovakia (Preambula). Due to the influence of Christianity, the demand to accept a greater number of Muslims in Slovakia has provoked a sense of threat to the Christian-national culture in a large part of society. This sense of threat has been reinforced by the fear of a surge in crime and violence, of terrorist acts by Muslim fanatics, and by doubts about the ability of Muslims to integrate into the national community.[62]

This negative perception of Islam and Muslims is exacerbated by a growing number of current and historical factors on both sides (Štefančík 2011, 2). As a first factor, it is necessary to highlight the extremely negative representation of Muslims in the media. Added to this are the problems of integrating the increasing number of Muslim immigrants and refugees in Western Europe, military conflicts in the Middle East, plus the terrorist attacks on civilian targets in Europe and the US, with 11 September 2001 as a major factor. It is in this context that one must read Robert Fico's statement addressed to the Federal Republic of Germany, in which

---

61 On the Christian orientation of Slovakia see Staško1982, 71-78, 131.
62 At this point, concern about financial burdens also reappears (Webnoviny 2015; Štefančík 2011, 3, 11).

he underlined the issue of safety: *"I do not want to wake up in this country and have 50,000 people we do not know anything about. I do not want to be held accountable for a possible terrorist attack just because we have underestimated something"* (Fico 2015; Rogalska 2016, 46).

Although Slovakia has (as yet) not been affected by these problems, there is an aura of negativity about them in the country. Western Europe is more visible in the Slovak press than is Slovakia in the Western European press.[63] What is more, public opinion is affected by the personal experience of Slovak working migrants and students in Western Europe. Although the number of Muslims in Slovakia is relatively low (approx. 5,000 including converts), they are well integrated, and their religious service is in the Slovak language (Štefančík 2011, 16-18; Drobný 2015, 142), parallel societies existing in Germany or France are causing fear of further mass immigration of Muslims to Slovakia. Robert Fico's anxiety derives from his perception of Germany; he expresses concern that, following the influx of more Muslims, their integration will be more complicated as they may create parallel societies (Fico 2016). Right-wing extremists from the People's Party Our Slovakia (ĽSNS) deny that Muslim immigrants have the ability to adapt. Muslims are presented as hordes that "refuse to comply with Slovak legislation and social standards," "commit crimes, and create a huge burden for the domestic population." What is more, Muslims would push Christianity and European culture out of Europe and would thus drastically *"change society according to their own ideas."*[64]

One clear form of concern about European Islamization was thematized by the Slovak National Party in 2012. *"Islam wants to change the cultural face of Europe. We state firmly: 'No' to the Islamization of the European Union, 'no' to Turkey's membership in the EU. We will initiate the creation of European cultural heritage against this form of multiculturalism, which could alienate us from our essence and could plunge [Europe] into ethnic conflicts. We protest against the*

---

[63] In its electoral program, the ĽSNS touched on the events in Cologne, Germany on New Year's Eve 2015. (ĽSNS 2016, 2.) Robert Fico also expressed his views on these events (Fico 2016).

[64] ĽSNS 2016, 2. A similar view is presented in the KDH party program (KDH 2016).

violent suppression of Christianity" (SNS 2012). A year earlier, the current chairman of the party Andrej Danko said the following regarding the Christian character of the state and of Europe: *"We must [...] create a mechanism that will guarantee us that Sharia will not be introduced in Slovakia to replace the Criminal Code. The Slovak National Party [...] will always consistently defend the interests of Christian Slovakia and Europe"* (Štefančík 2011, 23). For this reason, the SNS wants to prohibit by law the wearing of burkas and the building of minarets (SNS 2015, 26). Another party, OĽANO, sees political Islam as an "unprecedented threat," referring to the terrorist attacks that have been carried out "in the name of Islam" (OĽANO 2016, 128ff).

Such images and offers of interpretation are tangled in Slovak socio-culture, which associates its deep historical experience of Muslim culture and religion; these are considered foreign to it. They reinforce the negative perception of Islam and the sense of threat. At the same time, however, they confirm that the perception of contemporary Islam and Muslims is similar to the historical perception. At this point, it is worth mentioning that Ottoman Muslims had been present in the territory of today's Slovakia in the latter half of the sixteenth century and also during the seventeenth century. Muslims considered Slovakia a "holy war" territory, which was to be under their permanent control (Štefančík, Lenč 2012, 88). Unlike France or England, which actively dominated many Muslim countries as European colonial powers, Slovakia had a rather passive experience. The presence of Turks, or, more particularly, Ottomans, in the southern parts of contemporary Slovakia over a span of one and a half centuries influenced the Slovak view of the Muslims (Štefančík, Lenč 2012, 111, 116). During their conquest expeditions in the latter half of the sixteenth century, the Turks presented themselves as a population of looters and marauders that caused injustice to the civilian population in the occupied territories of their empire (Štefančík, Lenč 2012, 95). In fiction as well as in scientific books and war chronicles from the period of national revival, Islam was presented as enemy number one (Wheatcroft 2006, 292-305). This historical view of bloodthirsty Muslims as the archenemy of European Christianity and an apocalyptic threat to European society, which has existed in Slovakia since the sixteenth century, has its roots in the Slovak collective memory and has become part of the Slovak political socio-culture (Štefančík, Lenč 2012, 88). It is on this ground that the current national and Christian-oriented political parties can build their policies on the negative representation of Islam, although Slovak society currently has no direct contact with the Islamic world, unlike, for instance, neighboring Austria.[65]

The occupation of the territory of current southern Slovakia by the Ottoman Muslim troops was strongly instrumentalized by the current Slovak political parties during the discourse on the reception of refugees. As an example, the KDH invited the public to the re-enactment of the Battle of Vezekény on 20 January 2017. The invitation to this event stated that the event was of great symbolic importance even today, thereby clearly indicating that Europe is Christian.[66] The Catholic association Magnificat Slovakia and its chairman, former dissident Anton Selecký, a supporter of right-wing extremists from the ĽSNS, called on the director of the Public Radio and Television of Slovakia (RTVS), Václav Mika, to broadcast the Polish-Italian co-production film *The Day of the Siege: September Eleven 1683* (in the Polish original, "Bitwa pod Wiedniem").[67] Events such as the "Turks are coming" thematize the Turkish-Ottoman invasion of the sixteenth and seventeenth centuries into the territory of contemporary Slovakia (Tamo 2014).

To sum up, Slovakia rejects mandatory quotas for refugee admission because of its negative image of Islam, which has deep roots in its political socio-culture. It is precisely this negative image of Islam that is now also instrumentalized by national, conservative

---

65 Štefančík 2011, 16. In 1964, in order to tackle a labor shortage, Austria entered into an agreement with Turkey to engage new workforce. There have been several waves of labor migration from Muslim Turkey to Austria. That is why Austria has had both long-term and current experience with Muslims.
66 KDH 2017. This battle took place on 26 August 1652, and ended with the victory of Hungary over the Ottoman Empire. Even in its electoral program, the KDH referred to European values and European and Slovak traditions (KDH 2016, 76).
67 RTVS 2016; Magnificat 2016. For more details about the discussion of the film, see Morvay 2017, 11.

and Christian-orientated parties such as SNS, ĽSNS and OĽANO, as well as by the left-wing Smer-SD and liberally-oriented SaS. This historically inherited and now rearticulated level of socio-culture is associated with the fear of an asymmetric relationship between the EU and the Slovak Republic. In the understanding of a large part of Slovak society, the European Union is forcing Slovakia and its population to accept the migrants despite the fact that the Slovaks perceive them as a threat to their national and cultural identity and, as such, refuse to admit Muslim refugees into their territory.

Slovak migration experience

In addition to the sense of threat, the feelings of inequality, a sense of EU paternalism, and concerns about Islam, there is one more important reason why the Slovak population and its government refuse to accept the number of refugees prescribed by the European Union. Here, however, a seeming paradox must be mentioned. Between 1898 and 1913, approximately 430,000 Slovaks emigrated to North America (Bosák 1991, 69). In the latter half of the twentieth century, thousands of Slovaks sought and found protection from persecution by the Communist regime in Western European countries and across the ocean. First to leave Czechoslovakia were high representatives of the Slovak State (1939-1945), who fled the country soon after the end of World War II. Their exodus was followed by a second wave of emigration when the Communists took power in February 1948. The third large wave of emigration was triggered by forced suppression of the reform process, the Prague Spring, in August 1968 by the armies of the five Warsaw Pact countries. Many Slovaks left their homeland also in the 1980s (Štefančík, Lenč 2012, 60). After 1989 and following the Slovak Republic's accession to the European Union, many Slovaks found work abroad, and most of them no longer plan to return to their country of origin.[68] The main reasons behind economic migration after 1989 were high unemployment, associated low wages, and problems with the consolidation of democracy during the Third

---

68 At the end of 2015, their number was about 300,000 (Pluska 2015b).

Government of Vladimír Mečiar (1994-1998) (Štefančík, Lenč 2012, 70).

The answer to the question of why the state is reluctant to accept refugees can be found in the history of Slovak society, which was affected, among other things, by emigration. It can be said that Slovakia has only had experience with emigration. In other words, in the Slovak perception, migration is mostly associated with emigration abroad, rather than with immigration into Slovakia. It is in this aspect that this Central European country is different from the Western European countries. Unlike France or England, Slovakia had no colonial territories from which the local population would emigrate to the colonial power. At the same time, Slovakia is not highly developed economically and its demographic situation is not so bad as to rely on the recruitment of workers from other countries, as was the case in Germany or France after World War II. In these countries, as in other countries of Western Europe, North America, or Australia, and unlike in Slovakia, part of creating the national identity was the idea that their country was an immigrant state. Notwithstanding the period of National Socialism, Germany has had no experience with large emigration waves over the past 120 years. The same applies to the Benelux and Scandinavian countries. Emigration from England and France had ceased even earlier. Slovakia's experience is rather similar to that of southern Europe, to countries like Italy and Greece, which originally attempted to send migrants to the states of Northern Europe without delay (Sosnovska 2016, 16).

Until 1989, international migration was not a subject of public debate. The possibilities of labor migration, as well as of migration of refugees, were extremely limited. If immigration did occur, it was mainly to the Czech part of the Czechoslovak federation, where migrants arrived mainly from other countries of the Eastern Bloc, as well as from some of the affiliated African and Asian countries. In addition, the migration of Africans and Asians was mostly temporary, either for education purposes or for gaining work experience. However, the systemic transformation of political and economic conditions in 1989 brought about change in this area as well. In the early 1990s, first war refugees from the disintegrated

Yugoslavia and later from Iraq and Afghanistan arrived in the territory of Czechoslovakia or Slovakia. Higher rates of economic migration were recorded in Slovakia especially after Slovakia's accession to the European Union in May 2004 (Štefančík, Lenč 2012, 60-64, 67). Between 2004 and 2017, the number of foreigners with permanent or long-term residence in Slovakia more than quadrupled. Yet their number still accounts for only 1.92 percent of the total population of the state.[69] Most of them, however, come from European countries, or rather from the EU member states. This means that they have similar culture, traditions, a similar legal system, and thus are not perceived by the domestic population as a security threat. Moreover, foreigners from Western European countries are mostly highly qualified workers, such as managers or scientists. Less qualified economic migrants come mainly from Romania and Ukraine. In addition to these migrants, immigrants from East Asian countries such as Vietnam, China and Korea live in Slovakia as well (Štefančík, Lenč 2012, 60-64, 68-70; IOM 2018).

As a result of these developmental trends, the topic of migration was not the focus of public attention or a concern of the political elite (Štefančík 2010, 19). For example, the government's policy statement for 2016 and 2020 reported the problem of international migration only in connection with haphazard and illegal mass migration, protection of EU external borders and international terrorism (Vláda SR 2016b). The concept of the 2011 migration policy of the Slovak Republic refers only to the interest of the state authorities to pay greater attention to this policy (MVSR 2011, 5).

To sum up, the Slovak Republic has little experience with immigrants, especially refugees. On the other hand, since many of its inhabitants have left the country for various political and/or economic reasons, a large part of the population cannot understand why their own homeland should become a new home for refugees in general and for migrant workers in particular.

---

[69] From 22,108 in 2004 to 104,451 persons in 2017 (IOM 2018).

Summary conclusions

This chapter has presented an answer to the question of why Slovakia rejects mandatory quotas for the reception of refugees proposed by the European Commission and approved by the Council of the European Union. The answer draws on the concept of political culture, pioneered by the German political scientist Karl Rohe. According to Rohe, political culture is composed of basic attitudes to, and opinions on, the political world and associated operative ideas. Rohe distinguishes between political socio-culture and political culture of interpretation (Rohe 1996, 1). According to Rohe, socio-culture consists of everyday realities and denotes "*a sort of political and cultural normality*" (Dörner 2003, 604). It is the result of handed-down traditions and presents the collective memory of a political society. It is an internalized framework of action, which has socially crystallized as a way of life. Political culture of interpretation includes political theories, ideologies and ideas and images presented by politicians and intellectuals who seek to influence society's development. It describes suggestions by means of which a society should change or, on the contrary, should be preserved. However, these offers must pass muster before the population and its assessment criteria. The requirement of mandatory quotas on the part of the EU is such an offer of interpretation that, if were to be accepted, must pass the muster of the socio-culture of the Slovak population and its political representatives. However, the EU offer does not conform to the ideas that would correspond with the historical experience of the Slovaks who create the Slovak political socio-culture. As a result, this offer is rejected by both the Slovak population and the political elite. On the other hand, the population accepts those critical offers of interpretation criticizing the EU that will pass the muster of the Slovak socio-culture. The EU has failed to win over the Slovak population at large, particularly the Slovak politicians and Slovak political parties which have adapted to the methods and criteria of assessment of the Slovak population. Their offers of interpretation can thus measure up to the existing evaluation criteria.

The responsibility for rejecting the offer of interpretation of "refugee quotas" proposed by the EU should be sought in the experience with the historical hegemonic behavior of some countries toward Slovakia, in the experience with asymmetric relations between the Slovak nation and the Hungarian state, or between the Slovak nation and the Czech and German nations in the nineteenth and twentieth centuries. These historical circumstances have been used as reference points by political parties when justifying their attitudes to quotas, particularly by Smer-SD (Robert Fico and Ľuboš Blaha) and Sloboda a solidarita (Richard Sulík). Another reason behind the rejection is a diffusely positive image of the European Union, which, despite the criticism, is perceived as a framework for the Slovak emancipation process. Another factor to be taken into account is the historical experience with Islam in the territory of contemporary Slovakia in the sixteenth and seventeenth centuries, coupled with the awareness of the current terrorist attacks by militant Muslims on civilian targets in European cities, or in the U.S.A., and problems with integrating Muslims into European societies. This experience is shaping the Slovaks' negative image of Islam, which is especially perpetuated by SNS, ĽSNS, KDH, OĽaNO and the left-wing party Smer-SD. Finally, Slovakia, unlike Western European countries, has had a rather different experience with the phenomenon of international migration. Migration is perceived by the Slovak population as a movement of the population out of the state, i.e., as emigration, rather than immigration.

Confrontation with the EU's proposal to accept refugees under binding quotas substantiates the discourse on the process of national self-awareness. Its outcomes are "succinct formulations and patterns" of "self-perception and self-problematisation" (Kleiner, Nieland 2006, 143), which describe the "meaningful world" of the nation (Voegelin 1991, 84). These succinct formulations or patterns, which elucidate the internal structure of society and its members to external and unbiased observers as well, include the Slovak auto-stereotype of a small and oppressed nation and at the same time an effort to be recognized by the European Union as an equal and equivalent partner, a mature country driven to extremes by the system of binding quotas. Statements made by Robert Fico, Ľuboš Blaha (both Smer-SD), Richard Sulík (SaS) and Andrej Danko hide fears that the nation will not be recognized as an autonomous entity, but merely as a province or dependency of large political structures.[70] Mandatory refugee quotas are also perceived by the Slovaks as a return to the system of asymmetric relations with larger and stronger nations, in other words, to the painful past.

Yet these offers of interpretation, presented by official policy, are not embraced by the intellectuals. Not all Slovaks are unconditionally trapped in the Slovak political socio-culture as outlined above. As an example, political scientist Jozef Bátora believes that the perception of the Slovaks as a small and oppressed nation is obsolete. As a member of the European Union, Slovakia has assumed the role of an equal and equivalent state and has adopted EU rules, which, at the level of the Council of the European Union, are transformed into a common consensus of all nation states. In this context one should also read Jozef Bátora's offer of interpretation presented to the Slovak population in general and to the political representatives in particular; according to this offer, Slovakia is part of the "mature world" and as such acts according to its valid standards (Bátora 2007, 362-364). This also means compliance with the established rules, although it is questionable whether the binding reception of refugees does not mean real interference in our national and state sovereignty, a circumstance that makes it an extremely sensitive issue. Slovakia would like to decide on its own who it should consider a refugee and how many it will receive in its territory. This in particular can be interpreted as an expression of Slovak self-confidence, based on economic and political achievements as well as on renewed cooperation within the Visegrád Group (Poland, Hungary, the Czech Republic and the Slovak Republic).

---

70   Efforts at equality and equivalence are common features of national statehood. This also applies to other Central European countries (the Czech Republic, Poland and Hungary), to the Baltic States and also to Britain, which rejects EU dictatorship. Last but not least, Russia is also struggling with the US dictate.

With regard to the role of Christianity in Slovak history, Slovak historian Ivan Kamenec, an intellectual representative of Slovak socio-culture like Jozef Bátora, even though maintaining some detachment, states that this auto-stereotype cannot be explained solely by the national-emancipatory and state-building efforts and struggles of Slovak society (Kamenec 1998, 124-125). Such self-perception is as obsolete as the self-image of a small oppressed nation. Both views, simply put, stand in the way of the Slovak effort to be recognized as a modern, yet economically and culturally attractive country.

7. Slovak National Interest and the Hungarian Minority in the Post-Integration Period

Tibor Szentandrási

The core of my argument is simple: Slovakia's national and state interests[71] have a lot in common with those of its Slavic and non-Slavic neighbors despite all their differences and contradictions; moreover — *horribile dictu!* — they even show a similarity with the interests of the Hungarians, the alleged age-long enemies of the Slovaks (Weiss 2013).

I think that a considerable part of the public and the political elite believes that apart from global threats like climate change, the energy crisis, and immigration, Slovakia's nation-state interests, our safety, are at continuous risk — maybe ever since we gained sovereignty and became an independent republic — from our southern neighbor Hungary, or more precisely from Hungarians in general, including the Hungarian minority living in Slovakia. However, we do not much talk about this publicly because of the amicable neighborly relations we officially claim to maintain and because of the interests we share more or less since having lived under a socialist regime.[72] The historical reasons behind the

---

71 Not nation-state interests. I think that connecting them is risky and dangerous. If we connect them, it is easier for us to argue for and to act toward subordinating one part of society to another, or sacrificing the interests of the minority (or, in some cases, the majority) in favor of the interests of the other party.

72 In this case, what is being proclaimed officially might not always be honest, but at least it realistically represents the objective interests of the country and its citizens, unlike what certain individuals say out of historical prejudice or existential fear. This is well illustrated by some of the infamous phrases uttered by certain public servants and politicians, the best-known being Ján Slota (See "Výroky Jána Slotu." Dôležité, www.dolezite.sk/old/Vyroky_Jana_Slotu_118.html. Accessed 13 December 2016). Regardless of whether these statements were actually made, they can have a huge impact on public opinion and polls. For instance, in a poll surveying attitudes toward foreigners (or those perceived as such), Slovak citizens were asked what neighbors they would not

negative attitude Slovaks take toward Hungarians is fairly well-known; until the end of World War I, Slovakia's present-day territory and the Slovak nation's place of birth belonged to the Kingdom of Hungary. Even though the basic tenet of Slovak nationalism is that the Hungarians have been oppressing the Slovaks for a thousand years, historical documents do not support this assertion (see, e.g., Veczán 2015; Surján 2016; Ábrahám 2012). Hungarians started to make a concentrated effort to assimilate other ethnic groups only starting in the nineteenth century, after the notion of modern nationalism had been born in the French Revolution. This was when the Hungarian political elite set itself the belated — and rather inconvenient — goal of catching up with the more developed Western European states by creating a nation-state through the assimilation and homogenization of large ethnic groups living in the Kingdom of Hungary (who actually outnumbered the ethnic Hungarian population) (Koller 2006; Katus, Nagy 2016).

As laid down by the Treaty of Versailles (1919), the territory of Upper Hungary, occupied mostly by Slovaks, was attached to the newly-formed Czechoslovak Republic, together with a great number of non-Czechoslovaks and the territories they occupied.[73] The main endeavor of this new Czechoslovak state was to reduce the potential threat that the members of the previously ruling nations might present to them. Even if their ethnic brothers, now living on the other side of the newly drawn political borders — which, in most cases, were not determined by the ethnic makeup of

---

like to have and who they considered dangerous. Hungarians and Roma occupied the top places. Only a Hungarian poll produced worse results more than a decade ago, when Hungarians thought that the made-up "Piresians" posed the greatest danger to their country (the Slovaks did not even reach a position that would deserve special mention). See SÍK E., 2007. Nőtt a „pirézekkel" szembeni elutasítás [online] 2007. TÁRKI, www.tarki.hu/hu/news/2007/kitekint/20070308.html. Accessed 13 December 2016. Interestingly, ethnic Hungarians in Slovakia think almost the opposite of their Slovak neighbors. See Lampl 2013; also: www.aktuality.sk/clanok/188975/komentar-mpiresiansadari-sa-identifikuju-so-slovenskom/.

73 They were predominantly ethnic Germans (more than three million) and Hungarians (about one million) (cf. Vígh, 46; Popély 2003).

the population or by their will but rather by strategic, natural, economic, communication-related, and other aspects—tried to take some steps, their hands were tied by the guarantees of the Treaty of Versailles (A versailles-i békeszerződés 1919) and the other treaties that favored the same subjects, including the Treaty of Trianon (A trianoni békeszerződés 1921).[74]

The Treaty of Versailles also set certain human rights requirements in relation to the new ethnic minorities. However, the victorious parties often bypassed and violated them in their narrow-minded safety concerns; for instance, they obligated them to take an oath of loyalty to the new state (i.e., not simply to abide by the laws), adopted tax and estate reforms, and introduced political, cultural, and administrative changes and measures that discriminated against ethnic minorities, many of whose members were forced to leave their homes. Meanwhile, those who decided to stay were discriminated against by the government, which curtailed their economic, political, cultural, and other opportunities and restricted their rights. Nevertheless, we can confirm that with the exception of these anti-minority practices, the first Czechoslovak Republic was both formally and factually a democratic and legal state; much more so than Romania or Hungary, for instance. The state could not give any more opportunities and grant collective rights to its largest ethnic minorities, because even Slovaks did not receive them; they were regarded by the anti-revisionist Czechoslovak ideology as part of a joint state-building nation. Were they to act differently, it could break up the new state, which, in fact, did happen as a result of the political changes that occurred in Europe in the 1930s prior to the outbreak of World War II (Simon 2014; Vígh).

---

74 Even today, the majority of Hungarians sees these "peace treaties" as dictates, similarly to the way the Czech and Slovaks regard the Munich Agreement, because while the non-Hungarian nations of the Kingdom of Hungary were allowed to establish their own state or join neighboring nation-states, Hungary lost two thirds of its historical territory and a third of its ethnic Hungarian population (who used to live in a predominantly ethnically homogeneous territory). And the Hungarians had absolutely no say in the matter. See Szentandrási 2009.

In case of problems, it is always easier to put the blame on others rather than admit one is at fault (Loewenstein 1997). This is also what happened after the first Czechoslovak Republic fell apart and World War II broke out, which we generally ascribe to German Nazism and the disinterest of the Western allies (quite rightly) together with the collaboration between the Sudeten Germans and irredentist Hungarians. Speculating about historical what-ifs is rather meaningless; however, certain facts, circumstances, and parallels indicate that events could have unfolded completely differently and with much less bloodshed (Szabó 2006; Szentandrási 2011). It is more than likely that not all ethnic Germans would have supported Hitler and Nazism if they had felt at home in their own country and if they had been given equal rights and opportunities. When discussing the expansion of Nazism, it usually does not come up that the majority of Swiss Germans and Alsatians did not want to join the German Reich because they felt freer in Switzerland and France.

Upper Hungarians argued similarly when the Vienna Award allowed them to return to Hungary, their ethnic state; once the primary euphoria subsided, they also objected to the imperious manner of the Hungarian civil servants. Despite all the injustices and grievances they had had to endure under Czechoslovak rule because of their ethnicity, if they disregarded the lack of linguistic and cultural rights—and the resulting absence of economic and political opportunities—they had to admit that they felt better and more at home in the former, non-maternal, and occupant state.[75] However, after World War II, ethnic Hungarians had it even worse. Once the borders of the Czechoslovak state were re-established based on the Beneš decrees, all Germans and Hungarians were considered war criminals and collectively guilty for breaking up the republic; therefore, they were deprived of their rights, murdered, banished, "exchanged," deported to gulags, and sent to perform

---

75 See Simon 2014. To learn more about the current problems, misunderstandings, and conflicts that ethnic Hungarians experience in successor states and the constitutional efforts of their mother country to support them, see Öllös 2008.

forced labor in the Sudetenland. They even had to renounce their language by undergoing "re-Slovakization."[76]

So how is it possible that even though the totalitarian regime is over and we now live in a democratic legal state, those who consider themselves Hungarian are still not seen as citizens with equal rights, especially when it comes to linguistic and cultural matters? If they wish to be seen as equals, they have to master the official language (ideally at a native-speaker level) and speak it in public because if they do not, they could suffer disadvantages, like not getting employed, not receiving medicl treatment, not being accepted to universities, or not getting through to the authorities; moreover, they may even be harassed on the street or in public areas for speaking Hungarian. And why would they carry on using their mother tongue at home if they do not even need it? After all, everything is in Slovak, including the majority of product labels.[77]

The borders are open, and if someone does not like it here, they are free to leave, move to Hungary or somewhere else, go to the West, find a job there, and settle down. "What are you, Hungarian?!", "Slovakia belongs to the Slovaks!", and "Speak Slovak in Slovakia!" are just some of the self-affirming and legitimizing phrases that can be heard from the mouths of the members of the national majority. The Hungarian minority in Slovakia is decreasing every year by ten thousand inhabitants, the size of a small town; in a decade there will be a hundred thousand fewer of them, and the process will continue to quicken. Their assimilation is voluntary, since they realize that it is better to be a Slovak than a Hungarian in Slovakia.

As a result, the risk of the emergence of a fifth column—that is, potentially subversive agents who could break up the nation-state—is gradually diminishing, and we can assume that in a few decades, after this process of assimilation speeds up, there will only be a couple of insignificant textbook examples of folkloric Hungarians whose ancestors had at some point moved to our

---

[76] A few years ago, these decrees were still considered untouchable despite the fact that they were already said to be invalid (Horváth, Korom 2014).

[77] Even on products imported from Hungary, the Slovak label is plastered over the Hungarian one so that it cannot be read.

country, as indicated by our history books. Is this what we should see as a "positive, hopeful scenario"? Is this where the cultural and political system of our nation-state, the Slovak Republic, is discreetly but resolutely heading? While some ethnic Hungarians might not find this progress desirable or convenient, what can a handful of unsatisfied individuals — or even a whole minority — do against the majority that can count on the support of its national, political, and state elite? The members of the "state-building" majority usually reject the idea of meeting the subordinate minority, whose ancestors are said to have oppressed the Slovaks in the past, somewhere in the middle. It is as if this was some kind of reciprocal revenge: today the descendants of the former oppressors have to adapt to the majority for their own good. Or they could just leave. And let us hope that history will not repeat itself!

Is there any other way to increase the national and state interests — but not the nation-state interests! — of the country, apart from the above-mentioned method based on national supremacy, homogenization, assimilation, and unequal rights? One that would not be characterized by notions of superiority and inferiority which, sometimes unintentionally, result in animosity and conflicts, adding fuel to the fire and suggesting that the horrible, conflict-ridden history our parents and grandparents had to live through will repeat itself?

Can Slovaks and Hungarians be equal not only on an international and bilateral level but also on a domestic one? Can they work together toward their shared and individual goals? Can both sides feel secure without the fear of being subjugated by the other and losing themselves (Bauman 2006; Kymlicka 1994; Szentandrási 2011)? What can both sides do to achieve this? Are there any patterns or examples they could follow, at least to a certain extent?

Nations and states can only truly count on the support of citizens who are able to identify with the state — but not necessarily the nation! — and consider its goals their own. Such citizens regard the state as their home, feel safe in it, and can fulfill their potential without hindrance even if their ethnicity is different. Otherwise, states and nations can only coerce and pressure their ethnic citizens into giving them support; but such support will never be real, sufficient, or permanent, and therefore states will constantly have to keep an eye on these citizens. As a result of such ever-increasing control, ethnic citizens will either rise in revolt or, as the Slovak anthem says, "disappear."

Can ethnic minorities feel at home in a state established and controlled by a different majority? If the majority does not present a threat to their existence or identity, if they both enjoy the same opportunities, and if the majority will not be privileged to the minority's disadvantage, then why not? However, post-war experiences suggest that individual human rights are not enough to achieve this; the minority must be granted some collective rights but in a way that would not restrict their individual rights (Kymlicka 1995).

But what can be done with the historical prejudices that quite a few members of a certain community—like the Slovaks, for instance—hold against other communities, leading them to consequently be intolerant of their particularities, opportunities, independence, and autonomy? Why are so many Slovaks opposed to the efforts at autonomy by Hungarians living in Slovakia? Is it because of the voluntarism of "the founding fathers"—the state-building politicians—on both sides? After all, throughout their history Slovaks have also fought a remarkable fight for their own national equality, they also struggled to earn autonomy, and with some external help they eventually managed to establish the absolute sovereignty of their nation in their own nation-state.

During Habsburg rule in the middle of the nineteenth century, Slovak nationalists strove to obtain political autonomy for Slovakia within the Kingdom of Hungary,[78] and a strong autonomous movement existed in the era of the first Czechoslovak Republic as well. These efforts eventually resulted in Slovakia becoming independent. Besides the alleged irredentism of the Hungarians

---

78 They sometimes escalated into Pan-Slavic efforts to join tsarist Russia and were excessively persecuted and punished by the Austrian and Hungarian authorities.

(Zeidler 2002), these experiences might be another reason why Slovaks assume such a negative attitude to any endeavors that ethnic Hungarians make in order to gain autonomy in southern Slovakia, even though it is clear that current state borders would not change as they are guaranteed by international treaties. We have a lot to learn before we can work together toward our mutual interests, and to do so by means of trust and tolerance rather than authoritative, majority-based decisions.

How does theory address these questions? Many theorists claim that in pluralistic societies, it is extremely difficult—if not impossible—to establish and maintain a stable democratic government. The Dutch theorist Arend Lijphart seconds this opinion, asserting that the national homogeneity of a community is the precondition for political consensus and a stable democracy (Lijphart 1977). Margaret Moore also believes that democracy cannot function in a country if there are two separating, antagonistic political communities in it (Moore 2001). Karmela Liebkind presents this problem in the form of a question: Can we be equal and different at the same time (Liebkind 1985)? In addition, Gilbert Gottlieb maintains that "homogeneous national entities may be more likely to evolve into peaceable democracies than states rent by harsh linguistic and cultural antagonisms" (Gottlieb 1994, 101).

Michael Lind asserts that in linguistically and culturally differentiated societies, democracy has almost never lived up to the expectations that were placed on it. He says that from the few dozen multinational states, only three could be seen as successful examples of a multinational democracy.[79] On the other hand, states with low or insignificant ethnocultural differentiation tend to have much better organizational performances.

Therefore, ethnic, cultural, and religious differentiation might hinder democratization for multiple reasons. Under these conditions, representative democracy can achieve only modest results. In such cases, Gottlieb and Lind find the peaceful disintegration of oppressing multinational states perfectly

---

79 Such as Switzerland, Belgium and Canada. See Lind 1994.

justifiable, provided that democratic states are built on their ruins (Gottlieb 1994; Lind 1994).

The main reason why the democratic coexistence of various ethnic groups and cultures tends to fail lies in the fundamental non-constructability of human matters — that is, the impossibility to rationally organize them — because of the open anthropological characteristics of humans and their communities; a facet that is, in fact, rather fortunate. If democracy flounders in a multiethnic society, it paves the way for segregation; if negotiations will not yield an agreement regarding an acceptable institutional framework for the coexistence of all subjects, it makes the latter outcome all the more possible.

Similarly, there are two more forms of strategic dilemmas — failed attempts at communication and a lack of trust provoked by broken promises and pledges — that compel the members of opposing communities to look for a solution in segregation in order to prevent their conflicts escalating further. When communities try to negotiate via their representatives and reach an agreement regarding the conditions of their participation in a given political society, they habitually end up in a vicious cycle as the members of the majority refuse even the most basic demands of the minority, fearing that it might lead to secession; whatever proposition the majority puts forward, the minority finds it unacceptable, believing that it is just another attempt to assimilate them. Such cases cannot be resolved by mediators or arbitral interventions.

In multiethnic societies, the well-known shortcomings of democracy, known as "democratic deficits," become much more apparent. According to Rainer Bauböck, even the most inclusive political communities are characterized by such democratic deficits, together with the "liberal deficits of ethnic inequality and intolerance of diversity." This means that even such communities find it insufficient to simply integrate foreign ethnic groups into their society and insist on assimilating and homogenizing them; however, the difference is that they do it more successfully and in a more "acceptable" manner (Bauböck 1998).

Another somewhat different example of successfully resolving and regulating conflicts between majorities and minorities is presented by such destination countries for migration as the USA and Australia, and other countries with a long history of democracy like Great Britain, Sweden, Denmark, and Finland. They managed to do so mainly by establishing open deliberative democratic institutions that enable negotiations between conflicting parties. We can see a gradual shift in attitudes toward minorities even in countries like France, with its strong centralizing Jacobin traditions. These states are also marked by progressive decentralization and the transfer of the central government's functions to lower levels of self-governing administration.

These cases also show that neither the institutional system of a representative democratic majority nor the prosperity and homogenization connected with modernization has automatically reduced the tendency toward ethnopolitical mobilization. However, we can see these problems in a positive and optimistic light. According to Philip Payton, ethnicity can become an important tool to solve various problems of another nature that are caused by the "democratic deficit" of representative systems (Payton 1999, 34). One merely has to look at the experiences of the "Europe of regions" that complements the scope of nation-states (Grúber 2002; Glatz 1997). Saul Newman called attention to the fact that Belgian ethnic policy has managed to peacefully eliminate the centralized state without disposing of or undermining other democratic rights. Newman believes that this might eventually lead to the expansion of political participation in Belgium (quoted in Payton 1999, 34).

The ability of consolidated democracies to adapt despite their ethnocultural differentiation is based on generally respected norms that can be successfully applied even when it comes to regulating and solving interethnic conflicts. The possibility of peaceful segregation is also not entirely ruled out. (The former Czechoslovakia provides an example of this.) While historically less common, there is another option besides secession that also works—multinational federalism, which can offer a solution especially to the problems of autochthonous minorities. The multiculturalism model has not exhausted all its possibilities. While it mainly seems to work in countries with a high immigration rate, it does not really provide an answer to the problems of the domestic residents.

Will Kymlicka believes that there are three basic requirements for ethnocultural fairness: (1) recognition of citizenship, (2) plurality and tolerance of political national identity, and (3) allowing minorities to maintain their cultural particularities and develop their nation-building efforts. Although Kymlicka currently sees the fulfillment of these three requirements as an ideal, he thinks that there is a visible tendency toward their general acknowledgement. Nevertheless, the majority of states are far from putting his suggestions into practice, since they use double standards when it comes to dealing with their own issues and those of other states (or their own minorities) (quoted in Silat 2001, 311). There is an evident lack of international consensus regarding the fundamental principles of ethnocultural fairness.

We can still consider Adam Burgess's words valid when he stated that the *"treatment of minorities is the touchstone of democratic progress."*[80] Many countries are reluctant to accept and apply such principles and commit themselves in any way to their minorities, believing that it would undermine their sovereignty. In particular, states with non-consolidated and unstable democratic institutions refuse to accept the fact that preserving and institutionally anchoring ethnocultural diversity are fundamental rights and preconditions of liberal democracy. According to a UNESCO committee report from 1996, only consolidated democracies can afford to acknowledge plurality without fearing it might threaten their integrity (Perez de Cuellar et al. 1996, 20).

It seems contradictory that multiethnic societies with a short democratic tradition should follow these rules, since building and strengthening their own nationality and statehood should be their priority. These are usually young democracies with new institutions and the residues of totalitarianism in their institutional mechanisms (and in their citizens' psyches); therefore, such rival

---

80 See Burgess 1999, 49. Similar statements were made by the founder of Bolshevik totalitarianism, Vladimir Lenin, and by Zoltán Fábry, a prominent leftist Hungarian journalist in Slovakia in the twentieth century (see Lenin 1978; Fábry 1991).

communities with opposing cultural, economic, and other interests (concerning mainly their political participation, of course) cannot agree on consolidated ways to solve or regulate their mutual conflicts. They fear that accepting and institutionalizing the liberal standards of ethnocultural otherness — that is, rival nation-building efforts — would present a threat to the integrity and stability of their budding democracy. This is known as nation-state system failure (Zartman 2007).

The four fundamental norms of the modern world system — sovereignty, democracy, national self-determination, and human rights — are thus becoming contradictory (Krejčí 2007). The principles of state security, the protection of territorial integrity, and the inviolability of borders are becoming controversial in relation to the principle of national self-determination, while the unconditional recognition of statehood is incompatible with the guarantee of human rights and internationally accepted norms regulating the relation of states with their minorities. By accepting these rules, the international community *"had to steer a tortuous course between the Scylla of insufficient action and the Charybdis of overly intrusive interventions that might further weaken the very foundations of state legitimacy they intended to stabilize,"* as noted by the American authors Henry Farrell and Gregory Flynn (Farrell, Flynn 1999, 525).

When democratizing ethnoculturally differentiated countries, we should keep an eye on two mutually opposing goals: building statehood and ensuring sovereignty by balancing internal structures and communities in accordance with international requirements while also establishing ethnocultural diversity by officially recognizing the competing efforts of rival communities and respecting the internationally accepted recommendations regarding ethnic minorities, which to some extent goes against the principle of a nation-state's sovereignty. Is it possible to maintain both?

Many believe that the nation-building efforts of a community can only succeed if they suppress the exact same efforts by its minorities. However, minorities will never feel safe in such a country, even if their members are granted individual rights, since the majority will not officially acknowledge their right to build their own independent culture in parallel with them. In this vicious cycle, the majority and minority feel mutually threatened by one another, which prevents the consolidation of an authentic democracy. Kymlicka and Straehle observe that *"it becomes almost a matter of life or death whether one's group controls the state"* (Kymlicka, Straehle 1999, 84).

The authors furthermore maintain that if the existence of democracy in a multicultural society depends on the exclusive success of one of the rival nation-building groups, then there are two possibilities: (1) splitting up multinational states so as to enable all national groups to form their own nation-state through secession and the redrawing of boundaries or (2) enabling the largest or most powerful national group to use state-nationalism to destroy all competing national identities (Kymlicka, Straehle 1999).

According to Allen Buchanan, *"[e]ither we must acknowledge that some nationalities will not have their own states, but will be submerged to create mono-national states so that democracy can flourish, or we must forgo progress toward democracy in the name of equal consideration for nations by recognizing the multinational character of most existing states"* (Buchanan 1998, 301). Yet we cannot agree with the claim that minorities would necessarily undermine the democratic institutions of a state. However, Buchanan finds it lamentable that *"until very recently there have been almost no serious attempts to develop democratic states that recognized a plurality of nations"* (Buchanan 1998, 302).

Farrell and Flynn emphasize that the new interstate order enables certain "mechanisms of constructive intervention" that do not offend the sovereignty of states. National self-determination therefore would not have to threaten the inviolability of a state's borders; on the contrary, it could be *"directly and exclusively related to creating political institutions that would protect cultural and ethnic differences within common frameworks, rather than using these differences as a basis in themselves for separation"* (Farrell, Flynn 1999, 527-528).

The reasons for ethnopolitical mobilization will persist until the principles of ethnocultural fairness became generally accepted and applied, just as with the Universal Declaration of Human

Rights, and until ethnocultural communities are granted equal rights (Barša, Strmiska 1999). While one nation can enjoy moral privileges that are denied to others, the stability of a state can be only ensured by denying minorities the political, cultural, and economic rights that the majority retains. The best framework to overcome such a state of affairs is provided by the European Union's integrationist society, despite all its non-democratic, centralistic, and bureaucratic deficiencies.[81]

Mutual mistrust and animosity can be decreased primarily by means of knowledge, communication, and working together toward common goals. Such hostile feelings can also be minimized by cooperating at an international and regional level within a wider community like the European Union. In Western Europe, such forms of regional economic cooperation extending beyond borders have existed since the 1960s. In 1975, the European Regional Development Fund was created to support such endeavors. Hungary and Slovakia have also similarly cooperated on various occasions.[82]

What is the point of all these efforts? As a small country, we can only face global problems and threats like other small states all across the globe do — by joining forces (Gombár, Hankiss et al. 1996; Glatz 1997; Korten 2001). To reach our goals and ensure our safety, we should cooperate and act together in the name of equality and mutual benefit. In order to do so, we need to build up mutual trust and overcome our atavistic and obsolete historical prejudices by opening up to other cultures and getting to know them (Allport 1977; Bibó 1996).

---

[81] The analysis of these connections is beyond the scope of this work. To learn more, see Brhlíková 2014; Vaubel 2004.
[82] These pacts either bear the name of rivers (Váh, Danube, Ipeľ, Hron, Slaná, and Rimava) or historic counties (Novohrad). Such cooperation also exists between various cities (e.g., Košice and Miskolc), as pointed out by Mezei 2008.

8. Slovakia's National Interests and Slovak-Russian Bilateral Relations in the Context of the Ukrainian Crisis (2013-2018)[83]

Juraj Marušiak

Slovakia's relations with the countries of Eastern Europe, especially with the Russian Federation and Ukraine, constitute a multifaceted phenomenon. If Ukraine is Slovakia's largest neighbor in terms of size and population, the Russian Federation represents a global power, possessing nuclear weapons and considerable economic potential, where what is particularly relevant from Slovakia's perspective is the supply of strategic raw materials.

The debate on relations with Russia has affected domestic policy since the mid-nineteenth century. If Slovak-Hungarian, or rather Slovak-Czech relations were crucial to the dilemma as to whether Slovakia should exist as an independent state or merely as a part of a larger whole, and thus as a "political nation" constructed by it, Slovak-Russian relations present the dilemma of where, beyond considerations of security and the economy, Slovakia belongs from the cultural and civilizational perspective.

The aim of this chapter is to identify the role of relations with the Russian Federation (RF) in shaping the national interests of the Slovak Republic (SR). Furthermore, we will attempt to identify whether and to what extent the "Eastern policy" debate in the SR, especially the debate on the relations with the Russian Federation, constitutes a cleavage in Slovak politics. In view of the scope of the issue under consideration, we will focus on the post-2013 period, i.e., the period following the outbreak of the so-called Ukrainian crisis.

Alongside the fall of the communist regime, the constitution of an independent Slovak Republic (SR) and elections to the

---

[83] This chapter is the result of APVV Grant No. 16-0062 „Priorities of the Central and Eastern European Countries in the Context of the Energy Union".

National Council of the SR in 1998, which ended the period of "Mečiarism," marking a change not only in foreign policy but also in Slovakia's civilizational course by strengthening its resolve to join the European Union and NATO, one could define the period after the 2011 EU financial crisis and the outbreak of the Ukrainian crisis "as a potential formative moment in the political development of the SR," sparking a new debate about Slovakia's identity and the focus of its foreign policy. The aim of the present study is to identify the extent to which national interest issues, i.e., long-term interests shared consensually by decisive political forces, are reflected in the political discourse of the SR in the context of the Ukrainian crisis.

Even after Slovakia's accession to the European Union and NATO, the "Eastern dimension" still played an important part in its foreign policy. Relations between the SR and the RF have been characterized by high dynamism, primarily because of economic factors such as the dependence of Slovak exports on Russian markets and, conversely, the reliance of Slovakia on energy raw material supplies from the Russian Federation. On the other hand, even during the period of Slovakia's partial international isolation in the latter half of the 1990s, none of the major political parties questioned the SR's orientation toward European and Euro-Atlantic structures; however, the real impact of the steps taken by the ruling HZDS, such as the failed referendum on Slovakia's NATO membership or the unconstitutional stripping of two deputies to the National Council of the SR, František Gaulieder and Emil Spišák,[84], of their mandate, the SR was not invited to talks on its entry into the two structures in 1997. Only minor coalition parties—the Slovak National Party and the Slovak Workers' Association—officially contemplated the possibility of Slovakia's neutrality, guaranteed by the RF, even though Slovak President Michal Kováč admitted at that time that Vladimir Mečiar "had

---

84 Malová, Láštic 2001, 103-128. Resolution on the case of František Gaulieder, Member of the Slovak Parliament. B4-1389 and 1419/96. Official Journal C 020, 20/01/1997 P. 0145 http://eur-law.eu/EN/Resolution-case-Frantisek-Gaulieder-Member-Slovak-Parliament,168400,d.

never been convinced of Slovakia's need to join NATO. However, he was aware that the bulk of the population wished integration with the West, so the above goals appeared in his electoral program," even accusing Mečiar of "deliberately frustrating Slovakia's chance to join NATO" (Kováč 1997). On the other hand, the period 1994-1998 was characterized by the strengthening of political and security cooperation with the RF, Slovakia at that time acting as a country whose identity in the European space was not consolidated, as there was no consensus on this issue at the level of political elites.

A consensus on Slovakia's foreign policy existed, to a greater or lesser extent, especially following the accelerated NATO and EU accession process, and after the HZDS unambiguously expressed its position in favor of joining the two integration groups in 2000.This consensus lasted until the outbreak of the conflict about Slovakia's share in increasing the funds allocated to the European Financial Stability Facility (EFSF), leading to the break-up of the government coalition in October 2011. This conflict resulted in the formation of a relatively strong segment of "soft Euroskeptic forces" among Slovak political parties, which, however, despite their disapproval of some aspects of the development of the EU, did not question Slovakia's membership in it. These parties included, in particular, Sloboda a Solidarita ("Freedom and Solidarity," SaS), Obyčajní ľudia a nezávislé osobnosti ("Ordinary People and Independent Personalities," OĽaNO) and, in terms of sovereignty in "cultural-ethical issues," human rights and tax policy issues, also Kresťansko-demokratické hnutie ("Christian-Democratic Movement," KDH).

Relations between the SR and the RF did not change significantly despite the change of governments in 2006, 2010 and 2012, although the administrations controlled by the Smer – sociálna demokracia Party showed greater openness to RF interests in sCentral and Eastern Europe and were willing, especially in their rhetoric, to accept some of Russias arguments concerning international policy. Even Prime Minister Robert Fico, who subscribed to the idea of Slavic mutuality in the spirit conceived by

Ján Kollár,[85] in his address during the celebrations of the 62nd anniversary of the end of the World War II, did not question Slovakia's belonging to the West. Indeed, until 2016, the program of the Slavic identity of Slovakia as dominant in its relations with other countries was advocated exclusively by the Slovak National Party, while the Communist Party of Slovakia (KSS), represented in the National Council of the SR in 2002-2006, clearly rejected the SR's membership in NATO jointly with SNS, but avoided taking an official stance on its membership in the EU. The changes that occurred in Slovakia's foreign policy following Robert Fico's first administration taking office in 2006 only occurred at a symbolic level, and thus did not have a major impact on Slovakia's participation in the Eastern Partnership program or on the support of Eastern European countries in their efforts at rapprochement with the EU or on the transition inspired by the Central European countries, even though the establishment of the Eastern Partnership was seen by the RF as a hostile move. The RF's negative attitude toward the Partnership was, at least for a time, mitigated by the gesture made by Minister of Foreign Affairs Miroslav Lajčák when, during his visit to Moscow in September 2009, he did not rule out the possibility of RF's participation in certain projects within the program (MZV SR 2009). However, in terms of Slovakia's identity, this gesture confirmed its position as an EU member, while at the same time demonstrating Slovakia's interest in maintaining a positive atmosphere of bilateral relations with Russia.

Similarly, in later years before autumn 2013 and the outbreak of the Ukrainian crisis, as a result of the decision of then-President of Ukraine Viktor Yanukovych not to sign the Association Agreement with the EU, Slovakia's Eastern policy was primarily focused on developing friendly relations with individual Eastern European countries. The double-edged, or, more precisely, multi-vector nature of Slovakia's "Eastern policy" was shown, for instance, by the establishment of the Slovak Embassy in the Republic of Moldova in July 2013 (MZVaEZ SR 2013). The SR's efforts to present itself as a successful example of post-communist

---

85 TASR, 9 May 2007.

transition, one able to pass on its experience with the transition process and EU orientation to other countries, played a much larger part in this decision than economic interests. The process of creating closer ties with Moldova can be dated from the visit of the country's Foreign Minister Iurie Leanca to Bratislava in the February of 2010, i.e., following the formation of a pro-European coalition in Chisinau in 2009. This process went on continuously, even though Robert Fico's social democratic government, with the dominance of the Smer-sociálna demokracia Party was replaced in 2010 by a center-right coalition with Iveta Radičová (Marušiak 2012, 45) at its head, and held power until March 2013.

In a similar vein, Slovakia continuously pursued a policy of nurturing democratic and pro-Western forces in Belarus, regardless of the change of governments, although in 2003, Prime Minister Fico, still an opposition politician at that time, visited Belarus, where he met with Chair of the House of Representatives (Lower House of the Belarusian Parliament) Vladimir Konoplev (NARB).

Although, following Viktor Yanukovich's successful presidential election in 2010, Ukraine gradually abandoned the outwardly still-declared goal of convergence with the EU, Slovakia, together with Poland—countries that actively participated in the Eastern Partnership Project—spoke in favor of maintaining the EU-Ukraine dialogue despite the deterioration of democracy in the country. On 12 May 2012, following the cancellation of the planned meeting of Central European Presidents, President of the SR Ivan Gašparovič, jointly with Polish President Bronisław Komorowski, held talks with Yanukovych in Yalta (Minarechova 2012). At the same time, Slovakia continued its visa liberalization policy towardUkraine. On the one hand, the SR acted as an EU member state, but, on the other, together with Poland, it voiced its interest in preventing the isolation of a major EU partner, which was one the top priorities of Slovakia's European policy. The Europeanization of Slovak diplomacy, confirmed by Slovakia's share in the shaping of the common EU foreign and security policy, and also by harmonizing its own priorities with the other EU member countries, became apparent in relations with Russia after Slovakia joined the EU.

Although at the level of official public discourse, the RF respected Slovakia's status of an independent country, it had a particularly negative view of the process of NATO enlargement in the 1990s. Between 1994 and 1998, there emerged a new opportunity of security cooperation with the RF, or rather a guarantee of neutrality by the RF, as one of the alternatives to Slovakia's orientation toward the EU and NATO. Such an alternative to Slovakia's development was also hinted at by some of the Russian representatives (Duleba 1996). It was most enthusiastically supported by two parties in the then governing coalition—Slovenská národná strana ("Slovak National Party," SNS) and Združenie robotníkov Slovenska ("Slovak Workers' Association," ZRS) (Wolf 1997b); the idea of neutrality also appealed to some of the deputies of the strongest ruling party HZDS (Hlucháňová 1998, 97-104). SNS, led by Ján Slota, was especially inclined to support cooperation among the Slavic states, under the dominance of the RF, and even maintained contacts with the Serbian Radical Party and the Liberal Democratic Party of Russia (Wolf 1997a). It advocated this alternative even after 1998, while verbally supporting Slovakia's integration into the EU (Kopeček, Urubek 2000, 94). The RF's interest in the SR's continuing such domestic and foreign policy, which would cast doubt on Slovakia's integration into the EU and NATO, was also made clear during Mečiar's visit to Moscow in May 1998, i.e., shortly before the elections to the National Council of the SR, when Russian President Boris Yeltsin openly expressed his support forMečiar and HZDS (Sme 1998).

Alongside foreign policy, however, Slovakia was also faced with the question of its domestic policy. In the 1990s, due to the weakness of democratic elites, elements of what is sometimes (Dulebatermed the Russian or Eastern European, i.e., strong-personality-based model of transformation (Duleba 1998), began to assert itself in place of one based on the key role of formally defined rules and democratic institutions. This model, put forth by Mečiar's administration (1992-1994 and 1994-1998), was characterized by the policy of building a regime driven by personal power and an oligarchic model, i.e., a model directly linking the emerging layer of large-scale entrepreneurs and political power. While formally abiding by the principles of political pluralism, repressive forces and public service media were abused in the power struggle. At the same time, the ruling majority worked toward the weakening of control bodies, whether the secret service or the public media. These structures often violated laws, as imperfect as they were, with the intention of protecting the privileges of the new elites. What is more, resolutions of the government majority rendered a number of democratic institutions inoperative; such was the case when František Gaulieder was stripped of his parliamentary mandate after leaving HZDS, the party he represented when elected, in November 1996.[86] That this was not a singular case is evidenced by frustration of the referendum on the direct election of the President of the SR in 1997 (cf. Bútora, Mesežnikov 1997; Láštic 201) and the ignored resolution of the Constitutional Court of the SR, which defined this step as a violation of voters' rights (Leška 2011, 76). The coalition of political parties, which, following the 1998 parliamentary elections, replaced the HZDS-led administration, was politically oriented toward cooperation with EU and NATO member states, and also with political parties associated in European party groupings such as the European People's Party, the Liberal International and the Party of European Socialists. They committed themselves to the Western European political model and also to cooperation with those countries of Central and Eastern Europe that defined embracing a market economy and liberal democratic forms of government as the main goals of the post-communist transition. At the same time, they chose Western Europe and North American political model to be their standard of civilization.

The alternative model that was gaining ground in the RF following Vladimir Putin's election as President of the country was invoked by Robert Fico, leader of the Smer Party, as an inspiration

---

86 Resolution on the case of František Gaulieder, Member of the Slovak Parliament. B4-1389 and 1419/96. In Official Journal C 020, 20/01/1997 P. 0145. Available at: http://eur-law.eu/EN/Resolution-case-Frantisek-Gaulieder-ember-Slovak-Parliament,168400,d.

for domestic policy between 1999 and the parliamentary elections of 2002. He called it a *"program of order and the rule of law,"* which is *"close to the program values of the Smer Party"* (Leško 2016). In later years, however, Fico advocated the policy of Western European social democrats.

Meanwhile, the RF's political elites continued to see the growth of NATO's influence as a security risk, as confirmed by the RF's National Security Strategy, approved by President of the RF Vladimir Putin on 31 December 2015. According to Paragraph 15 of this document, "NATO's growing potential and its acquiring the status of a global authority, exercised in violation of the norms of international law, the stepping up of military action by the countries of the bloc, further enlargement of the alliance and bringing its military infrastructure closer to the Russian borders pose a threat to national security" (Strategia nacionaľnoj 2015).

Reflection on the recent past shows another difference in the perception of foreign policy orientation. That Slovakia is one of the EU member states that appreciate the role of the USSR in the defeat of Nazism in 1945 was demonstrated by the participation of Slovakia's Prime Minister Fico in the celebrations of the 70th anniversary of the end of World War II. However, Russia's state-controlled media issue controversial statements, such as those justifying the invasion of Czechoslovakia by the Warsaw Pact troops in August 1968 by alleging that NATO intended to invade Czechoslovakia (MZVaEZ SR 2017).

The events of 1968 present the only significant confrontational aspect in the history of Slovak-Russian relations; as a rule, representatives of both countries emphasize much more the positives. A statement made by Foreign Minister Miroslav Lajčák (2009-2010 and 2012-) during his visit to Moscow on May 10 2016 will illustrate. He pointed out that Slovak-Russian bilateral relations *"have good foundations built on long-term partnership and cooperation, even though today they are affected by the general atmosphere of the EU's relations with Russia"* (MZVaEZ SR 2016). Nevertheless, even Slovakia's state authorities admit that the two countries' state interests are different; for example, the report of the Ministry of the Interior of the SR of June 2016 admits that, like the other countries of Central and Eastern Europe, Slovakia is *"subject to the informational influence of the so-called structures of influence of the Russian Federation,"* regarding it as an *"interference in the internal affairs of the Slovak Republic."* According to the Ministry, the propaganda, whose task is to put Slovakia's membership in the EU and NATO in doubt, presents one of the hybrid threats (Bariak 2016).

Slovakia's example demonstrates that the choice of internal political model and foreign policy orientation are conditional on each other. The shaping of the political identity of a country also influences the definition of its interests and thus also the practical steps taken in its foreign policy. The decision to adopt the model of liberal democracy, inspired by that applied in the EU member states, immediately after the fall of the communist regime and confirmed by the 1998 elections to the National Council of the SR, had a significant impact on the formulation of Slovakia's policy toward the RF—but, naturally, this does not rule out the existence of specific interests pursued by Slovakia in its policy toward the RF.

These specific interests, mostly pertaining to the country's economy, such as the imports of energy raw materials (oil, natural gas, nuclear fuel), differ from those of other EU member states. Before 1990, over 30 percent or, more exactly, almost 40 percent of Slovakia's industrial capacity, including its arms industry, relied on Soviet markets (Duleba 2009b, 14). Although this reliance on the former USSR dropped considerably after 1990, Slovakia continues to show a long-term passive balance of foreign trade with the RF; meanwhile, it is in the long-term interests of the political elites to reduce the latter. Economic cooperation between the SR and the RF has been coordinated by the bilateral Slovak-Russian Intergovernmental Commission for Economic, Scientific and Technical Cooperation, whose activities fall under the Ministry of Economy of the SR and the Ministry of Industry and Trade of the RF. The Commission constitutes the supreme forum of bilateral Slovak-Russian cooperation at the government level. Traditionally, the most important part in bilateral Slovak-Russian relations has been played by the meetings between the Slovak Prime Minister and the RF's President or Prime Minister. In public communication, the Prime Minister of the SR is also the chief actor in formulating the political agenda of bilateral Slovak-Russian relations, something that has been particularly true of Mečiar and Fico. Another significant actor is the Slovak-Russian Business Council, whose members are business entities cooperating with their RF partners. These structures currently represent the key actors that support cooperation between the SR and the RF.

Slovak exports to the RF have been dominated mostly by passenger cars, spare parts and motor car accessories, pharmaceutical products, television sets, medical equipment, telecommunications equipment and accessories, flat-rolled iron and steel. Slovakia imports from the RF mostly petroleum oils, natural gas, coal, iron ore and concentrates (Slovenský exporter 2016). Slovakia's interest in maintaining a steady supply of oil and natural gas recognizes its strategic importance for the country. As demonstrated by the steps taken by the coalition and opposition parties during the Russian-Ukrainian dispute in January 2009, resulting in the suspension of natural gas supplies to Slovakia (Duleba 2009a, 4-6), it represents a consensual priority, and thus can be defined as a national interest.

During 2015 and 2016, one can speak of a positive dynamic in Slovak-Russian trade relations, as the volume of Slovakia's passive balance dropped from EUR 2,025 million in 2015 to EUR 1,281.7 million in 2016 (Štatistický úrad 2016; Štatistický úrad 2017). The decline in trade exchange is due in part to economic sanctions imposed by the EU on the RF as a result of the annexation of Crimea and Russian support for the separatist forces in Eastern Ukraine; the RF's share in the total exports from the SR has decreased continuously since 2012 (MZVaEZ SR 2015). Where, in 2014, Russia's share in Slovak imports was 8.4 percent, ranking third after Germany and the Czech Republic (MH 2013), it dropped to 4 percent in 2016, with Russia going down by three places, ranking sixth (Štatistický úrad 2017).

Decline in the volume of imports from the RF was caused by a fall in the prices of energy raw materials after 2014. In terms of exports, RF ranks tenth, its share in the total exports of the Slovak Republic accounting for 2 percent (Štatistický úrad 2017). Farmers and food producers were among those who complained about the negative consequences of the downturn in trade exchange with the RF (Stupňan, Ružínska 2016). In 2015, the Ministry of Agriculture and Rural Development of the SR estimated the losses associated with sanctions imposed by the RF on imports of agricultural products from EU countries at EUR 8 million, a relatively small amount in terms of the total volume of trade between the two countries (MZVaEZ SR 2015). Hence, in contrast to the situation in Poland, sanctions against Russia have had no significant impact on the exports of food products from the SR, and the agrarian sector does not greatly affect policy-making toward the RF (PSL.PL). However, the consequences of sanctions in the form of a decline in trade with the RF were felt by small and medium-sized enterprises. While the automotive industry was able to offset the decrease in exports to the RF by exports to other markets, cancellation of the RF order for railway carriages brought about layoffs in Railway Casted Components (Krajanová 2015), something also experienced by CSM Tisovec, which had been exporting road and building mechanisms to Russia (Nemec 2017). The decline in trade between the SR and the RF cannot be blamed exclusively on the sanctions imposed on Russia as a result of its interference in Ukraine's affairs. Even Fico, Prime Minister of the Slovak Republic, admits, despite his repeated criticisms, that the situation is due to *"a number of objective factors"* (Vláda SR 2016a), such as the adverse economic development of the RF after 2012.

In the course of 2016, Slovakia and Russia were also split over the construction of the Nord Stream 2 gas pipeline. Slovakia was the strongest critic of the project, which would mean a further decline in natural gas transport through the territory of Ukraine and the SR, bringing about a loss in revenues for Slovakia. Slovakia's position on the issue was backed by the Visegrád group, Romania, Croatia and the Baltic States, while the RF and Germany took an opposing stance (V energetike.sk 2016; Ružinská 2016).

Another dimension in Slovak-Russian relations was an effort to enhance Slovakia's international standing, namely by winning the post of UN Secretary General for Miroslav Lajčák, Minister of

Foreign and European Affairs of the SR. To this end, the SR sought support from the RF in 2016, which, however, limited itself to declaring support for preserving the established rotation principle based on regional affiliation, which stipulates that the office should pass to a candidate from Central or Eastern Europe (Furik 2016). Nevertheless, the RF had never been clearly in favor of Lajčák's candidacy, as there were a number of other candidates from the region who applied for the post (such as Serbia's former Foreign Minister Vuk Jeremić or Bulgarian politician and UNESCO Secretary General Irina Bokova). What is more, the RF did not block the election of Lajčák's rival candidate, former Portuguese Prime Minister Antonio Guterres.

If, in the 1990s, the development of trade relations with the RF was a top priority for textile and footwear industries and also for the sectors involved in the processing and transit of raw materials from the RF—such as Slovnaft, Slovenský plynárenský priemysel (Slovak Gasworks Industry) and Východoslovenské železiarne (East Slovakia Ironworks)—at present the dependence on RF markets has decreased. In addition to a part of Slovak industrial business circles, some representatives of state-owned enterprises in the RF, such as Russian Railways, were interested in economic and political cooperation as well. The project of extending the broad-gauge railway line across the territory of the SR to Bratislava, or to the future terminal in Austria, allowing the transport of goods from the RF, or, more specifically, from China to Europe, received support from Prime Minister Fico and the Slovak Chamber of Commerce and Industry (Sme 2015a), was criticized by the center-right parties and halted in 2015 on the grounds of cost and the ongoing conflict between Russia and Ukraine (Sotník 2013). In terms of the dynamics of economic relations between the SR and the RF, despite the continued dependence of the SR on the supply of energy raw materials from the RF, Russia's economic relevance for Slovakia is on the decline.

The decision of the Ukrainian government to withdraw from the forthcoming EU-Ukraine Association Agreement in November 2013 initially came as a surprise to Slovakia, as did the protests which broke out subsequently in Kiev and other Ukrainian cities, and official Slovak representatives expressed their reservations. Only later, on 13 December 2013, did the National Council of the SR adopt a declaration that called for the peaceful resolution of the newly erupted political crisis and express support for the policy directed at Ukraine's integration into the EU (NRSR 2013), thereby indirectly showing support for the demands of the protesters. At the same time, Slovakia's Prime Minister Fico criticized EU policy, saying that the decision on integration should remain with Ukraine alone (Sita 2015). In supporting the peaceful resolution of the internal political conflict in Ukraine, Slovakia took a similar stance to other EU members and joined the other V4 countries (Visegrád Group 2014a). On the other hand, Slovakia, like other countries of the Visegrád Group, recognized potential risks flowing from the expected wave of refugees from Ukraine (Visegrád Group 2014c). V4 representatives, including the Slovak Republic, at the same time endorsed the newly emerging Ukrainian government and its territorial integrity (Visegrád Group 2014b). Peaceful conflict resolution and openness to dialogue with Ukraine has been Slovakia's consensual priority both in terms of internal policy and in terms of relations with its closest allies in the EU, including the Visegrád Group. The fear of illegal migration in the given context acted as a partial and short-term interest, reflected primarily as a particular interest of the V4 countries.

Slovakia demonstrated its national interest by rejecting the forcible change of state borders, without the consent of all countries affected by such a change, in the resolution of the National Council of the SR denouncing the occupation and subsequent annexation of Crimea by the RF. In this case, Slovakia acted consistently with its position on the recognition of independence of the Serbian province of Kosovo and the Georgian territories of Abkhazia and South Ossetia. Like other EU member states, Slovakia defined Crimea's annexation to the Russian Federation as *"a violation of international law by the Russian Federation."*[87]

---

[87] Vyhlásenie NR SR k situácii na Ukrajine Uznesenie č. 1060. Statement of the National Council of the Slovak Republic on the situation in Ukraine. Resolution No 1060. Bratislava: National Council of the Slovak Republic, 18 March 2014.

If some Slovak politicians, mostly from the right-wing parties, viewed the ongoing conflict in Ukraine as a dispute over values (e.g., the NOVA party leader Daniel Lipšic, who joined the protesters in Kiev [Piško 2014]), Prime Minister Fico explained the conflict in Ukraine in geopolitical terms, i.e., in terms of the conflict of power interests between Russia and the USA. Where the interpretation of the conflict in Ukraine is concerned, whether during the protests from November 2013 to February 2014, or later, during the annexation of Crimea and the outbreak of conflict between the armed separatist groups in the Donetsk and Luhansk regions, no consensus has been reached by the political elites.

Slovakia was not among the EU member states actively supporting the policy of sanctions against the RF or their strengthening; on the other hand, it has not attempted to block or boycott them (Mikušovič 2014; Aktuality.sk 2014). Regarding potential economic sanctions against the RF, Prime Minister Fico said in June 2014 that *"tougher sanctions would significantly curb our accelerating growth"* and refused steps that would *"severely harm our businesses, industry and eventually people and their jobs."* He called this position *"the national interest"* of the SR (HN 2014). In August 2014, he said he did not rule out the use of the veto if the sanctions *"impaired the national interests"* of Slovakia, referring to the similar view expressed by the Czech Prime Minister Bohuslav Sobotka (Sme 2014) — however, without specifying the nature of "national interests" in the given context. Fico drew attention to the negative economic consequences of the sanctions imposed by the EU on the RF, particularly in 2014 and 2015, and called for their mitigation. At the same time, he expressed the interest of the SR in preserving the EU's integrity (Pravda 2016a). Cooperation with the EU and protection of its integrity, and the declared interest in including the SR in the EU's core (Sme 2017), suggests that, even if the current Slovak administration attaches great importance to economic cooperation with the RF and its further growth, Slovakia's EU membership still remains its priority. What is more, criticism of the sanctions against the RF would not be expressed openly by other political parties, so in this case the concept of "national interest" is instrumentalized as an alibi for particular priorities.

On the subject of the sanctions imposed on the Russian Federation, there are potential partners of the SR that maintain active political and economic contacts with the RF, namely, Austria, Hungary and (at least in part) the Czech Republic. The informal grouping of the Slavkov Triangle, comprising Slovakia, the Czech Republic and Austria, looks to distance itself from Poland and its confrontational relations with Russia (Palata 2015). However, as yet, the so-called Slavkov Triangle has not actively participated in the European debate on relations with Russia.

Slovakia´s participation in granting financial aid to Greece in 2011 violated, as already mentioned, the existing foreign-policy consensus of the decisive political powers in the SR, and resulted in the emergence of "soft Euroskeptics represented mainly by SaS, OĽaNO, and, to a lesser degree, KDH. The rise of the extreme right-wing National Party Naše Slovensko (Our Slovakia — ĽSNS), following the victory of its chairman Marián Kotleba in the 2013 regional self-government elections, winning the post of chairman of the Banská Bystrica Region, and the party's subsequent entry into the National Council of the SR in the 2016 elections, where it won 8.04 percent of the votes (Volbysr.sk 2016), created a new line of conflict in Slovak politics. In 2014, during the protests in Kiev, when Chairman of the Banská Bystrica Self-governing Region, Kotleba wrote a letter to the then Ukrainian President Viktor Janukovych, in which he expressed his support for his administration as well as for the policy of the RF toward Ukraine. The protests, he said, aimed to bring Ukraine closer to NATO (Vražda 2014). In the runup to the March 2016 parliamentary elections, his party declared that Slovakia´s withdrawal from NATO was part of its program, and also announced that it would launch a referendum on Slovakia´s withdrawal from the EU. The party program advocated replacement of a one-sided orientation towars the West *"with a balanced cooperation with all countries of the world"* (ĽSNS 2016. The RF's foreign policy is also openly supported by the extra-parliamentary Communist Party of Slovakia.

The official position of Smer-SD, the strongest political party in Slovakia, on the Ukrainian crisis is in keeping with the line pursued by the EU and NATO. On the other hand, with an eye to its voters, it speaks against escalating tensions in relations with the RF. Smer-SD's Chairman and Prime Minister Fico dismisses speculation about Ukraine's entry into NATO (Pravda 2014a). At the same time, Slovakia was among the first EU member states to ratify the EU-Ukraine Association Agreement (following Bulgaria, Latvia, Lithuania, Malta and Romania), with 132 out of 134 present deputies voting in favor of the ratification, where, in the sixth electoral term of the National Council (2012-2016), Smer-SD enjoyed an absolute majority in parliament. What is more, the government, composed exclusively of Smer-SD nominees, consented to reverse the flow of natural gas via the Vojany-Uzhorod pipeline, which allowed Ukraine to minimize their dependence on natural gas supplies from the RF (Webnoviny 2014a). On the other hand, Slovakia, like Germany and the Czech Republic, is reticent about Ukraine's demand for supplies of deadly weapons, even though Slovakia provides Ukraine with military training of and humanitarian aid in the wake of the armed conflict in Donbass (Glváč 2014; Čaplovič, Stupňan 2014).

Some politicians from the party, such as Chairman of the Committee of the National Council of the SR for European Affairs Ľuboš Blaha, actively criticized EU and NATO policy against the RF while voting to adopt the EU-Ukraine Association Agreement. The coordinated European Affairs Committee of the National Council of the SR, headed by Blaha, took note of the proposal to introduce visa-free travel for citizens of Ukraine visiting the EU for a three-month stay, thereby allowing its adoption (NRSR 2016). At the same time, Blaha pointed to the role of extreme right-wing Ukrainian political groups in the Maidan protests and in Ukrainian post-2014 policy, accusing the West of orchestrating the coup in Ukraine. With regard to the Crimean events, he has said that the population of the peninsula had the right to civil disobedience (Blaha 2014). He has spoken against the policy of isolating Russia, expressed criticism of the current Ukrainian leadership, and maintained contacts with representatives of the RF. Gradually, he has begun to show attitudes that run counter to critical dialogue with the RF, as advocated by the Slovak government, despite being a member of the deputy club of the strongest government coalition party (Smer-SD). He has often stressed not only that he regards Russia as *"a culturally related nation and very close to ours,"* but also that *"to us, Russia is a friend that liberated us from fascism and it is in our interests to have the best possible relations with the country"* (Kapusta 2018). He has also spoken against "Russophobia," i.e., anti-Russian sentiments, in international forums, such as the Parliamentary Assembly of the Council of Europe, where he is head of the delegation of the SR. At a session in January 2018, he dismissed the view that the RF is an enemy, blaming the conflict in East Ukraine on both parties equally and refusing the policy of sanctions against the RF (Council of Europe 2018).

In a similar vein, the Smer-SD EP deputy Monika Flašíková-Beňová interpreted the Crimea referendum of 2014 as a decision of the local population, breaking from the position held by Slovakia's government and the parliament majority (Webnoviny 2014b). Later, however, she adopted a more critical stance on the RF and its Ukrainian policy.

Slovakia's government policy implies that, while being based on the common position of the EU and NATO, it is not interested in escalating conflict with the RF but in achieving security and stability.Maintaining favorable relations with Russia still remains the government's objective, as testified by the role that Smer-SD played in organizing the Road to Peace on 6-7 March 2015 in Košice, initiated by the German-Russian Forum headed by the former leader of the German Social-Democratic Party (SPD) Matthias Platzek, considered a pro-Russian politician. The conference was attended by representatives of the pro-Russian separatists from Donbass. The Smer-SD chairman cancelled his attendance just before the conference began (Slovak Spectator 2015a; Slovak Spectator 2015b). Mitigating or lifting the sanctions against the RF was the main message of the "Capitalism in the 21st century — Europe without future?" conference organized by Smer-SD in December 2015 in Bratislava, attended by Slovakia's Prime Minister Fico, members of SPD who advocated close cooperation between Germany and the RF (M. Platzek, Gerhard Schröder), and the EU deputy for ČSSD Jan Keller (Teraz.sk 2015).

The parties with a more pronounced stance on the issue of Slovak-Russian relations in 2014-2015 were NOVA, headed by Daniel Lipšic, and Sloboda a Solidarita ("Freedom and Solidarity," SAS) led by Richard Sulík, who even called Fico a threat to national security for his soft stance on Russia (SaS 2014) and criticized Fico's decision to take part in the celebrations of the 70th anniversary of the end of World War II in Moscow, saying that it called Slovakia's European credibility into doubt (Webnoviny 2015b). Unlike Sulík, representatives of other opposition parties did not condemn Fico's visit to Moscow, but supported his decision not to take part in the military parade in Red Square due to Russia's involvement in the Ukrainian crisis (Webnoviny 2015a).

During the presidential elections of 2014, the issue of relations with Russia and attitudes to the Ukrainian crisis played only a minor part. Candidates who openly expressed their support for the RF's policy did not succeed. The former Prime Minister of the SR (1991-1992) and Chairman of the Christian-Democratic movement (KDH) (1990-2000) Ján Čarnogurský, who termed Crimea's annexation "a return of historical territories" to the sovereignty of the RF (Čarnogurský 2014), won 12,207 votes in the presidential elections (0.64 percent), while another pro-Russian candidate Ján Jurišta, backed by the Slovak Communist Party (KSS), won 12,209 votes (Štatistický úrad 2014).

Likewise, during the parliamentary elections of March 2016, the question of relations with the RF was not a main issue of the election campaign. Apart from the Kotleba—ĽSNS Party mentioned above, the other pro-Russian groupings received considerably fewer votes. KSS won 0.62 percent while Odvaha (Courage)—a large nationalist and pro-Russian coalition—a mere 0.13 percent (Štatistický úrad 2016). The result of the parliamentary elections confirmed Fico's position as the Prime Minister of the SR. Alongside Smer-SD, the government coalition included the Slovak National Party (SNS) and Most-Híd. Although in the runup to the election SNS presented itself as a pro-Russian party, calling the sanctions against Russia an act of aggression (Rafaj 2014), it stopped questioning Slovakia's foreign policy when it joined the government. By contrast, another coalition partner—Most-Híd—

pursues an openly pro-Atlantic course. Its deputy to the National Council František Šebej accuses Russia of efforts to undermine EU's integrity (Teraz.sk 2016). While most of the center-right parties perceive the RF's current policy as a security risk, the position of the ruling Smer-SD, but also of a part of the opposition, uses softer rhetoric. In November 2016, Chairman of SaS Sulík, with five other European Parliament deputies elected for the Slovak Republic (Monika Flašíková-Beňová, Vladimír Maňka, Monika Smolková – Smer-SD; Branislav Škripek – OĽaNO; Anna Záborská – KDH) abstained from voting on the resolution that denounced the information activities of the RF and Islamic terrorist organizations aimed at undermining trust in democratic values, calling upon the EU to support free media in the post-Soviet countries and to fund the activities whose aim is to challenge the said propaganda and disinformation (such as a group of experts of the European Commission East StratCom). Most center-right EP deputies, but also Boris Zala, elected for Smer-SD, backed this resolution (Pál Csáky – SMK; Eduard Kukan – SDKÚ-DS; József Nagy –Most-Híd; Jana Žitňanská – NOVA; Miroslav Mikolášik and Ivan Štefanec – KDH). The PES Group proposed different wording; however, Maňka's claimed that their intention was not to block the adoption of the resolution. Sulík argued primarily on the grounds of freedom of speech while Záborská objected to lumping Russian and Islamist propaganda together (Európsky parlament 2016).

In the post-election period, Andrej Kiska, President of the SR, criticized Slovakia's policy towards the RF, saying that the Slovak administration has been sending "mixed signals" by, on the one hand, supporting sanctions against Russia, while on the other it criticizes them and questions their relevance. He also said that the RF's leadership *"has grossly violated the fundamental principles of the post-war respect for the sovereignty and territorial integrity of Europe. Crimea's annexation and the military support for the separatists in East Ukraine are unacceptable moves that cannot be left without response"* (Prezident.sk 2017a) . In response, Prime Minister Fico argued for the steps taken by the SR government to stabilize the situation in Ukraine (Pravda 2017).

A new factor in the political debate on Slovak-Russian relations is the emergence of some extra-parliamentary pro-Russian political formations, which have announced their intention to enter actively into politics, such as Slovenské hnutie obrody ("Slovak Revival Movement," SHO) with a strong Pan-Slavic bent or a potential party of the unsuccessful presidential candidate Štefan Harabin (SHO 2016). As a follow-up to the Pan-Slavic Congress in Moscow held 26 May-2 June 2017, the editor-in-chief of the Zem a vek (Earth and Era) journal announced jointly with Mladá Matica, Slavica (which took part in the Pan-Slavic Congress with the Matica slovenská representatives) and Slovenskí slobodní motorkári ("Slovak Free Bikers"), that a celebration of Slavism and statehood would be held on the Jankov Vŕšok Mountain on 29 August 2017. The purpose of the event was not only to "find a new integration potential among the V4 countries, particularly in a Slavic Europe of 300 million," but also to submit a proposal for a new candidate for the post of the President of the SR (Oslavy Slovanstva 2017). This statement was in line with the spirit of the Congress, whose declaration called for the establishment of a Commonwealth of Independent Slavic States (Trinitas.ru 2017).

During the years 2015 and 2016, the relevance of the Ukrainian crisis in Slovak politics and especially in party discourse diminished. The political crisis in Ukraine, which broke out in November 2013 and which, due to its internationalization, escalated into perhaps the most violent crisis in the relations between the West (i.e., EU and USA) and the RF since the end of the Cold War, stirring considerable emotions in Slovak society, has not so far contributed to reshaping the Slovak political scene. Despite the tensions between the Slovak government and the EU regarding mandatory refugee quotas, most relevant political parties in the SR do not regard political and security cooperation with Russia as an alternative to Slovakia's membership in NATO and the EU. When the extreme right-wing ĽSNS, under the influence of a successful referendum in the UK, launched a campaign to leave the EU and NATO, it failed to gain support from other political parties, including the Eurosckeptic group Sme rodina ("We Are Family") led by Boris Kollár (Kyseľ 2016). However, during the years 2017 and 2018, the mood of the party discourse on the relations between the SR and the RF changed., The Chairman of the National Council and leader of the coalition SNS Andrej Danko, in his address in the Russian State Duma on 15 November 2017, recognized the role of the RF in maintaining world peace and advocated the idea of Slavic mutuality (SNS 2018). This was met with disapproval from Slovakia's Minister of Foreign and European Affairs Miroslav Lajčák (Lajčák 2017), who had criticized the EU and USA sanctions against the RF since 2017. Although the three highest state officials of the SR announced in their joint declaration of October 2018 their support for *"a clear continuation of the pro-European and pro-Atlantic orientation"* as a *"strategic interest of the Slovak Republic"* (Prezident.sk 2017b), in reality their interpretation of current relations between the SR, or the EU, and the RF is fundamentally different. For this reason, it is not possible to regard the policy of the SR toward the RF as a product of consensus of political forces. One example of the absence of this consensus is the fact that SNS spoke against submitting the proposal of two key documents — Defence Strategy of the SR and Security Strategy of the SR — to the National Council of the SR, even though both documents were approved by the SR government in October 2017. Representatives of this party disapprove of the fact that both documents allegedly define the RF as an enemy.

In 2018, the issue of Slovak-Russian relations once more became the focus of conflict in the government coalition in connection with the case of poisoning of the former federal intelligence officer of the Russian Federation Sergei Skripal and his daughter Yulia in Salisbury, UK. According to the official investigation, both were poisoned by the chemical substance called Novichok. British Prime Minister Theresa May blamed Russia's military agency GRU (the Main Directorate of the General Staff of the Armed Forces of the Russian Federation) for the attack, which led to the expulsion of 23 Russian diplomats from the United Kingdom. This step was followed, in varying degrees, by 21 EU member countries (including Hungary, which has the closest ties to Russia of all V4 countries), the USA and Ukraine. By contrast, Slovakia, like Austria, Slovenia, Bulgaria, Cyprus, Luxembourg,

Greece and Malta, did not follow their example, limiting itself only to the removal of ambassador Peter Priputen from his office in Moscow (Wróbel 2018). State Secretary of the Ministry of Foreign and European Affairs of the SR Lukáš Parízek summoned Russian Ambassador Alexei Fedotov, and described Russia's act as a *"straightforward violation of international law"* (MZVaEZ SR 2018). The decision not to expel Russian diplomats sparked discontent among the opposition parties Sloboda a Solidarita (SaS) and Obyčajní ľudia a nezávislé osdobnosti (OľaNO), but also a conflict between the Most-Híd and its coalition partners in Smer-SD and SNS. Chair of the Foreign Committee of the National Council of the SR Katarína Cséfalvayová (Most-Híd) described the behavior of the coalition partners as "ambiguous." According to her, Slovakia should have followed the example of the other V4 countries (Dennikn 2018).

***

Although the subject of Slovak-Russian relations is not a matter of consensus at the level of political parties and is often a focus of political conflict, conflict was more palpable in the civic sector than in the political parties. What is more, the political discourse reveals the rather weak position of openly pro-Russian, identity-driven attitudes. A more radical change was only accomplished by SNS, by transforming the dispute over the form of Slovak-Russian relations into one between the ruling coalition and the opposition, and within the ruling coalition itself, where SNS's positions are shared by Ľuboš Blaha (Smer-SD), Chairman of the Committee of the National Council of the SR for European Affairs.

While opponents of the official position of the EU and NATO against Russia present their criticisms without putting forward viable alternatives, it cannot be ruled out that this question will become the focus of party debate, given the broad readership of such periodicals as Zem a vek. For the time being, due to the absence of relevant pro-Russian political parties, with the exception of ĽSNS, one cannot speak of a new cleavage in Slovak society able to affect electoral competition. Still, given the policy of SNS and its chairman after 2017, one could say that a new line of division is beginning to form.

In relations with the RF, the preservation of EU and NATO integrity still remains the key national interest of the SR. Membership in the latter organizations is also a matter of the country's political identity. In terms of the choice of the nature of political regime, it is clear that closer cooperation with the RF in political and security areas, at the expense of its membership in the EU and NATO, is mostly advanced by the political parties that claim the legacy of non-democratic regimes in the past, such as ĽSNS, the Slovak National Revival Movement and the Communist Party of Slovakia. In this regard, the decision to form a strategic alliance with Russia would cast doubt upon the current internal political identity to which most of the political forces in the SR, represented in the National Council of the SR, have subscribed.

All in all, Slovak political parties differ from each other in their formulation of political priorities in relation to the RF and in the degree of criticism directed at its policies. While Smer-SD, as the strongest political party in the SR, seeks to maintain both friendly relations with the RF and the current level of economic cooperation, some other political parties, as well as President Andrej Kiska, express their reservations about the RF's foreign policy in stronger terms, beyond what is usually termed "critical dialogue," which does not contradict the European stance, as presented by the Minister of Foreign and European Affairs of the SR Miroslav Lajčák (Lajčák 2016).

It is in the permanent interest of the SR, one shared by all relevant political parties, to preserve smooth flow of energy raw materials, especially of oil and natural gas, as well as of the transit of natural gas through the territory of the SR. This interest, however, is of secondary importance to the RF, as is increasing the volume of bilateral trade. To be exact, security of energy supplies for the SR may be described as an interest with a high degree of relevance, as viewed by the political elites of the SR. One of the long-term priorities of the SR is respect for the principle of the territorial integrity of states and the inviolability of borders without the consent of the relevant parties. Following Crimea's annexation by the RF and after unilateral recognition of the independence of the Georgian regions of Abkhazia and Southern Ossetia, Russia can hardly be regarded as a relevant partner of the SR on this issue, which is a major national security concern for the SR. Another long-term interest of the SR, shared by the majority of the relevant political parties, is maintaining close cooperation with Ukraine, its rapprochement with the EU and its political stabilization.

Based on the above facts, we may conclude that in the context of the Ukrainian crisis, the national interests of the SR are not in line with the steps taken by the RF toward Ukraine. Although one cannot speak categorically of a consolidated position of the SR toward the RF, especially given the difference between the rhetoric of some of government officials of the SR when addressing a domestic public and the practical steps taken in the area of foreign policy, including SR strategy at the level of the EU structures, one can safely state that the key priority of the foreign policy of the SR, its key national interest, is integration into the EU, while efforts at a dialogue with the RF present an interest of secondary importance.

9. Slovak National Interest: A Difficult Pursuit. The Three Key Blockages to the Attainment of National Interest

David Reichardt

The relatively small country of Slovakia was formed in 1993 with the formal partition of the Czechoslovakia into the Czech and Slovak Republics. In the first twelve years of its existence, it made major strides in crafting its own independent identity. It joined the Council of Europe in 1993, and NATO and the European Union (EU) in 2004. From 1998 until roughly 2006, it brought a wealth of foreign direct investment into the country, ensuring thousands of new jobs.

Yet in spite of these major accomplishments, Slovakia appears not to have done much since to advance. One is hard pressed to point to any accomplishments comparable to those mentioned above. The result has been governments that have settled for "muddling through," simply fulfilling the tasks of the day to day running of government, rather than anything more ambitious. There almost appears to be a lack of awareness of the national interest, or a paralysis in regards to articulating or advancing it.

The question of this chapter is: why? Why has Slovakia not visibly advanced its national interests in the past twelve years relative to the previous twelve? This chapter argues that the reasons are largely threefold. They reflect more or less structural blockages in three key areas of government and society: a) Ideology; b) Corruption; and c) Short-term decision-making. In order to advance these explanations, this chapter begins with a definition and discussion of the core concept of "national interests."

"National interests" is a disputed concept in the scholarly field of international relations. It is basically taken to imply the desires of a particular country. In this understanding, the "National" of National Interests is somewhat of a misnomer, as it is not intended to refer to the "Nation," but rather to the "State." Thus, any discussion of National Interests today—particularly in "Western" academic journals—invariably implies the interests of the state. However, beyond that there is little academic or political consensus on the precise meaning of the term. This is highlighted tellingly by Scott Burchell in his book, *The National Interest in International Relations*. As he writes, there are those who hold national interests to be objectively "discoverable," like scholars such as Joseph Frankel, while others view them as always subjective or contextual, as did the British scholar Martin Wight in his now famous 1950s lecture series on international relations (Burchill 2005, 3-5).

This relatively small chapter, will not engage the debate, but rather recognize that national interests may have varying interpretations. Here, national interests will simply be defined as those things which all states need or perceive that they need for their survival and advancement. Joseph S. Nye puts it more generally: "National Interests are a state's perceptions of its goals in the international system." National Interests can be more universal—such as Security—or more particular to one state—such as improved relations with a hostile neighbor, additional grain imports, or access to a specific waterway. As such, national interests are often contrasted with "Identity," "Ideals," or "Ideological objectives" which states also pursue—sometimes in contradiction to their national interests. The United States, for example, has often been blamed for confusing the two, in part by pursuing costly, extensive wars intended to advance the values of democratic liberalism, while resulting in no concrete advantages to the US in and of themselves—and often to US detriment. The Vietnam War and the second Gulf War were both cast in this light at times. An even more extreme example of a country obfuscating interests due to its ideals is National Socialist Germany and the way it doggedly pursued its racist ideology at the expense of actually winning the war. Thus, it is a delicate business for any government to pursue National Ideals while keeping their eyes clearly on the National Interest, working hard not to neglect the latter in its pursuit of the former.

However, national interests, even when unencumbered by ideological blindness, can still be difficult to perceive. A classic example is the national interest of the United Kingdom in 1938 vis-à-vis an increasingly aggressive, demanding Germany. Prime Minister Neville Chamberlain obviously felt he was pursuing British national interests of stability in Europe when he engaged in "appeasement" of the Germans at Munich, and if they had lived up to that agreement, he might well have been proven correct. However, as the world soon learned, he was very, very wrong. In this case, "knowing the adversary" was critical to knowing the best approach to the national interest, and Chamberlain, who clearly had little idea as to the true character of his opponent, ultimately made a decision that ran directly counter to British national interests.

Indeed, regarding the complex nature of national interests, Nye makes this observation:

> *It is important to bear in mind that the National Interest is almost always contested. People who would agree at an abstract level that power and security are important national interests very often disagree about the concrete policies that promote them. Sometimes policy preferences are completely opposite and incompatible. During the period between the two world wars, there was a vibrant debate in the United States between those who believed that the best way to promote American security was to avoid becoming entangled in the thorny power politics of Europe and East Asia, and those who believed that American security depended upon actively working with others to check the rising power and imperial ambitions of Germany and Japan* (Nye, Welch 2013, 52).

Thus, national interests—as regards their articulation, formulation in policy, and striving for them—are contextual. They depend on the best information, on knowing the general situation, and on knowing one's adversary at any given time and place.

National interests are also subject to clashes among themselves. This is particularly true in the sense of short- versus long-term national interests. Short-term interests are those whose goals one immediately desires, while long-term interests are those for which it is worth to forgo the immediate gain to wait for fulfillment of a longer term objective. The problem here is that the two may be completely incompatible, with pursuit of the short-term jeopardizing the realization of the long-term and vice versa. This can be clearly seen even in personal human relations. A verbal argument, for example, between two marriage partners is just such a case. It may be in the short-term interest of the partner with the better reasoned argument to aggressively drive home his or her point—thus winning "the battle," potentially leaving the other partner demoralized or upset. However, is this really the best long-term approach in the interest of loving mutual relations, especially as the "marriage game" continues for life? One sees similarities in international relations. Is it really in the long-term interests, for example, for either the Israelis or the Palestinians to score a quick victory, humiliating the other, knowing that their futures are tied indefinitely and intimately together on a narrow strip of Middle Eastern land? As will be seen later in this chapter, all of these dimensions of national interests have affected Slovakia since its independence from the state of Czechoslovakia in 1993.

Slovakia, a country of roughly five and a half million people, is one of the smaller countries in Central Europe. As such, like all states, it has interests related to its size and location, but also to its particular political circumstances. First, upon separating from Czechoslovakia in 1993 and forming an independent state, it was critical for Slovakia to cultivate good relations with states that could assist it. Its entry into the Council of Europe in 1993 showed that it was a serious state with democratic credentials that wished to further them. In terms of security, as a country literally bordering "Western and Eastern" Europe, Slovakia needed a firm security arrangement. This involved advancing the physical security of the country, and the Slovak government attended to this through joining NATO and regularly participating in its exercises. Since that time, it has worked hard to "catch up" to its fellow NATO partners militarily. It entered NATO's integrated command structure, upgraded its material capabilities, and participated in a number of training exercises and actual military missions (e.g., Afghanistan, Albania, Angola, Bosnia and Herzegovina, East Timor, Ethiopia and Eritrea, Iraq, Kosovo, Kuwait, Liberia, Macedonia, Moldova, Rwanda, Sierra Leone, Sudan/Darfur, Uganda, etc.).

To advance itself politically, Slovakia joined the European Union. After successful ratification of the Accession Treaty, the

Slovak Republic became an EU member state on 1 May 2004. In doing so, it accepted the EU's Treaties, adopted the Acquis Communautaire, or Body of Laws of the organization, and placed itself under the authority of EU institutions, such as the Court of Justice. Slovakia also acceded to the United Nations (1993), the World Trade Organization (1995), and the International Criminal Court (2002). Economically, Slovakia accepted the Euro currency (2009), the EU's trade policy, and opened up its economy to foreign direct investment (FDI). The latter has involved multinationals such as Kia, IBM, Samsung, US Steel and Volkswagen moving major parts of their operations to Slovakia, creating thousands of new jobs within the country.

These were all major accomplishments of the young Slovakia's early formulation in the 1990s and the early part of the new millennium, and each was a huge step in the direction of the country's national interests.

However, in the more recent past, Slovakia has been backsliding or, at a minimum, stagnating in terms of any further recognizable advancement in its key interests. For example, since 2006, foreign direct investment has slowed. A high-profile symbol of this has been the departure of US Steel. The giant steel concern pulled out of Slovakia in 2017, selling off its major holdings to the Chinese He Steel Group. Though the current Slovak government apparently tried to halt this move with a five-year memorandum between the Slovak government and US Steel, it allowed it to expire without offering further concessions to the steel corporation to remain (Slovak Spectator 2017b). It is feared the new controlling Chinese group will cut jobs, skimp on investment, and pay less attention to environmental concerns.

Figure 2

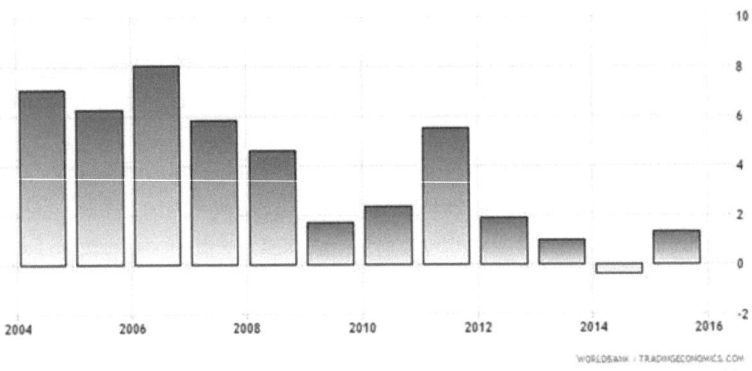

(Trading Economics, 2017)

The above chart shows, relatively, the dramatic falling-off in foreign direct investment in Slovakia in the past years. It is important to remark here that what was achieved earlier was largely due to the efforts of an activist government, namely the "Dzurinda government" which held office from 1998-2006. It actively sought out international firms to relocate to Slovakia and to keep them there with enticements such as tax incentives, low wages, and the promise of industrial parks. A lack of similar vision and energy has characterized subsequent Slovak governments.

Additionally, there are any number of international projects of material benefit to Slovakia that have been neglected. One of the most recent is a plan to extend the broad-gauge rail line from eastern Slovakia to Vienna, to enable the smoother transport of goods from China via Russia and Ukraine. This project has been "on the table" in Slovakia for several years, but so far not even a feasibility study for the project has been completed (Slovak Spectator 2017a). It is entirely possible that such projects will be picked up again by subsequent governments; however, taking important steps and furthering them are two different things, and so far little of the latter has been in evidence.

Given this background, this chapter turns now to explain some of the reasons why Slovakia has been so slow to realize the development of its national interests in the past twelve years, focusing on the three key blockages referred to earlier: 1) Ideology; 2) Corruption; and 3) Short-term decision-making.

Ideology is often a "killer" of a country's national interests, particularly when it clashes with or becomes entwined in its foreign policies. This need not always be the case. For example, the "democracy promotion" emphasis of the early post- World War II United States government certainly enhanced American prestige and economic relations abroad (e.g., democratic peace, the securing of allies, dollar dominance, free trade benefits, etc.). However, it is far from certain that ideology will always work this way. As mentioned previously, the United States democracy-promotion emphasis also got it into considerable trouble in Vietnam and the Middle East. It is rarer for a country's ideology to be in sync with its national interests than to be aligned with them. In terms of the latter, the extreme example of this is again National Socialist Germany—which undermined its own war effort by imprisoning and murdering hundreds of thousands of its own citizens and relegating its women largely to the home rather than to the factory.

As a relatively new state in Central Europe, the situation of Slovakia requires a clear vision (if not strategy) for identifying and securing its national interests. However, within the country the "politics of ideals" or ideology appears to have repeatedly overshadowed if not actually trumped the "politics of interests." A variety of factors have combined to cause this. First, there was the lag in attaining democratic liberalism following the communist period; countries that experienced highly ideological socialism emerged in a much different form than their Western European counterparts when released from its bonds after 1989. For one, the nature of their political parties took on a different character—at once more parochial (i.e., less attached to their sister parties abroad), and, secondly, more ideological. Take, for example, the KDH—or Christian Democratic Party of Slovakia. Only with difficulty could one even begin to compare it its mission and perspective with that of the CDU of Germany. The latter is today a broad-based conservative party, with only the loosest ties to any Christian denomination or dogma. The KDH, by contrast, remains closely in tune with core Christian principles and aligned with the

Catholic Church. This has included a strong focus on moral/political issues such as abortion, divorce, same-sex marriage, and Vatican relations. Likewise the right wing Slovak National Party—or SNS—has tended to be much more blatantly ideologically "nationalist" than its counterparts in the "West," openly challenging and picking fights with the parties of Slovakia's Hungarian minority, sparring partners on which its *raison d'être* ultimately depends. Meanwhile the Slovak center-left has remained further to the left than most mainstream "Western" center-leftist parties (one thinks here of the British Labour Party or Germany's Social Democratic Party). Finally, the SaS, or Slovak Liberal party harkens back to the Liberals of the nineteenth century in its radical laissez-faire agenda, and can in no way be compared to the moderate Liberals of Germany or the British Liberal Party.

Figure 3

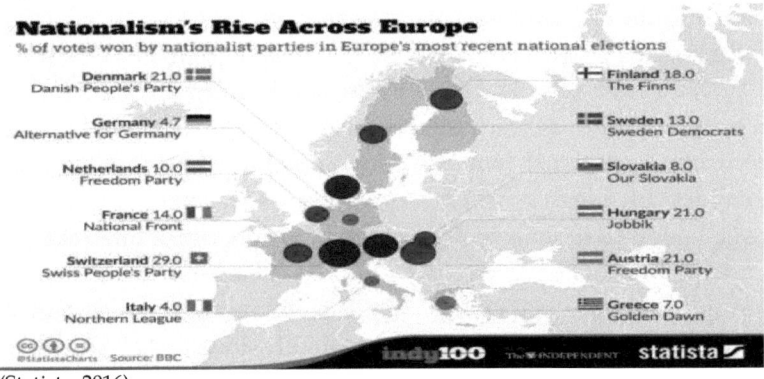

(Statista, 2016)

The argument here is that the narrower ideological focus of Slovakia's political parties prevents policy makers in these parties from concentrating on the larger issues of Slovak national interests. A very good example of this is the SNS protesting Slovakia's NATO membership. It has been joined in this—though less assertively—by some members of the dominant SMER party, despite that party's official recognition of NATO membership. In terms of the SNS, the explanation is clear: Slovak nationalists distrust foreigners, and that includes, of course, the Americans who are perceived as unduly controlling NATO. Meanwhile, the left-leaning SMER nostalgically looks back to the socialist solidarity that once obtained between Czechoslovakia and Russia, a country it still views as a friend, despite the conflicted and confused politics of the present Russian government.

Perhaps the ultimate example of ideology in party politics trumping interests involved the SaS, a government coalition partner in 2006, which committed political suicide by strictly adhering to its radical liberal principles and demanding a rejection of the EU's financial bailout plan for Greece. The government of which it was a part subsequently fell on the issue and new elections were held. The SaS lost and was not included in the new coalition.

A further case is that of Slovakia's membership in the European Union. One would think that a small country like Slovakia would work harder to cultivate ties with neighboring post-communist states like Hungary, in order to increase its lobbying power within the constructs of the EU. But here again it appears that ideology trumps national interest. Slovak nationalism, once more, played an influential role. Politicians of the SNS and other parties have made a career of extolling Slovak national virtues at the expense of better relations with Hungary. Perhaps a low point was in 2009, when no less a figure than the Hungarian President Laszlo Solyom was prevented from completing a private visit to the ethnically Hungarian town of Komarno, there to unveil a statue of King Stephen I of Hungary. The Slovak government said that he was not welcome in Slovakia on this day and that his planned visit was a "provocation" (European Court of Justice 2012). Since that time Slovak nationalism has worked against better relations with Hungary that would advantage Slovak national interests.

These examples highlight the fact that "coalition government" magnifies the effects of ideological nationalism and detracts from a focus on national interests. This is primarily due to two factors. First, much of the energy of government is spent in simply holding the coalition together. Pleasing—or at least not overly upsetting coalition partners—is a primary objective. A unified national interest focus often takes second place to this all-important task.

This has been all the more true in Slovakia, due to its rather odd mixtures of coalition partners in the past several governments. For example, the 2005 government consisted of the center-left SMER party, the rightist nationalist SNS party, and the former ruling party—the populist (and suspect) Movement for a Democratic Slovakia. The government of 2008 included the secular conservative SDKU, the highly Catholic KDU and the radical Liberal SaS. Finally, the government formed in 2012—which still governs today—includes the center-left SMER, the rightist nationalist SNS and the Hungarian dominated MOST-HID party!

Second, in order to hang together, a coalition needs to compromise—sometimes creating an ideological mess. Concretely, this means that the country is often mired in domestic infighting and coalition politics built around coming to terms with "who" rather than "what it wants to accomplish for the country." In such a situation, national interests once again get pushed into the background.

A second consideration that detracts from national interests in Slovak government is "corruption." Corruption eats away at the national interests of a country, due to diversion from the public good and toward the enrichment of particular individuals and concerns in society. Countries heavily burdened by corruption make very little economic, social or political progress relative to countries that are not so heavily burdened. According to the 2016/17 Global Competitiveness Report of the World Economic Forum, Slovakia is one of the most corrupt countries in Europe with a score of 3.7 (Slovak Spectator 2016d). Finland was the least corrupt with a score of 6.3. In fact, the country report for Slovakia shows that corruption, tax rates and inefficient government bureaucracy are the three most problematic factors for doing business in Slovakia. Financial scandals abound. According to the World Economic Forum:

> *Political corruption in Slovakia remains a huge problem. The "Gorilla scandal" that rocked the country in 2011 indicated that politicians, business leaders, and officials routinely take bribes in exchange for private contracts* (Business Insider 2016).

Figure 4 gives a good comparative view of the relative corruption problem plaguing Slovakia:

Figure 4

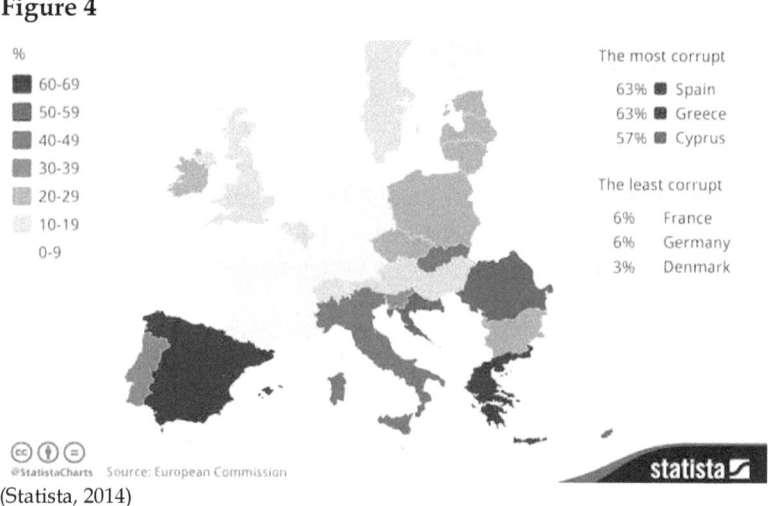

(Statista, 2014)

The "Gorilla Scandal" — the largest of the scandals in Slovakia of the recent past — refers to a wiretap file from the years 2005-2006 which leaked to the internet in December 2011, and which contained information about politicians, officials, and business executives discussing kickbacks in return for government contracts (Financial Times 2012). It resulted in some of the largest public protests yet seen in the young country. More recent scandals include those of the high-profile financial affairs involving Slovak Interior Minister Robert Kaliňák (Slovak Spectator 2016c) and the Minister of Education Peter Plavčan (Slovak Spectator 2017d), but there have been dozens more. In fact, Slovakia and Ukraine share the second worst position in the World Economic Forum's "corruption index" where they both scored 2.72 (Slovak Spectator 2016d). The dire situation of corruption in Slovakia provoked large public protests again in Slovak cities in 2017. The most recent protests have been led by a group of very young urban activists who, according to an article in the journal Foreign Policy, *"have riled up the status quo and antagonized plenty of older Slovaks; part of the first generation born and raised inside the European Union, they have a different set of expectations about what their government is meant to be"* (Foreign Policy 2017). It goes almost without saying that a society that must turn its attention to addressing widespread corruption is simultaneously crippled in terms of articulating and pursuing its larger national interests.

The third key blockage to a focus on national interests in Slovakia is the government's decision-making. Specifically, it is its "short term decision-making proclivity." The differences in short-term vs. long-term decision-making in foreign policy were nicely articulated by Ernest Petričin his book, *Foreign Policy: From Conception to Diplomatic Practice*, in which he notes:

> Sometimes, short-term and temporary goals and the vision of the political elite, or the interests of other elites, such as leading economic groups, are identified as the national interest. These "national interests" usually bear no relation to the actual national interest. Frequently, such partial interests which do not coincide with the real national interest are presented to the public as the "national interest" (Petrič 2013, 108).

In this context, the Slovak government has been increasingly conflicted in reconciling its short-term interests with its longer term national interests. For example, the illegitimate invasion by Russia into the sovereign territory of Ukraine in 2014, which was recognized as such by the United Nations, caused the government of Slovakia no small degree of confusion. Should it side with its member organizations, the United Nations, the European Union, and NATO, all of which condemned the invasion and annexation of Crimea, as well as Russian incursions into eastern Ukraine (the "Donbass region")? Or should it ignore the UN, EU and NATO stances, and side with Russia, from which it gets the vast majority of its oil, natural gas, and nuclear fuel for two power plants? The government initially chose the latter. During a visit of Russian Foreign Minister Sergai Lavrov to celebrate the 70th anniversary of the liberation of Slovakia from Nazi occupation by the Soviet Army,Lavrov stated that that *"Moscow and Bratislava share a common position on Ukraine"*(Wall Street Journal 2015). For its part, the Slovak government called for greater diplomatic efforts toward a peace treaty between Ukraine and Russia. Thereafter, the Slovak government at first ignored pleas from the European Commission for a show of unity on the Crimea situation. Practically, this meant delaying support for a first round of EU economic sanctions against Russia as well as a second round, while complaining about them most of the way. Slovak Prime Minister Robert Fico was quoted at his August 2016 meeting with President Putin in Russia as saying:

> *Personally, I think it is time to view the sanctions rationally and to say that they harm both the EU and Russia. They have brought absolutely nothing to (solving) the sensitive questions which they were supposed to influence. We agreed with Vladimir Putin that our common pursuit is to revive our mutual trade again* (Reuters 2016).

He reiterated these feelings again after the EU Summit meeting in Brussels on 21 October 2016 saying, "*the European Union's sanctions against Russia are pointless and do not work*" (Slovak Spectator 2016a). Slovak foreign Minister, Miroslav Lajčák, has been fully supportive of such views and has worked to advance them in policy, to the frustration of EU and NATO leaders.

The result has been a murky Slovak policy simultaneously aimed at appeasing Russia and Solvakia's member state organizations. According to commentary by Euractiv, Slovakia is engaged in:

> *...an awkward balancing act ...preserving the economic benefits of being close to Russia while also belonging to a European Union set on punishing the Kremlin for annexing Ukrainian territory* (Euractiv 2014).

Clearly, this approach, which has been seen by some as "disloyal" or even "cowardly," was in Slovakia's short-term national interests. Russian gas and oil—if denied to other EU member states by Russia due to the economic sanctions—might still be supplied, uninterrupted, to the Slovak state. However, was this in the longer term national interests of Slovakia? Was it wise to break with both EU and NATO partner states and go with short-term gain at the expense of longer term solidarity and support? One is reminded here of the classic "Stag Hunt" in game theory, in which a hunter goes for the short-term gain of capturing the hare as opposed to remaining with the group, which is necessary to ensnare the much larger stag. As the Ukraine conflict worsens, is such a strategy by the Slovak state sustainable? At what point, does it become a danger to good relations with the EU and NATO, so that those organizations and their members will deny support to Slovakia when she is in need?

These are questions that it appears the Slovak government has not, to date, taken fully into consideration. One is painfully reminded of the short-term decision-making of a much earlier Slovak government—that of the first Slovak Republic under President Tiso—in which Slovakia cooperated with the wartime Nazi regime of Germany with apparently little thought to the outcome of the war—which even at the outset was far from certain. The well-known disastrous results led to the loss of sovereignty of the young independent state and the execution of its president.

While much has changed since the 1940s, the similarities regarding both governments' inability to avoid the temptations of short-term benefits at the risk of long-term ruin are inescapable. The clear lesson is that, while short-term interests certainly need to be taken into account, they may be pursued only at the risk of a state's longer term interests, which may include its very survival.

A second example of Slovakia's short-term decision-making tendency involves its behavior in the European Union itself. Slovakia has presently been a member state for almost 14 years. In that time, the country has been a net beneficiary, reaping the benefits of a relatively poorer member state in the first part of the new millennium. Objectively, one might very well deem this a national interest victory for the small state. Yet when one considers the longer term interests of the country, the situation becomes more disturbing. Slovakia has largely subsisted without any remarkable contribution to the EU's ongoing formation. What has Slovakia contributed to the EU's vision? How has it helped to improve the organization, in a way that would further Slovakia's own future interests? One would be hard pressed to list any accomplishments in any specific area of EU policy where Slovakia led the way. To adapt a phrase, Slovakia has acted as a proverbial "free rider," eschewing a leadership role.

This was set to change in the second half of 2016, as Slovakia assumed the six-month rotating presidency of the Council of the European Union. In this role, each member state has a real opportunity to shape EU policy and advance its own interests, as it assumes the chairmanship of each of the Council's ten individual councils. However, few policy initiatives of any magnitude were initiated by the young country during its six month reign. Rather, at the outset of the presidency, the Slovak government itself was teetering on the edge of collapse due to the above-mentioned Kaliňák scandal. It finished the presidency with yet another scandal, this one involving Slovak Foreign Affairs Minister Miroslav Lajčák (Slovak Spectator 2016b).

Opinions differ on the overall "success" of the Slovak EU Presidency. Slovak Prime Minister Fico and a number of political pundits proclaimed it a resounding success (Slovak Spectator 2017a) and indeed, on short-term interest issues, one could support that claim. For example, the 2017 EU Budget was completed, mobile telephone roaming fees were eliminated across EU states, and the Paris Climate Agreement ratification process was sped up.

On the key longer term interest issues of immigration, security and defense, however, there was no significant movement forward during Slovakia's presidency. Thus, while the presidency was certainly not a "failure," it was much less successful on the larger issues than on a flurry of smaller ones, highlighting again the shorter term vision of the Slovak government.

Finally, related to Slovakia's short-term decision-making tendency is the example of the Visegrád Group, now known as the Visegrád Four. It was initially formed in 1991 as the "Visegrád Three" in the Hungarian town of Visegrád, availing itself of the symbolism of a historical cooperative meeting of medieval Central European kings. With the breakup of Czechoslovakia into the Czech and Slovak Republics, the Visegrád Four ("V4") was born. From the outset, this loosely structured coalition was a prescient idea. It involved a cluster of post-communist Central European states, each with similar national interests due to their proximity, size and post-communist concerns. However, since its inception there have been relatively few concrete initiatives that could be firmly placed in a "national interests" category. Two of note are the 2011 Defense Cooperation Agreement, involving meetings of V4 defense ministers to discuss common security concerns and to advance regular V4 exercises under the control of the NATO Response Forces (Visegrád Group 2014d); and the Expert Working Group on Energy, which meets once or twice a year to discuss proposals of the Visegrád country energy ministers. The topics discussed by the latter have included considerations concerning the creation of new gas and oil pipelines.

Yet instead of building a solid platform from which to lobby within the confines of organizations such as the EU and NATO, the group has floundered. Short-term thinking and concern eventually replaced a longer term strategic vision. One regional commentator highlighted the "political hollowness" of the group by remarking that at a recent V4 meeting, "*a lengthy discussion ensued on opposition to the soft drink Sprite, which is flavored with fructose syrup instead of the sugar used in Germany or Austria*" (Slovak Spectator 2017c). In sum, from a long-term interests perspective, the V4 represents a missed opportunity, as the idea of a cluster of states with similar national interests working together to lobby for concrete long-term goals in the EU, NATO, and other regional and global governmental forums is certainly a worthy one.

This chapter has centered on national interests and the structural and non-structural barriers to the Slovak government advancing them. The question of the chapter was, "why has Slovakia not visibly advanced its national interests beyond the first several years of the new millennium?" This chapter argued that the reasons involve blockages in three key areas: a) Ideology; b) Corruption; and c) Short-term decision-making. The first argument stressed the great difficulty of a country focusing on its national interests in an ideologically charged political environment, particularly one which affects governing coalitions. Slovakia has been no stranger to this phenomenon, and Slovak national interests have often been ignored or overshadowed by ideological concerns. The second key factor inhibiting a national interest's focus in Slovakia was argued to be its high level of economic and political corruption. Corruption—by definition—takes focus away from the common good and places it on the personal, the private. It "suffocates" the national interest and has almost certainly had this effect in Slovakia, though—as with ideology—the precise degree is not empirically measurable. The third key argument was that Slovakia—when it has avoided such structural blockages—has often been a victim of non-structural factors—in particular, its decision-making approach. This implies that the Slovak government, in recent years, has considered its national interests imperfectly and, at times, recklessly, reaching for expedient short-term interests at the expense of the pursuit of the more important longer term. This is not untypical of many governments in the world, but tends to explain much of what has been happening in regards to policy focus in the country.

Overall, the pattern emerges that national interests in Slovakia have been increasingly swept aside due to these key blockages. They have acted as distractions and diversions. As two of them—ideological nationalism and corruption—may be more structurally endemic to the political and social system, it is not at all sure a change of government will necessarily alter the situation. However, more frequent changes of government would certainly provide the context for re-evaluation and possible re-orientation toward those national interests that best serve the public good.

CONCLUSION

In this book, the authors surveyed the institutional, political, and philosophical aspects of the formation of the Slovak Republic's national interests since its accession to full membership in the European Union and NATO. The research focused on analyzing the civil, national, and transnational actors that impact on the development and implementation of Slovakia's national interests. The chapters looked at the current international security environment in which the Slovak Republic promotes its interests and examined the theoretical aspects of forming national interests amidst the growing mistrust in national and translational authorities. The research focused on analyzing security as a fundamental state interest, comparing its definitions in the strategy papers of the Slovak Republic and the European Union. The book looked at the way Slovak political parties and movements define the country's national interests while also examining Slovakia's preparations for assuming its historically first Presidency of the Council of the European Union, presented as a huge diplomatic success, which earned Slovakia much publicity not only within the European Union, but also in the global community. The authors have also examined the migration crisis and the related domestic political discussion in the context of Slovakia's national interests and obligations to the European Union, the question of granting development aid to fulfill its foreign policy objectives and commitments, and the national minorities' lack of participation when it comes to establishing the country's national interests.

During the research, finding the correct term to denote a country's "national" or "nation-state" interests proved to be something of a linguistic challenge. In general, a state's interests comprise a set of requirements whose fulfillment is imperative to its sovereignty. The problem lies not so much in defining this notion as in finding the right term to denote it, something illustrated in this book. The authors of the individual chapters used various adjectives to describe a state's interests: state, national, national state, and nation-state. All of these terms are used in academic literature and European strategic policy documents, but they might become problematic once we try to define them.

What Anglo-American literature calls "national interest" is usually translated into Slovak literally as *národný záujem*, but while in Anglo-American diction the expression denotes the interests of a political nation-state that are shared by all of its ethnic groups, in the European—and especially Central and Eastern European—context, the term "national" tends to refer to ethnic groups. Therefore, "national" often denotes the interests of a particular nation or ethnic group, and in general it is used in relation to the foreign policy and external affairs of a state. Where "state interests" are concerned, they are usually related to the domestic policies of a country. The term might occasionally carry negative connotations, when "state interests" clash with individual rights (for instance, when it comes to expropriating private property to build infrastructure).

Finally, the adjective *národnoštátny* ("nation-state" or "national state") was coined to indicate that the nation and state are seen as one; however, in multiethnic states this can sometimes refer only to the national majority, excluding any minorities. This problem should be addressed in more detail in the future. Similarly, the formulation, implementation and application of a state's national interest in the broader globalized community should also remain a highly topical issue, since the collision of various national interests might either result in cooperation, lead to conflict, or even escalate into war.

References

A TRIANONI BÉKESZERZŐDÉS. 1921. [online] Available at: https://inter matrix.hu/samples/trianoni_beke.pdf

A VERSAILLES-I BÉKESZERZŐDÉS.1919. [online] Grotius-dokumentomok. Available at: http://www.grotius.hu/doc/pub/UPKVVT/2013-02-06_a-versailles-i-bekeszerzodes.pdf

ÁBRAHÁM, B. (2012): "Cselekedjetek jól vagy rosszul, csak tudja a világ, hogy a szlovákok élnek" [online], www.prominoritate.hu/folyoiratok/1999/ProMino99-1-03-Abraham.pdf.

AKTUALITY.SK (2014): *Fico nesúhlasí s novými sankciami voči Rusku. Chýba mu objektívny obraz o dianí na Ukrajine.* (Fico objects to new sanctions against Russia. He lacks a true picture of the doings in Ukraine) Aktuality.sk, 31 August 2014.

AKTUALITY.SK (2015): *Róbert Fico: Pri plyne zosúladíme európske aj národné záujmy krajín.* Aktuality.sk, 29. 1. 2015.

ALLPORT, G. W. (1977): *Az előítélet.* Budapest: Gondolat, 1977. 743 s. ISBN 963-280-450-3

ALMOND, G.A. – VERBA, S. (1963): *The civic culture. Political attitudes and democracy in five nations.* Princeton: Princeton University Press, 1963, p. 562.

ANDROVIČOVÁ, J. (2016): *The migration and refugee crisis in political discourse in Slovakia: Institutionalized securitization and moral panic.* In: Acta Universitatis Carolinae Studia Territorialia, 2016, No. 2, pp. 39-64.

Áno a nie Jána Čarnogurského v rozhovore s Ivou Kernou. Bratislava: Vydavateľstvo Spolku slovenských spisovateľov 2015.

BALIBAR, É. (2004): *We, the People of Europe. Reflections on Transnational Citizenship.* Princeton University Press, Princeton and Oxford, 2004.

BARGEROVÁ, Z. – DIVINSKÝ, B. (2008): *Integrácia migrantov v Slovenskej republike. Výzvy a odporúčania pre tvorcov politík.* Bratislava: IOM.

BARIAK, L. Jr. (2016): *Kaliňákov rezort priznáva: Slovensko je predmetom pôsobenia ruského vplyvu.* (Kaliňák's department admits: Slovakia is a target of Russian influence). Aktuality.sk, 6. 6. 2016.

BARNARD, F. M. (1988): *Self-Direction and Political Legitimacy – Rousseau and Herder.* Oxford, Clarendon Press, 1988.

BARŠA, P. – STRMISKA, M. (1999): *Národní stát a etnický konflikt.* Brno: CDK, 1999. 330 s. ISBN 80-85959-52-6.

BARŠOVÁ, A. – BARŠA, P. (2005): *Přistěhovalectví a liberální stát. Imigrační a integrační politiky v USA, západní Evropě a Česku.* Brno: Masarykova univerzita v Brně. 2005. ISBN 80-210-3875-6.

BARŠOVÁ, A. (2005): *Integrace přistěhovalců v Evropě: od občanské integrace k multikulturalismu a zpět?* [online]. Konference Soudobé spory o multikulturalismus a politiku identit, p. 1. Available at: http://www.varianty.cz/download/doc/texts/4.pdf.

BÁTORA, J. 2004. Identita a štátny záujem? O čo ide v slovenskej zahraničnej politike. (Identity and state interest? What is the point of foreign policy? In SZIGETI, L. (ed.). *Slovenská otázka dnes.* Bratislava: Kalligram, 2007, pp. 359-366.

BÁTORA, J. 2004a: *Identita a štátny záujem v slovenskej zahraničnej politike.* Medzinárodné otázky, Vol. 13, 2004, No. 2, p. 39-53.

BAUBÖCK, R. (1998): Sharing history and future? Time horizons of democratic membership in an age of migration. In: Constellations. Vol. 4, 1998, No. 3. ISSN 1467-8675. pp. 320-345.

BAUMAN, Z. (2006): *Komunita – hľadanie bezpečia vo svete bez istôt.* Bratislava, Vydavateľstvo Spolku slovenských spisovateľov, 2006. 122 s. ISBN 80-8061-225-0.

BELLAMY, R.: Sovereignty, Post-Sovereignty and Pre-Sovereignty: Three Models of the State, Democracy and Rights within the EU. In: WALKER, N. (ed.): *Sovereignty in Transition.* Oxford: Hart, 2003, pp. 167-190.

BEZPEČNOSTNÁ STRATÉGIA SLOVENSKEJ REPUBLIKY schválená Národnou radou Slovenskej republiky 27. septembra 2005. Available at: http://www.mosr.sk/data/files/833.pdf or https://www.vlada. gov.sk//zakladne-dokumenty-riesiace-bezpecnost-slovenskej-repu bliky/.

BIBÓ, I. (1986): *Válogatott tanulmányok II.* Budapest: Magvető Könyvkiadó, 1986.

BIBÓ, I. (1996): *Bieda východoeurópskych malých štátov.* Bratislava: Kalligram, 1966. 578 s. ISBN 80-7149-148-9.

BILLÝ, Ľ. (2012): Immigration issues in Slovak politics. In Contemporary European Studies, č. 1, 2012. ISSN 1802-4289, pp. 53-64.

BÍRÓ, G. (1995): *Az identitásválasztás szabadsága.* Budapest: Osiris, 1995. 289 s., ISBN 963-8384-99-9.

BIRSL, U. a kol. (2003): *Migration und Interkulturalität in Großbritannien, Deutschland und Spanien. Fallstudien aus der Arbeitswelt.* Opladen: Leske+Budrich. 2003. ISBN 978-381-00379-1-6.

BLAHA, Ľ. (2014): *Kríza na Kryme. Netlačme Rusko do kúta.* Noveslovo.sk, 2. 3. 2014.

BLAHA, L. (2015): *Kvóty sú podvod – o čo ide Západu v skutočnosti?* (Crisis in Crimea. Let's not corner Russia). Noveslovo.sk, 2 March 2014. [online] Available at: http://www.noveslovo.sk/c/Kvoty_su_podvod_o_co_ide_Zapadu_.

BODIN, J.: *The Six Books of the Commonwealth.* Book I. Oxford: Basil Blackwell 1955.

BOLEČEKOVÁ, M.–OLEJAROVÁ, B. Migration as a Political and Public Phenomenom: The Case of Slovak Republic. In: ŁOŚ, R.– KOBIERECKA, A. (eds.): *The V4 Towards Migration Challenges in Europe,* Lodz: Wydawnictwo Uniwersitetu Lodzkiego 2017 pp. 191-226.

BOOKER, Ch.–NORTH, R. (2006): *Skryté dějiny evropské integrace od roku 1918 do současnosti.* Barrister & Principal, Společnost pro odbornou literaturu, 2006.

BOSÁK, E. (1991): Slovaks and Czechs: An uneasy coexistence. In SKILLING, H. G. (ed.): *Czechoslovakia 1918-88. Seventy Years from Independence.* New York: Palgrave Macmillan UK, 1991, s. 65-81.

BRATISLAVSKÁ DEKLARÁCIA A BRATISLAVSKÁ CESTOVNÁ MAPA. 2016. Available at: http://www.eu2016.sk/data/documents/160916-bratislava-declaration-and-roadmap-sk-1.pdf

BRHLÍKOVÁ, R. (2014): *Bezpečnosť a Európska únia.* Nitra: UKF, 2014. 208 s. ISBN 978-80-558-0717-1.

BRHLÍKOVÁ, R. (2009): *ESDP – respond to 21st century security challenges according to the new treaty?* In. Panorama of global security environment. Bratislava: Centre for European and North Atlantic Affairs. 2009.

BROCKHAUS ENZYKLOPÄDIE, 20. Band, Mannheim: F. A. Brockhaus 1993, p. 231.

BROŽÍK, I. (2012): Slovakia needs to think and act more in the Slovak interest. Slovenské národné noviny (Slovak National Newspaper), 29. 10. 2012.

BUCHANAN, A. (1998): What's so special about nations? In: Couture, J., Nielsen, K., Seymour, M. (eds.): *Rethinking Nationalism.* Calgary: University Press, 1998, 709 s. ISBN 978-0-919491-22-9, s. 283-310.

BURGESS, A. (1999): Critical reflections on the return of national minority rights regulation to East/West European affairs. In: Cordell, K. (ed.) *Ethnicity an democratization in the new Europe.* London–New York: Routledge, 1999. 214 s. ISBN 9780-415-17312-4, s. 44-54.

BURCHILL, S. (2005): *The National Interest in International Relations Theory.* United Kingdom. Palgrave Macmillan. ISBN: 978-1-349-52596-6.

BUSINESS INSIDER (2016): *These are the 11 most corrupt countries in the developed world.* Business Insider, 29 September 2016. [online] Available at: http://uk.businessinsider.com/wef-corruption-index-the-most-corrupt-countries-in-the-oecd-2016-9/#8-latvia-4.

BÚTORA, M.—MESEŽNIKOV, G. (eds.) (1997): *Slovenské referendum '97: zrod, priebeh, dôsledky* (The Slovak referendum: origin, evolution and consequences). Bratislava: IVO 1997.

BUZALKA, J (2001): *Vybrané otázky teórie krízového manažmentu a civilná ochrana*, Bratislava: Akadémia policajného zboru, 2001, s. 35.

BYSTRICKÝ, V. (1997): Štátnosť darovaná, či vnútená. (Statehood presented as a gift or enforced) In SZIGETI, L. (ed.). *Slovenská otázka dnes*. Bratislava: Kalligram, 2007, pp. 50-59.

CARLSNAES, W.—SJURSEN, H.—WHITE, B. (2004): *Contemporary European Foreign Policy*. London: SAGE 2004.

CIA: *The World Factbook*. [online] Available at: https://www.cia.gov/library/publications/the-world-factbook/geos/ke.html.

CÍSAŘ, O.—FIALA, P (2004): Obhajoba zájmů a transnacionální vztahy. Úvod do studia. In: CÍSAŘ Ondřej—FIALA Petr (eds.): *Obhajoba zájmů a transnacionální vztahy*. Brno: Masarykova univerzita.

CLEVELANDSKÁ DOHODA 1915. *Clevelandská dohoda*. (The Cleveland Agreement) In Dokumenty slovenskej národnej identity a štátnosti I. Bratislava: Nár. Lit. Centrum, 1998, pp. 445-448.

CLINTON, W. D. (1994): *The two faces of national interest*. Baton Rouge: Louisiana State University.

CONSTITUTION OF THE SLOVAK REPUBLIC, 1 September 1992, nr. 460/1992. [online] Available at: https://www.prezident.sk/upload-files/46422.pdf.

COUDENHOVE-CALERGY, R. (1988): *Pan-Europe*. Paris, Presses Universitaires de France, 1988.

COUDENHOVE-CALERGY, R. (2004): PÁNEURÓPA. In: SZÉNÁSI Éva (eds.): *Elméletek az európai egységről II*. L'Harmattan, Zsigmond Király Főiskola, Budapest, 2004.

COUNCIL OF EUROPE: *2018 Ordinary session*. Report. Fourth sitting, Council of Europe, 23 January 2018. [online] Available at: http://assembly.coe.int/Documents/Records/2018/E/1801231530E.htm (accessed on February 19, 2019).

CROCKER, CH. A.—HAMPSON, F. O.—AALL, P. (eds.) (1997): *Managing global chaos: Sources and responses to international conflict*. Washington: United States Institute of Peace Press, 1997. 640 p. ISBN 978-1-878379-58-0.

CUPRIK, R. (2017): *Referendum o EÚ spojilo aj Mečiara s Kováčom. Fico politikárčil.* Sme, 22. 12. 2017.

ČAPLOVIČ, M.–STUPŇAN, I. (2014): *Slovensko pomohlo ukrajinským vojakom* (Slovakia helps Ukrainian sodiers). Pravda, 12 September 2014.

ČARNOGURSKÝ, J. (2003): *Nech rozhodnú občania.* In Sme, 10. 1. 2003. [online] Available at: https://www.sme.sk/c/779602/nech-rozhodnu-obcania.html#ixzz5XFtY2Jzy.

ČARNOGURSKÝ, J. (2013): *Denník 1994-2007.* Michal Vaško – Vydavateľstvo: Prešov 2013.

ČARNOGURSKÝ, J. (2014): *Krym patrí Rusku.* (Crimea belongs to Russia). Blog.sme.sk, 21 March 2014. [online] Available at: http://carnogursky.blog.sme.sk/c/352012/Krym-patri-Rusku.html.

ČERVOV, N.–MOROZOV, V. (1984): *O bezpečnosti v jaderném věku.* Praha: Naše vojsko, 1984.

COUDENHOVE-KALERGI, R. (1988): *Pan-Europe.* Paris, Presses Universitaires de France, 1988.

DANIŠKA, J. (2007): *Fico proti slovenským záujmom.* Impulz revue, No. 3, 2007. [online] Available at: http://www.impulzrevue.sk/article.php?222.

DECLARATION ON EUROPEAN IDENTITY (Copenhagen, 14 December 1973).

DENNIKN (2018): *Slovensko stiahne veľvyslanca z Moskvy. Nestačí to, hovorí aj prezident Kiska,* [Slovakia pulls its ambassador from Moscow. It's not enough, says President Kiska] DennikN, 28 March 2018. [online] Available at: https://dennikn.sk/1079087/slovensko-stiahne-velvyslanca-z-moskvy-vyhostit-ruskych-diplomatov-sa-nechysta/.

DER DERIAN, J.: *The Pen, the Sword and the Smart Bomb: Criticism in the Age of Video.* Alternatives 19:1 (1994), pp. 133-40.

DIVINSKÝ, B. (2005): *Zahraničná migrácia v Slovenskej republike. Stav trend. Společenské súvislosti.* (Foreign migration in the Slovak Republic – status, trends and social context). Bratislava: FES 2005.

DLF 2015: *Flüchtlingsdebatte.* [online] Available at: http://www.deutschlandfunk.de/fluechtlingsdebatte-es-gibt-keine-pflicht-fluechtlinge.694.de.html?dram:article_id=328736.

DOMINO FORUM (2000): *Ľudovcom nestačí Šefčovičovo vysvetlenie.* Domino Fórum, 19. 1. 2000 -- 25. 10. 2000.

DOMINO FORUM (2000): *Průběh „grilování" potenciálních komisařů se vyostřil.* Domino Fórum, 14.1.2010 – 25.10. 000.

DOMINO FORUM (2000a): *Správy STV.* Domino Fórum, 25.5.2010 – 25.10.2000.

DOMINO FORUM (2000b): *Udalosti z Európskeho parlamentu majú dohru doma*. Domino Fórum, 22. 1. 2010 — 25. 10. 2000.

DÖRNER, A. (2003): Politische Kulturforschung. In: MÜNKLER, H. (ed.). *Politikwissenschaft. Ein Grundkurs*. Reinbeck bei Hamburg: Rowohlt, 2003, pp. 578-618.

DREZNER, D. W. (1999): *The Sanctions Paradox: Economic Statecraft and International Relations*. Cambridge Studies in International Relations, 1999, ISBN 978-0521644150.

DROBNÝ, J. (2015): *Moslimská populácia na Slovensku*. (Muslim population in Slovakia) In: Populačné štúdie Slovenska, 7, 2015, pp. 137-145.

DRULÁK, P. (2012): *Politika nezájmu: Česko a Západ v krizi*. Praha: SLON.

DRULÁK, P. (2010): How to Explore National Interest and Why. In: *The Quest for National Interest. A Methodological Reflection on Czech Foreign Policy*. Eds.: Petr Drulák — Mats Braun. Frankfurt am Main: Petr Lang 2010, p. 11-20.

DRULÁK, P. (2010): Úvod. In: DRULÁK Petr — Střítecký Vít a kol.: *Hledání českých zájmů. Mezinárodní bezpečnost*. Praha: Ústav mezinárodních vztahů.

DS (1998): *Zásady politiky Demokratickej strany*. Programové tézy Demokratickej strany ako vklad do volebného programu SDK.

DÚ A: *Ide o veľa. Ide o Slovensko*. Demokratická únia Slovenska.

DÚ B: *Občan na prvom mieste*. Volebný program, Demokratická únia Slovenska, február 1996.

DULEBA, A. (1996): *Slepý pragmatizmus slovenskej východnej politiky. Aktuálna agenda slovensko-ruských bilaterálnych vzťahov*. (Blind pragmatism of Slovakia's Eastern policy. Current agenda of Slovak-Russian relations) Bratislava: SFPA 1996.

DULEBA, A. (2009a): *Príčiny rusko-ukrajinského plynového sporu a poučenie pre Slovensko*. (The reasons behind Russia-Ukraine gas dispute and the lessons for Slovakia) Slovgas, Vol. 1, 2009, Issue 1, pp.4-6.

DULEBA, A. (2009b): *Slovakia's Relations with Russia and Eastern Neighbours. In EU-Russian relations and the Eastern Partnership — Central-East European Member-state interests and positions*. East European Studies. Eds. Gábor Fóti — Zsuzsa Ludvig. Budapest: MTA Világgazdasági Kutatóintézet 2009, pp. 7-60.

DULEBA, A. (1998): *From Domination to Partnership. The Perspectives of Russian-Central-East European Relations*. Final Report to the NATO Research Fellowship Program, 1996 — 1998. [online] Available at: http://www.nato.int/acad/fellow/96-98/duleba.pdf, p. 6.

DUNN, J. (1993): *Western Political Theory in the Face of the Future*. Cambridge University Press, Canto edition, 1993.

DURAY, M. (1999): *Önrendelkezési kísérleteink.* Somorja: Méry Ratio, 1999. 425 s. ISBN 80-88837-16-2.

ĎUROVIČ, L. (1997): Tá naša (slovenská) identita ...? Ako sa formovala politicky a teritoriálne? (Our (Slovak) identity...? How did it shape politically and territorially?) In SZIGETI, L (ed.). *Slovenská otázka dnes.* Bratislava: Kalligram, 2007, pp. 32-40.

EGYÜTTÉLÉS: *Választások – Voľby 1994.* Az EGYÜTTÉLÉS politikai mozgalom választási programja. Volebný program politického hnutia SPOLUŽITIA.

EICHLER, J.–HYNEK, N. (2010): Obnova Afghánistánu: bezpečnostní kontext české účasti. In: DRULÁK Petr–STŘÍTECKÝ Vít a kol.: *Hledání českých zájmů. Mezinárodní bezpečnost.* Praha: Ústav mezinárodních vztahů.

EICHLER, J. (2009): *Mezinárodní bezpečnost v době globalizace.* Praha: Portál, 2009. 328 s. ISBN 978-80-7367-540-0.

EICHLER, J. (2010): Mezi jestřábem a holubicí: Česko hledá demokratický mír. In: DRULÁK Petr–STŘÍLECKÝ Vít a kol.: *Hledání českých zájmů. Mezinárodní bezpečnost.* Praha: Ústav mezinárodních vztahů.

EURACTIV (2014): *Slovakia nurtures special ties to Russia, despite EU sanctions* [online] Available at: https://www.euractiv.com/section/central-europe/news/slovakia-nurtures-special-ties-to-russia-despite-eu-sanctions/.

EURACTIV (2015): *Slowakei klagt vor EuGH.* [online] Available at: https://www.euractiv.de/section/eu-innenpolitik/news/slowakei-klagt-vor-eugh-gegen-fluchtlingsquote/.

EUROPEAN COMMISSION (2015*): First measures under the European migration agenda: questions and answers.* [online] Available at: http://europa.eu/rapid/press-release_MEMO-15-5038_en.htm.

EUROPEAN COUNCIL MEETING IN LAEKEN 14 AND 15 DECEMBER 2001.

EUROPEAN COURT OF JUSTICE (2012): Press Release No. 21/12. Advocate General's Opinion in Case C-364/10, Hungary v. Slovakia: According to Advocate General Bot, the Slovak Republic did not infringe EU law when it refused to allow Mr Sólyom, the Hungarian President, to enter its territory. Availabe online at: https://europa.eu/rapid/press-release_CJE-12-21_en.htm.

EURÓPSKY PARLAMENT (2016): *Uznesenie Európskeho parlamentu z 23. novembra 2016 o strategickej komunikácii EÚ s cieľom bojovať s propagandou tretích strán zameranou proti Únii.* (Resolution of the European Parliament of 23 November 2016 on EU strategic communication to counteract propaganda against it by third parties) (2016/2030(INI)). European Parliament – official website, 23 November 2016.

FÁBRY, Z. (1991): *Merre vagy Európa? Kisebbségek a vádlottak padján.* Pozsony: Pannóna, 1991. 192 s. ISBN 80-900391-9-7.

FARREL, H. – FLYNN, G. (1999): Piecing together the democratic peace. In: International Organisation, Vol. 53, 1999, No. 3. ISSN 0020-8183. pp. 505-535.

FERENČUHOVÁ, B. 1998. Zmieri sa Slovensko so svojím nacionalizmom? (Will Slovakia reconcile itself to its nationalism?) In SZIGETI, L. (ed.). *Slovenská otázka dnes.* Bratislava: Kalligram, 2007, pp. 171-187.

FERRY, J. M. – THIBAULT, P. (2006): *Vita Európáról*, L'Harmattan, Zsigmond Király Főiskola, Budapest, 2006.

FICO, R. (2015a): *Kvótam hovorím nie. Nechcem niesť zodpovednosť za teroristický útok.* (I say No to quotas. I do not want to bear responsibility for a terrorist attack) [online] Available online: http://spravy.pravda.sk/domace/clanok/367102-fico-kvotam-hovorim-nie-nechcem-niest-zodpovednost-za-teroristicky-utok/.

FICO, R. (2015b): *Diktát odmietame, kvóty nebude Slovensko rešpektovať.* (We refuse the dictate; Slovakia will not respect the quotas) [online] Available online: http://spravy.pravda.sk/domace/clanok/368428-fico-povinne-kvoty-slovensko-nebude-respektovat/.

FICO, R. (2016a): *Fico o novom postoji vlády k téme migrácie.* (Fico on the new government's stance on migration) [online] Available online: http://www.vlada.gov.sk/tlacova-konferencia-predsedu-vlady-sr-roberta-fica-o-novom-postoji-vlady-k-teme-migracie-po-udalostiach-v-nemeckom-koline-nad-rynom/.

FICO, R. (2016b): *Podľa Fica nemá islam na Slovensku priestor.* (According to Fico, there is no room for Islam in Slovakia) [online] Available online: http://www.topky.sk/cl/100535/1549827/Podla-Fica-nema-islam-na-Slovensku-priestor--Moslimovia-su-pobureni--toto-je-ich-reakcia.

FIGEĽ, J. (2001): Bezpečnostné výzvy po ukončený studenej vojny a slovenská bezpečnostná politika, In: *Slovensko a NATO – bezpečnosť prostredníctvom spolupráce*, Prešov: Výskumné centrum SFPA, 2001.

FIJALKOWSKI, J. (1997): Integrationspolitik im europäischen Vergleich. In Angenendt, S. (ed.). *Migration und Flucht, Aufgaben und Strategien für Deutschland, Europa und die internationale Gesellschaft.* München. 1997. ISBN 978-389-33127-2-6, pp. 154-169.

FINDOR, A. (2013): Tisíročná poroba? (A thousand years of serfdom?) In KREKOVIČ, E. – MANNOVÁ, E. – KREKOVIČOVÁ, E. (eds.). *Mýty naše slovenské*. Bratislava: Premedia Group, 2013, pp. 71-76.

FOREIGN POLICY (2017): They spent months protesting corruption. Now what? Available at: https://foreignpolicy.com/2017/09/29/they-spent-months-protesting-corruption-now-what-slovakia-kalinak-bratislava/.

FREEMAN, G. P. (1995): *Modes of Immigration Politics in Liberal Democratic States*. In International Migration Review, Vol. 29, No. 4, 1995. ISSN 1747-7379, pp. 881-902.

FREEMAN, G. P. (2004): Political Science and Comparative Immigration Politics. In Bommes, M.; Morawska, E. (ed.). *International Migration Research: Constructions, Omissions and the Promises of Interdisciplinarity*. Aldershot. 2004. ISBN 978-075-46421-9-0, pp. 111-128.

FURIK, A. (2016): *Lajčák sa priblížil k postu šéfa OSN* (Lajčák closer to the post of the U.N. head). Euractiv.sk, 31 August 2016. [online] Available at: https://euractiv.sk/clanky/zahranicie-a-bezpecnost/lajcak-sa-priblizil-k-postu-sefa-osn/.

GARSZTECKI, S. (2001): Kulturkonzepte und politikwissenschaftliche Transformationsforschung. In: HÖHMANN, H.-H. (ed.). *Kultur als Bestimmungsfaktor der Transformation im Osten Europas. Konzeptionelle Entwicklung – Empirische Befunde*. Bremen: Ed. Temmen, 2001, pp. 52-71.

GIDDENS, A. (1985): *The Nation-state and Violence*. Oxford: Blacwkell Pubishers Ltd. 1985.

GILPIN, R. (1981): *War and Change in World Politics*. New York. Cambridge University Press. ISBN 0-521-27376-5.

GLATZ, F. (ed.) (1997): *Globalizáció és nemzeti érdek*. Budapest: MTA, 1997. 197 s. ISBN 963-508-020-4.

GLOB.ZOZNAM.SK (2018*): Štefanec hovoril o najväčšej výzve EÚ: Zladiť národné záujmy s európskymi*. Glob.Zoznam.sk, 29. 7. 2018. [online] Available at: https://glob.zoznam.sk/stefanec-hovoril-o-najvacsej-vyzve-eu-zladit-narodne-zaujmy-s-europskymi/.

GLVÁČ, M (2014): *Slovenskí vojaci budú v rámci pomoci pre Ukrajinu školiť odmínovačov*. (Slovak soldiers will train mine clearers to help Ukraine) Bratislava: Ministry of Defence SR, 25 September 2014.

GOMBÁR, Cs. – HANKISS E. et al. (eds.) (1996): *A szuverenitás káprázata*. Budapest: Korridor, 1996. 261 s. ISBN 963-85155-8-9.

GOTTLIEB, G. (1994): *Nations without states*. In: Foreign Affairs. roč. 73, 1994, č. 3. ISSN 2327-7793. s. 100-112.

GROSS, J.T. (2015): *Flüchtlingsabwehr: Die osteuropäische Schande.* In Blätter für deutsche und internationale Politik, Vol. 59, 2015, No. 10, pp. 41-42.

GRÚBER, K. (2002): *Európai identitások: régió, nemzet, integráció.* Budapest: Osiris, 2006. 245 s. ISBN 963-86244-0-X.

GYŐRY SZABÓ, P. (2006): Kisebbség, autonómia, regionalizmus. Budapest: Osiris, 2006. 586 s. ISBN 963-389-880-3.

HABERMAS, J. (2001): *Zur Verfassung Europas.* Berlin: Suhrkamp, 2011.

HAD, M. (1992): Státní zájmy. In: VALENTA Jiří a kol.: *Máme národní zájmy?* Praha: Ústav mezinárodních vztahů.

HANDL, V. (2007): *Vom Feindbild zum differenzierten Europabild? Tschechien, Ostmitteleuropa und die europäische Integration.* In: Integration. Vierteljahreszeitschrift des Instituts für Europäische Politik, vol. 30, 2007, No. 4, pp. 470-483.

HAUGHTON, T. (2001): HZDS: *The Ideology, Organisation and Support Base of Slovakia's Most Successful Party 2001.* Europe-Asia Studies, Vol. 53, No. 5 (Jul., 2001), pp. 745-769.

HECKMANN, F., TOMEI, V. (1997): Zur Dialektik von Kooperation und Nicht-Kooperation in der internationalen Migrationspolitik. In: Angenendt, S. (ed.). *Migration und Flucht. Aufgaben und Strategien für Deutschland, Europa und internationale Gemeinschaft.* München: Oldenburg Verlag. 1997. 978-389-33127-2-6, pp. 223-229.

HEY, J. A. K. (2003): *Small States in World Politics – Explaining Foreing Policy Behaviour.* Boulder. Lynne Rienner Publishers. ISBN 978-1555879433.

HILL, R. (1997): *We Europeans,* Europublic, Brussels, 1997.

HIRTLOVÁ, P. – SRB, V. (eds.) (2009): *Menšiny a integrující se Evropa.* Kolín: Nezávislé centrum pro studium politiky, 447 s. ISBN 978-80-86879-23-9.

HLINČÍKOVÁ, M. (2016): *Migrácia vo volebných programoch politických strán.* Denník N, 9. 2. 2016. [online] Available at: https://dennikn.sk/366597/migracia-vo-volebnych-programoch-politickych-stran/.

HLOUŠEK, V. – KOPEČEK, L. (2005): *Konfliktní linie v současné české a slovenské politice: mezi stabilitou a změnou.* Working Paper No. 10. Brno: IIPS, 2005, p. 4. [online] Available at: http://www.iips.cz/userfiles/file/wp_10_konfliktni_linie.pdf.

HLOUŠEK, V. (2004): *Proces europeanizace a politické strany v kandidátských zemích.* Sociální studia, 2004, Vol. 1, No. 1, p. 93-108.

HLUCHÁŇOVÁ, M. (1998): Vstup do NATO v slovenskom parlamente. (Entry into NATO in the Slovak Parliament) In: *Slovensko v šedej zóne? Rozširovanie NATO, zlyhanie a perspektívy Slovenska.* Eds. Martin Bútora – František Šebej. Bratislava: IVO 1998, pp. 97-104.

HN (2000): *HZDS změnilo stanovy i rétoriku*. Hospodářské noviny, 20. 3. 2000.
HN (2014): FICO, R.: *Priestor pre národný záujem*. (Room for the national interest). Hospodárske noviny, 3 June 2014.
HOFFMAN, S. (2003): *The crisis in transatlantic relations*. In *Shift or Rift. Assessing US/EU relations after Iraq*. Paris: European Union Institut for Security Studies, Transatlantic Book 2003.
HOLLIFIELD, J. F. (2000): The Politics of International Migration: How Can We 'Bring the State In'? In: Brettel, C. B., Hollifield, J. F. (ed.). *Migration Theory: Talking Across Disciplines*. New York a Londýn: Routledge. 2000. ISBN 978-041-59542-7-3, pp. 137-185.
HORVÁTH, A.—KOROM, Á. (2014): *A Benes-dekrétumok az Európai Parlamentben*. Budapest: Nemzeti Közszolgálati Egyetem, 2014. 79 s. ISBN 978-615-5491-10-8. [online] Available at: https://edit.elte.hu/xmlui/bitstream/handle/10831/30295/benes.pdf.
HURKA, T. (1997): *The Justification of National Partiality*. In: Robert McKim and Jeff McMahan (eds.): The Morality of Nationalism. Oxford University Press, USA, 1997.
HZDS A: *...bez falošných tónov. Slovensko do toho*. Programové tézy HZDS na VOĽBY 1994.
HZDS B: *Zmluva na 3. tisícročie medzi HZDS a občanmi SR*. Voľby 1998. Programové zámery HZDS na roky 1998—2002.
CHANGENET.SK (2002): *Prestaňte ohrozovať národnoštátne záujmy Slovenska*. Changenet.sk, 13 February 2002. [online] Available online: http://www.changenet.sk/index.stm?section=spr&x=20717.
CHMEL, R. (1997): Slovenská otázka v 20. storočí. (The Slovak question in the 20th century) In CHMEL, R. (ed.). *Slovenská otázka v 20. storočí*. Bratislava: Kalligram, 1997, pp. 5-34.
CHMEL. R. (1998): Slovenské nesúžitie so susedmi. (Slovakia's non-coexistence with its neighbours) In SZIGETI, L. (ed.). *Slovenská otázka dnes*. Bratislava: Kalligram, 2007, pp. 133-139.
INGLEHART, R. 1988. *The renaissance of political culture*. In The American Political Science Review, Vol. 82, 1988, No. 4, pp. 1203-1230.
IOM 2018: *Migrácia na Slovensku*. (Migration in Slovakia) [online] Available at: http://www.iom.sk/sk/migracia/migracia-na-slovensku.
IVANČÍK, R.—JURČÁK, V. (2014): *Kauzalita participácie ozbrojených síl Slovenskej republiky v operáciách medzinárodného krízového manažmentu a jej finančné aspekty*. Wyzsza Skola Biznesu i Przedsiebiorczosci w Ostrowcu Sw., 2014, 213 s. ISBN978-83-64557-05-7.

IVANČÍK, R. – KELEMEN, M. (2013): *Bezpečnosť štátu a občana: Energetická bezpečnosť*. Plzeň: Vydavatelství a nakladatelství Aleš Čeněk, s.r.o., 2013. 177 s. ISBN 978-80-7380-474-9.

IVANČÍK, R. (2012): *Teoreticko-metodologický pohľad na bezpečnosť*. In: Vojenské reflexie, 2012, roč. 7, č. 1, s. 38-57. ISSN 1336-9202.

JÁSZI O. (1918): *A monarchia jövője*. Budapest, 1918.

JUDT, T. (2002): *Európa – a nagy ábránd?* XX. Század Intézet, Budapest, 2002, str. 87.

JUZA, P. (2016): Zahraničná politika Slovenskej republiky a napĺňanie národnoštátnych záujmov Slovenska. In: PEKNÍK Miroslav a kolektív: *Pohľady na slovenskú politiku po roku 1989*. II. Časť. Bratislava: VEDA, vydavateľstvo SAV – Ústav politických vied SAV.

KAŁĄŻNA, K. – ROSICKI, R. (2013): *O interesie narodowym i racji stanu – rozważania teoretyczne*. In: Przegląd Politologiczny, vol. 1.

KAMENEC, I. (1998): Stereotypy v slovenských dejinách a v slovenskej historiografii. (Stereotypes in Slovak history and Slovak historiography) In: SZIGETI, L. (ed.). *Slovenská otázka dnes*. Bratislava: Kalligram, 2007, pp. 120-126.

KANCELÁRIA PREZIDENTA (1999): *Prejav prezidenta Slovenskej republiky Rudolfa Schustera v Národnej rade Slovenskej republiky dňa 2. novembra 1999*. Bratislava: Kancelária Prezidenta SR 1999.

KAPUSTA, P. (2018): *Ľuboš Blaha: Politici na Západe naivne verili, že z Ukrajiny bude druhé Švédsko*. (Politicians in the West naively believed Ukraine wiould turn another Sweden). Na palete, 15 January 2018. [online] Available at: https://www.napalete.sk/lubos-blaha-politici-na-zapade-naivne-verili-ze-z-ukrajiny-bude-druhe-svedsko/.

KATUS, L. – NAGY, M. (2016): *A Magyar Korona országainak nemzetiségei a 18-19. században*. Árkádia. [online] Available at: http://arkadia.pte.hu/tortenelem/cikkek/magyar_korona_orsz_nemzetisegei_1819sz.

KATZENSTEIN, E. (1996): *The Culture of National Security: Norms and Identity in World Politics*. New York: Columbia University Press, 1996.

KDH (1992): *Voľby '92*.Volebný program KDH 1992.

KDH (1994): *Spolu to dokážeme. Voľby '94. Voľte č. 15. František Mikloško (poslanec NR SR za KDH)*.

KDH (1994a): *Spolu to dokážeme. Voľby '94. Voľte č. 15. Ján Figeľ (poslanec NR SR za KDH)*.

KDH (2016): *Slovensko. Bezpečný domov, spokojné rodiny*. Volebný program KDH 2016. (Slovakia. Safe home, happy families. Election program of KDH 2016.) [online] Available at: http://kdh.sk/wp-content/uploads/2016/01/volebny_program_web.pdf.

KDH (2017). [online] Available online: https://www.facebook.com/ krestanskidemokrati/photos/a.220307418290.131563.163449818290/ 10155055965363291/?type=3&theater.

KEDURIE, E. (2000): *Nationalism*. Oxford, Blacwell Publishers, 2000.

KERSHAW, I. (2016): *Höllensturz. Európa 1914 bis 1949*. Deutsche Verlags- Anstalt, München, 2016.

KIPKE, R.—VODIČKA, K. (2000): *Slowakische Republik. Studien zur politischen Entwicklung*. Münster: Lit-Verlag 2000.

KIRSCHBAUM, S. (1994). Das slowakische Problem. In: BRUNNER, G.; LEMBERG, H. (eds.). *Volksgruppen in Ostmittel- und Südosteuropa*. Baden-Baden: Nomos, 1994, pp. 111-130.

KISSINGER, H. (1994): *Umenie Diplomacie*. Praha. Prostor. ISBN 80-7260- 025-7.

KLEINER, M.S.—NIELAND, J.-U. 2006. Diskurs und Praxis: Zur Institutionalisierung der Medienkritik in Deutschland. In: BECKER, B.; WEHNER, J. (eds.). *Kulturindustrie reviewed. Ansätze zur kritischen Reflexion der Mediengesellschaft*. Bielefeld: transcript Verlag, 2006., pp. 143-182.

KOLB, H. (2003): *Die „gap-Hypothese" in der Migrationsforschung und das Analysepontential der Politikwissenschaft: eine Diskussion am Beispiel der deutschen „Green Card"*. In IMIS-Beiträge, 22/2003. 2003. ISSN 0949- 4723, s. 13-38.

KOLLER, B. (2006): *Nemzet, identitás és politika Európában*. Budapest: L'Harmattan, 2006. 153 s. ISBN 963-9683-55-8.

KÖNIGOVÁ, L.: *Teorie státní suverenity a praxe intervence*. Mezinárodní vztahy, Vol. 36, 2001, No. 3, p. 41-58.

KONSOLIDOVANÉ ZNENIE ZMLUVY O EURÓPSKEJ ÚNII A ZMLUVY O FUNGOVANÍ EURÓPSKEJ ÚNIE. CHARTA ZÁKLADNÝCH PRÁV EURÓPSKEJ ÚNIE. Luxemburg: Úrad pre vydávanie publikácii Európskej únie, 2010, ISBN 978-928242589-3.

KOPEČEK, L.—URUBEK, T. (2000): Slovenská republika. In: *Zahraniční politika politických stran v České republice, Maďarsku, Polsku a na Slovensku*. Eds.: Břetislav Dančák—Miroslav Mareš. Brno: Masarykova univerzita—Mezinárodní politologický ústav, 2000, pp. 86-113.

KORTEN, D. C. (2001): *Keď korporácie vládnu svetu*. Košice: M. Hučko, 2001. 351 s. ISBN 80-968603-0-5.

KOVÁČ, M. (1997): *V Európe nie je miesto pre diktatúru*. (There is no room for dictatorship in Europe). Práca, 30. 7. 1997.

KRAJANOVÁ, D. (2015): *Zlievareň v Prakovciach prepustí vyše polovicu ľudí.* (The foundry at Prakovce to lay off over half of its workforce). DenníkN, 18 March 2015.

KRÁLIK, P.: V. Remišová: *Vláda poškodzuje národné záujmy pri správe eurofondov.* Eurorespekt.sk, 7. 6. 2018.

KRATOCHVÍL, P. (2010): Národní zájem a jeho legitimita. In: DRULÁK Petr — Střítecký Vít a kol.: *Hledání českých zájmů. Mezinárodní bezpečnost.* Praha: Ústav mezinárodních vztahů.

KRATOCHVIL, P. (2010a): National Interest and Its Legitimacy. In: *The Quest for National Interest. A Methodological Reflection on Czech Foreign Policy.* Eds.: Petr Drulák — Mats Braun. Frankfurt am Main: Petr Lang 2010, pp. 21–34.

KRATOCHVÍL, P. (2010b): *Původ a smysl národního zájmu. Analýza legitimity jednoho politického konceptu.* Brno: Centrum pro studium demokracie a kultury (Brno: Centre for the Study of Democracy and Culture), 2010.

KREJČÍ, O. (2001): *Mezinárodní politika.* Praha: EKOPRESS, druhé, aktualizované a rozšířené vydání.

KREJČÍ, O. (2007): *Mezinárodní politika.* Praha: Ekopress, 2007. 743 s. ISBN 80-86929-21-7.

KREJČÍ, O. (2014): *Medzinárodná politika.* 5 vydanie, Praha. Ekopress ISBN 978-80-87865-07-1.

KREJČÍ, O. (2000): *Geopolitika středoevropského prostoru.* Praha: Ekopress, 2000.

KREKOVIČOVÁ, E. (1998): Folklór a politika. Etnocentrismus a Slovensko. (Folklore and politics. Ethocentrism and Slovakia). In SZIGETI, L. (ed.). *Slovenská otázka dnes.* Bratislava: Kalligram, 2007, pp. 127-132.

KREKOVIČOVÁ, E. 2013. Mýtus plebejského národa. (The myth of a plebeian nation). In: KREKOVIČ, E. — MANNOVÁ, E. — KREKOVIČOVÁ, E. (eds.). *Mýty naše slovenské.* Bratislava: Premedia Group, 2013, pp. 86-93.

KRIVÝ, V., MANNOVÁ, E. (2013): Mýtus obete. (The myth of a victim) In: KREKOVIČ, E. — MANNOVÁ, E. — KREKOVIČOVÁ, E. (eds.). *Mýty naše slovenské.* Bratislava: Premedia Group, 2013, pp. 77-85.

KRPEC, O. (2009): *Národní zájmy v moderní demokracii — Česká republika.* Brno: Masarykova univerzita, Mezinárodní politologický ústav.

KRUŽLIAK, I. (1982): Tvorcovia nového Slovenska. (Creators of modern Slovakia) In STAŠKO, J. (ed.): *Tvorcovia nového Slovenska. The shaping of modern Slovakia.* Cambridge, Ontario: Friend of good books, 1982, pp. 3-61.

KULAŠIK, P. a kol. (2002): *Slovník bezpečnostných vzťahov*. Bratislava: Smaragd, 2002.

KULTÚRA (2001): *Štátna doktrína Slovenskej republiky (návrh)*. Kultúra, 2001, Vol. 4, No. 14–15.

KUNDERA, M. (1984): *A Kidnapped West or Culture Bows Out*. [online] Retrieved from https://granta.com/a-kidnapped-west-or-culture-bows-out/.

KUSÝ, M. (1998): *Čo s našimi Maďarmi?* Bratislava: Kalligram, 1998. 229 s. ISBN 80-7149-200-0.

KUSÝ, M. (2016): Žijú na Slovensku. (They live in Slovakia) In: KUSÝ, M. *Politika a menšiny*, Vol.II, Bratislava 2016, pp. 412-659.

KYMLICKA, W. (1995) *Multicultural Citizenship: A Liberal Theory of Minority Rights*. Oxford: University Press, 199 296 p. ISBN 978-0-19-8229091-3.

KYMLICKA, W. – STRAEHLE, C. (1999): *Cosmopolitaniasm, nation-states and minority nationalism*. In: European Journal of Philosophy, Vol. 7, 1999. No. 1, ISSN 0966-8373. pp. 65-88.

KYSEĽ, T. (2016): *Kotleba ostal sám. Odchod z EÚ nechce dokonca ani Kollár.* (Kotleba left alone. Even Kollár against withdrawal from the EU). Aktuality.sk, 28 June 2016. [online] Available at: https://www.aktuality.sk/clanok/351029/kotleba-ostal-sam-odchod-z-eu-nechce-dokonca-ani-kollar/.

LAJČÁK, M. (2016): *Vzťahy SR a Rumunska spája spoločná história a členstvo v EÚ* (Relations between the Slovak Republic amnd Romania are forged by a common history and EU membership). Teraz.sk, 30 August 2016. [online] Available at: http://www.teraz.sk/slovensko/lajcak-vztahy-sr-a-rumunska-spaja-s/214940-clanok.html.

LAJČÁK, M. (2017): *Nie je v poriadku, že so mnou ústavní činitelia nekonzultujú svoje prejavy*. (It is not in order that government officials do not seek advice on their public speeches.) In Pravda [online], 15 November 2017. Available at: https://spravy.pravda.sk/domace/clanok/448226-lajcak-nie-je-v-poriadku-ze-so-mnou-ustavni-cinitelia-nekonzultuju-svoje-prejavy/ [cit. 2018-11-20].

LAMPL, Z. (2013): *Sociológia Maďarov na Slovensku*. Šamorín: Fórum, 2013. 148 s. ISBN 978-80-89249-68-8.

LANG, K. O. (2015): *Rückzug aus der Solidarität*. In SWP-Aktuell, 84, Oktober 2015. [online] Available at: https://www.swp-berlin.org/publikation/visegrad-laender-und-fluechtlingspolitik/.

LÁŠTIC, E. (2011): *V rukách politických strán: Referendum na Slovensku 1993-2010* (In the hands of the political parties: referendum in Slovakia) Bratislava: Univerzita Komenského 2011.

LENČ, J. (2011): Islam a moslimskí migranti na Slovensku a v Európe. In Štefančík, R., Lenč, J. (eds.). *Migračná politika národných štátov*. Trnava: SSRP, 2011. ISBN 978-80-969043-3-4, s. 34-62.

LENIN, V. I. (1978): *Összes művei 25. kötet*. Budapest: Kossuth, 1978. 610 s. ISBN 963-09-1107-8.

LEŠKA, D. (2011): *Formovanie politického systému na Slovensku po roku 1989*. (Formation of the political system in Slovakia after 1989). Bratislava: Infopress, 2011.

LEŠKO, M. (1996): *Najlepší z výberu (podľa premiéra). Tandem Mečiar L Lexa: O vzniku a fungovaní politickej symbiózy vyššieho typu 1*. Sme, 12. 4. 1996.

LEŠKO, M. (2016): *Smer: strana predstieranej identity* (Smer: a party of pretended identity. Trend, 19 Febriary 2016.

LEŠKOVÁ, E. (2006): Slovensko. (Slovakia) In HAVLÍK, V. – KANIOK, P. (eds.). *Euroskepticsimus a země střední a východní Evropy*. Brno: IIPS, 2006, pp. 31-44.

LIĎÁK, J. (2016): International Migration from Asia and Africa – Issues and Challenges for Europe. In Asian and African Studies, Vol. 25, No. 2. 2016. ISSN 1335-1257, pp. 211-248.

LIEBKIND, K. (1985): Some problems in the theoryand application of cultural pluralism: The social psychology of minority identy. In: *Cultural pluralism and cultural identity. The experience of Canada, Finland and Yugoslavia*. Final Report of the UNESCO Joint Study on Cultural Development in Countries containing Different National and/or Ethnic Groups. Paris: UNESCO, 1985. pp. 91-97. [online] [cit.13.12.2016] Available at: http://unesdoc.unesco.org/images/0006/000651/065187eo.pdf.

LIJPHART, A. (1977): *Democracy in plural societies*. New Haven: Yale University Press, 1977. 248 p. ISBN 978-0-300-02494-0.

LIND, M. (1994): *In defense of liberal nationalism*. In: Foreign Affairs. Vol. 73, 1994, No. 3. ISSN 2327-7793. pp. 87-99.

LIPTÁK, L. (2013): Koniec mýtov na Slovensku? (The end of myths in Slovakia?) In: KREKOVIČ, E. – MANNOVÁ, E. – KREKOVIČOVÁ, E. (eds.). *Mýty naše slovenské*. Bratislava: Premedia Group, 2013, pp. 239-241.

LOEWENSTEIN, B. W. (1997): *My ti druzí*. Brno: Doplněk, 1997. 356 s. ISBN 80-85765-64-0.

ŁOŚ, R. – KOBIERECKA, A. (eds.): *The V4 Towards Migration Challenges in Europe*. Lodz: Wydawnictwo Uniwersitetu Lodzkiego 2017.

ŁOŚ, R. – NOWAK, T. (2000): *Stosunki międzynarodowe. Teorie – systemy – uczestnicy*. Wrocław: Wydawnictwo Universytetu Wrocławskiego.

ĽSNS (2015): *Výzva europoslancom, ktorí zradili naše národné záujmy – vzdajte sa mandátu.* Kotleba – Ľudová strana Naše Slovensko, 13 May 2015.

ĽSNS (2016): *10 Bodov za Naše Slovensko. Volebný program politickej strany Kotleba – Ľudová strana Naše Slovensko.* (10 points for our Slovakia. Election program of the political party Kotleba – People's Party Our Slovakia – official website. [online] Available at: http://www.naseslovensko.net/wp-content/uploads/2015/01/Volebn%C3%BD-program-2016.pdf.

LUKÁČ, P. (2003): Historická a politická identita Slovenska na prahu jeho integrácie do EÚ. (Historical and political identity of Slovakia at the threshold of its integration into EU) In SZIGETI, L. (ed.). *Slovenská otázka dnes.* Bratislava: Kalligram, 2007, pp. 336-345.

MACKERT. J. (2006): *Staatsbürgerschaft. Eine Einführung.* Wiesbaden: Verlag für Sozialwissenschaften. 2006. ISBN 978-3-531-14626-3.

MAGNIFICAT 2016. Film 11. september 1683. [online] Available at: http://www.magnificat.sk/vaclav-mika-film-11-september-1683-bitka-pri-viedni-je-sovinisticky-a-xenofobny-vyhlasenie-k-listu-vaclava-miku/.

MALOVÁ, D. – LÁŠTIC, E. (2001): *The Gradual Amending of the Slovak Constitution. Combating the Ambiguous Rules in 1992 – 2001.* Central European Political Science Review, Vol. 2, issue 4, Summer 2001, pp. 103 – 128.

MARTINIELLI, M. (2005): *Political Participation, Mobilisation and Representation of Immigrants and their Offspring's in Europe.* Willy Brandt Series of Working Papers in International Migration and Ethnic Relations, 1/05, Malmö University. 2005. ISSN 1650-5743.

MARTINKOVIČ, M. (2013): *Politické myslenie Novej školy. Občiansko-národný program Slovenských novín.* (Political thinking of the New School. Slovak national-civic program) Bratislava: Institute of Philosophy SAS, 2013.

MARUŠIAK Juraj (2013): *Zahraničná politika – od prežitia k lepšiemu svetu.* [online] Available at: http://www.jetotak.sk/europa/od-prezitia-klepsiemu-svetu.

MARUŠIAK, J. (2012): The Czech Republic and Slovakia: Partnership with Moldova for Transformation and Europeanization. In: Eds. Marcin Kosienkowski – William Schreiber: *Moldova: arena of International Influences.* Lanham, Boulder, New York, Toronto, Plymouth, UK: Lexington Books, 2012, pp. 35-50.

MEARSHEIMER, J. J. (2001): *Tragedy of Great Power Politics.* New York. W.W. Norton & Company. ISBN 978-0-393-34927-6.

MEDIENSERVICE 2017. *Relocations Program.* [online] Available at: http://medienservicestelle.at/migration_bewegt/2017/03/28/relocation-programm-oesterreich-hat-noch-keine-fluechtlinge-aufgenommen.

MEMORANDUM 1861. *Memorandum národa slovenského.* (Memorandum of the Slovak nation) In Dokumenty slovenskej národnej identity a štátnosti I. Bratislava: Nár. Lit. Centrum, 1998, pp. 336-343.

MEZEI, I. (2008): *A magyar-szlovák határmenti kapcsolatok esélye.* Budapest–Pécs: Dialóg Campus, 2008. 154 s. ISBN 978-963-7296-825-6.

MH (2013): *Zahraničný obchod Slovenska za rok 2013.* (Slovakia's foreign trade in 2013). Bratislava: Ministry of Economy SR 2013.

MH (2016): *Zahraničný obchod SR – za rok 2015 (v porovnaní s rokom 2014)* (Slovakia's foreign trade for 2015 (as compared with 2014)). Bratislava: Ministerstvo hospodárstva SR 2016.

MIKUŠOVIČ, D. (2014): *Fico sa pustil do sankcií: Sú nezmyselné a ohrozujú Slovensko.* (Fico attacks sanctions: they are pointless and may harm Slovakia) Sme, 9 August 2014.

MINARECHOVÁ, R. (2012): *Gašparovič faces Ukrainian challenge.* Slovak Spectator, 14. 5. 2012.

MINISTERSTVO OBRANY SR (2005): *Bezpečnostná stratégia SR.* [online] Available at: http://www.mod.gov.sk/data/files/833.pdf.

MINISTERSTVO OBRANY SR (2005): *Obranná stratégia SR.* [online] Available at: http://www.mod.gov.sk/data/files/832.pdf.

MINISTERSTVO OBRANY SR (2013): *White Paper on Defence of the Slovak Republic.* [online] Available at: http://www.mod.gov.sk/white-paper-on-defence-of-the-slovak-republic/.

MINISTRY OF DEFENCE: *History of Military Operations Abroad.* [online] Available at: http://www.mosr.sk/history-of-military-operations-abroad/.

MITRANY, D. (1966): *A working peace system.* Quadrangle Books. ASIN B0007DNROQ.

MOJŽITA M. (2004): *KŇAŽKO / DEMEŠ / KŇAŽKO. Formovanie slovenskej diplomacie v rokoch 1990 až 1993.* Bratislava: VEDA, vydavateľstvo SAV – Ústav politických vied SAV.

MOORE, M. (2003): *The ethics of nationalism.* Oxford: University Press, 2003. 272 p. ISBN 978-0198297468.

MORGENTHAU, H. J. (1951): *In Defense of the National Interest: A Critical Examination of American Foreign Policy.* New York: Knopf 1951.

MORVAY, P. (2017): *Kotleba ako Turčín Poničan.* (Kotleba as Turčín Poničan) In Dennik N, vol. 3, 2017, No. 72 (12.4.2017), p. 11.

MOS: *Program Maďarskej občianskej strany prijatý V. snemom MOS*. 26 October 1996 (Zhrnutie).

MŠVVŠ SR (2016): *Priority Ministerstva školstva, vedy, výskumu a športu SR*. 2016. [online] Available at: https://www.minedu.sk/priority-ministerstva-skolstva-vedy-vyskumu-a-sportu-sr/.

MVSR (2011): *Migračná politika Slovenskej republiky s výhľadom do roku 2020*. (Ministry of the Interior SK. Migration policy of the Slovak Republic—an outlook for 2020) [online] Available online: http://www.minv.sk/?zamer-migracnej-politiky-slovenskej-republiky&subor=10500.

MVSR 2017: Statistiky. (Statistics) [online] Available online: http://www.minv.sk/?statistiky-20&subor=219019.

MZV ČR (1993): ZAHRANIČNÍ POLITIKA ČESKÉ REPUBLIKY. Dokumenty. 6/1993. Ministerstvo zahraničních věcí.

MZV SR (2009): *Vystúpenie M. Lajčáka na Moskovskom štátnom inštitúte medzinárodných vzťahov*. (M. Lajčák's address at the Moscow State Institute of International Relations) Bratislava: Ministry of Foreign Affairs SR, 8 September 2009.

MZV SR (2010): *Zahraničná politika v roku 2010. Výročná správa 2010*. Ministerstvo zahraničných vecí Slovenskej republiky, s. 3. [online] Available at: https://www.mzv.sk/documents/10182/2365670/2010+Vyrocna+sprava+ministerstva.

MZV SR A: *Správa o plnení úloh zahraničnej politiky SR. Zameranie zahraničnej politiky SR*. Rok 1993—1994, 1994—1995, 1995—1996, 1996—1997. Ministerstvo zahraničných vecí Slovenskej republiky.

MZV SR B: *Správa o plnení úloh zahraničnej politiky SR. Zameranie zahraničnej politiky SR*. Rok 1997—1998, 1998—1999, 1999—2000, 2000—2001. Ministerstvo zahraničných vecí Slovenskej republiky.

MZVaEZ SR (2013): *Minister M. Lajčák navštívi Moldavsko* (Minister M. Lajčák to visit Moldova). Bratislava: Ministry of Foreign and European Affairs SR, 7 July 2013.

MZVaEZ SR (2014): *Zameranie zahraničnej a európskej politiky Slovenskej republiky na rok 2014*. [online] Available at: https://www.mzv.sk/documents/10182/2198827/2014+-+Zameranie+zahrani%C4%8Dnej+a+eur%C3%B3pskej+politiky+Slovenskej+republiky.

MZVaEZ SR (2015): *Sankcie medzi EÚ a RU—aktuálny stav a dopady. Informačný materiál na rokovanie Rady vlády SR pre podporu exportu a investícií* (Sanctions between EU and RU—current state and effects. Information material for the session of the Council of the Government of the Slovak republic for Export and Investment Support). 18 February 2015. Bratislava: Ministry of Foreign and European Affairs SR 2015.

MZVaEZ SR (2015): *Zameranie zahraničnej a európskej politiky Slovenskej republiky na rok 2015*. [online] Available at: https://www.mzv.sk/documents/10182/2198827/2015+-+Zameranie+zahrani%C4%8Dnej+a+eur%C3%B3pskej+politiky+Slovenskej+republiky.

MZVaEZ SR (2016): *M. Lajčák rokoval v Moskve s ruským ministrom zahraničných vecí S. Lavrovom.* (M. Lajčák holds talks with the Russian Foreign Minister S. Lavrov in Moscow) Bratislava: Ministerstvo zahraničných vecí a európskych záležitostí SR 10.5.2016.

MZVaEZ SR (2016): *Zameranie zahraničnej a európskej politiky Slovenskej republiky na rok 2016*. [online] Available at: https://www.mzv.sk/documents/10182/2198827/2016+-+Zameranie+zahrani%C4%8Dnej+a+eur%C3%B3pskej+politiky+Slovenskej+republiky.

MZVaEZ SR (2017): *Vyhlásenie hovorcu MZVaEZ SR k zavádzajúcemu dokumentu ruskej televízie o invázii.* (Statement of the Spokesperson of the Ministry of Foreign and European Affairs SR on the misleading document of the Russian television on invasion). Bratislava: Ministry of Foreign and European Affairs SR, 31 May 2017.

MZVaEZ SR (2017): *Zmeranie ekonomickej diplomacie v oblasti bilaterálnych vzťahov do roku 2020.* MZVaEZ SR. [online] Available at: https://www.mzv.sk/documents/10182/2663415.

MZVaEZ SR (2018): *Russian ambassador with State Secretary L. Parizek on Salisbury incident.* Ministry of Foreign and European Affairs of the Slovak Republic, March 27, 2018. [online] Available at: https://www.mzv.sk/web/en/news/current_issues/-/asset_publisher/lrJ2tDuQdEKp/content/rusky-velvyslanec-u-statneho-tajomnika-l-parizka-kvoli-incidentu-salisbury/10182?_101_INSTANCE_lrJ2tDuQdEKp_redirect=%2Fweb%2Fen%2Fnews%3Frok%3D2018%26mesiac%3D2%26strana%3D1.

NARB: *9 ijunia 2003 goda sostojalas´ vstreča slovackich parlamentarijev s deputatami Palaty predstavitelej Nacionaľnogo sobranija Respubliki Belarus* (On 9 June 2003, a meeting was held between Slovak parliamentarians and deputies of the House of Representatives of the National Assembly of the Republic of Belarus) Minsk: National Assembly of the Republic of Belarus — House of Representatives, June 9, 2003. [online] Available at: http://house.gov.by/index.php/,0,703,,,0,,,0.html.

NAROVINU. [online] Available at: www.centrumnarovinu.sk.

NEMEC, M. (2017): *Hladová dolina na Gemeri bojuje o zamestnávateľa.* (A hungry valley in Gemer struggles for an employer) Hospodárske noviny, 11. 7. 2017.

NÉMETH, Š. (ed.) (2011): *Politika, etnopolitika a identita.* Nitra: UKF, 2011. 112 s. ISBN 978-80-8094-931-0.

NEUBERT, S. – ROTH, H.-J. – YILDIZ, E. (2002): Multikulturalismus – ein umstrittenes Konzept. In Neubert, S., Roth, H.-J., Yildiz, E. (ed.). *Multikulturalität in der Diskussion. Neure Beiträge zu einem umstrittenen Konzept.* Opladen: Verlag für Sozialwissenschaften. 2002. ISBN 978-3-531-19431-8, s. 9-30.

NOS (2016): *Výskum verejnej mienky v oblasti pravicového extrémizmu* Nadácia otvorenej spoločnosti 2012. [online] Available at: http://cvek.sk/wp-content/uploads/2015/11/pravicovy-extremizmus.pdf.

NOVÁ ŠKOLA 1868. *Program politického zoskupenia Nová škola slovenská.* (New School 1868. The program of the political grouping Nová škola slovenská) In: Dokumenty slovenskej národnej identity a štátnosti I. Bratislava: Nár. Lit. Centrum, 1998, pp. 358-360.

NOVINY.SK (2015): *Fico v Moskve kritizoval sankcie, zdôraznil národné záujmy.* Noviny.sk, 2. 6. 2015.

NOVOMESKÝ, L. (1968a): Zmysel federácie. (1968a. The purpose of federation) In CHMEL, R. (ed.). *Slovenská otázka v 20. storočí.* Bratislava: Kalligram, 1997, pp. 391-395.

NOVOMESKÝ, L. (1968b): Slovenská štátnosť – ovocie demokratizácie. (1968b. Slovak statehood – the fruit of democratisation) In: CHMEL, R. (ed.). *Slovenská otázka v 20. storočí.* Bratislava: Kalligram, 1997, pp. 396-399.

NOVOSAD, F. (1998): Peripetie repolitizácie (Peripeties of repoliticisation) In Szgeti, László (ed.). *Slovenská otázka dnes.* Bratislava: Kalligram, 2007, pp. 140-150.

NOVOSÁD, F. (2010): *Útržky o Slovensku.* Bratislava: Kalligram 2010.

NOVOTNÝ, P. (2010): *Paľba Maďarov nás nepotopila.* Hospodárske noviny, 20- 1. 2010.

NRSR (1992): Stenografická správa o 2. schôdzi Slovenskej národnej rady, konanej 14. a 15. júla 1992. Available at: http://www.nrsr.sk/dl/Browser/Document?documentId=71564.

NRSR (1994): *Stenografická správa o 26. schôdzi Národnej rady Slovenskej republiky*, konanej 26., 27., 28. januára, 2., 3., 4., 16., 17. a18. februára 1994. [online] Available at: http://www.nrsr.sk/dl/Browser/DsDocumentVariant?documentVariantId=12498&fileName=zazn.pdf&ext=pdf.

NRSR (1996): *Stenografická správa o 16. schôdzi Národnej rady Slovenskej rady Slovenskej republiky*, konanej 19., 20., 21., 25. júna a 1., 2., 3., 4. júla 1996. [online] Available at: http://www.nrsr.sk/dl/Browser/Document?documentId=65839.

NRSR (1998): *Vyhlásenie NR SR z 1. decembra 1998 k integrácii Slovenskej republiky do EÚ.* Bratislava: NR SR 1998. [online] Available at: https://www.nrsr.sk/web/Static/sk-SK/NRSR/Doc/v_k-integracii-do-eu-19981201.htm.

NRSR (2001): *Ústavný zákon č. 90/2001 Z.z. z 23. februára 2001, ktorým sa mení a dopĺňa Ústava Slovenskej republiky č. 460/1992 Zb. v znení neskorších predpisov.* Zbierka zákonov No. 90/2001, pp. 1226–1236; Návrh skupiny poslancov NR SR na vydanie ústavného zákona, ktorým sa mení a dopĺňa Ústava SR č. 460/1992 Zb. v znení ústavného zákona č. 244/1998 Z. z. a ústavného zákona č. 9/1999 Z. z.(tlač 643) – tretie čítanie. Hlasovanie o návrhu ústavného zákona ako o celku. NR SR – hlasovanie poslancov [online]. Bratislava: NR SR, sitting no. 45, 23 February 2001. Available online: http://www.nrsr.sk/web/Default.aspx?sid=schodze/hlasovanie/hlasklub&ID=5779.

NRSR (2004): *The Constitutional Act no. 397/2004 Coll. on Cooperation of the National Council of the Slovak Republic and the Government of the Slovak Republic in matters concerning the European Union.* [online] Available at: https://www.nrsr.sk/web/Static/sk-SK/NRSR/Doc/zd_zalezitosti-eu.pdf.

NRSR (2007): *Vyhlásenie NR SR k riešeniu budúceho štatútu srbskej provincie Kosovo.* Uznesenie č. 309. Bratislava: NR SR, 28 March 2007 [online] Available at: https://www.nrsr.sk/web/Default.aspx?sid=schodze/hlasovanie/hlasovanie&ID=8825.

NRSR (2010): *Uznesenie NR SR č. 2075 k návrhu novelizácie zákona o štátnom občianstve, o ktorom rokuje Národné zhromaždenie Maďarskej republiky* (tlač 1543). NR SR 4. volebné obdobie NR SR, 52. schôdza.. NR SR, 25. 5. 2010.

NRSR (2013): *Vyhlásenie NR SR k situácii na Ukrajine.* (Statement of the National Council of the Slovak Republic on the situation in Ukraine) Uznesenie č. 956 (Resolution No 956). Bratislava: NC SR, 13 December 2013.

NRSR (2014): *Vyhlásenie NR SR k situácii na Ukrajine.* Uznesenie č. 1060. Statement of the National Council of the Slovak Republic on the situation in Ukraine. Resolution No 1060. Bratislava: National Council of the Slovak Republic, 18 March 2014.

NRSR (2015): *Vyhlásenie NR SR k riešeniu migračných výziev, ktorým aktuálne čelí Európska únia.* Uznesenie č. 1837. Bratislava: NR SR, 24 June 2015.

NRSR (2016): *Návrh nariadenia Európskeho parlamentu a Rady, ktorým sa mení nariadenie (ES) č. 539/2001 uvádzajúce zoznam tretích krajín, ktorých štátni príslušníci musia mať víza pri prekračovaní vonkajších hraníc členských štátov, a krajín, ktorých štátni príslušníci sú oslobodení od tejto povinnosti* (Ukrajina), KOM (2016) 236. In: Uznesenie Výboru NR SR pre európske záležitosti č. 17 z 9. júna 2016. 8. schôdza výboru CRD-1048-1/2016-VEZ. Bratislava: Národná rada SR 2016 (Draft Regulation of the European Parliament and of the Council, amending regulation (ES) No 539/2001 listing the third countries whose nationals must be in possession of visas when crossing the external borders of the Member States and those countries whose nationals are exempt form that obligation (Ukraine), KOM (2016) 236. In: Resolution of the Committee of the National Council for European Affairs No 17 of 9 June 2016. 8th Session of the Committee, CRD-1048-1/2016-VEZ).

NRSR (2017): *Migračná politika Slovenskej republiky s výhľadom do roku 2020.* Hlasovanie o návrhu uznesenia. Bratislava: National Council of the Slovak Republic 26. 33. 2017 14. December 2017. [online] Available at: https://www.nrsr.sk/web/Default.aspx?sid=schodze/hlasovanie/hlasklub&ID=16817.

NRSR (2018): *Uznesenie NR SR k z 29. novembra 2018 k dokumentu OSN Globálny pakt o bezpečnej, riadenej a legálnej migrácii.* 4, 1998, no. 3. Bratislava: National Council of Slovak Republic, 29 November 2018.

NRSR A: *Informácia o vzťahoch a možných negatívnych dopadoch inštitucionalizácie Fóra maďarských poslancov Karpatskej kotliny pri maďarskom parlamente na politický a spoločenský vývoj strednej Európy.* Hlasovanie o návrhu uznesenia. Bratislava: Peterburg 4 November 2017. [online] Available at: https://www.nrsr.sk/web/Default.aspx?sid=schodze/hlasovanie/hlasovanie&ID=8825.

NRSR B: *Návrh Vyhlásenia Národnej rady Slovenskej republiky k opakovaným nacionalistickým výrokom Viktora Orbána, predsedu FIDESZ-MPP a niektorých ďalších predstaviteľov počas volebnej kampane do Európskeho parlamentu smerujúcich k etnickej separácii, popieraniu suverenity susedných krajín, ako aj k spochybňovaniu územnej celistvosti Slovenskej republiky a podnecovaniu nestability v strednej Európe* (tlač 1125). Hlasovanie o návrhu uznesenia. Bratislava: Peterburg 26. 38. 2017 3. 6. 2017. [online] Available at: https://www.nrsr.sk/web/Default.aspx?sid=schodze/hlasovanie/hlasovanie&ID=8825.

NRSR C: *Návrh Zahraničného výboru Národnej rady Slovenskej republiky na prijatie Vyhlásenia Národnej rady Slovenskej republiky o Zákone o Maďaroch žijúcich v susedných krajinách* (tlač 248). Hlasovanie o návrhu uznesenia. NR SR – hlasovanie poslancov. Bratislava: Peterburg 26. 8. 2017 28. 3. 2017. [online] Available at: https://www.nrsr.sk/web/Default.aspx?sid=schodze/hlasovanie/hlasovanie&ID=8825.

NRSR D: *Návrh Zahraničného výboru Národnej rady Slovenskej republiky na prijatie Vyhlásenia Národnej rady Slovenskej republiky o Zákone o Maďaroch žijúcich v susedných krajinách* (tlač 1291). Hlasovanie o návrhu uznesenia. Bratislava: National Council of the Slovak Republic 26. 54. 2017 7. 2. 2017. 18. 12. 2001. [online] Available at: https://www.nrsr.sk/web/Default.aspx?sid=schodze/hlasovanie/hlasovanie&ID=8825.

NRSR E: *Vyhlásenie NR SR k riešeniu migračných výziev, ktorým aktuálne čelí Európska únia.* Hlasovanie o návrhu uznesenia. Bratislava: Peterburg 26. 53. 2017 24. 6. 2017. [online] Available at: https://www.nrsr.sk/web/Default.aspx?sid=schodze/hlasovanie/hlasklub&ID=35989.

NRSR F: *Základné ciele a zásady národnej bezpečnosti Slovenskej republiky.* [online] Available at: http://www.nrsr.sk/dl/Browser/DsDocumentVariant?documentVariantId=22424&fileName=nav_0424.pdf&ext=pdf.

NYE, J. (2011): *The Future of Power.* New York. Public Affairs. ISBN 978-1-61039-069-9.

NYE, J. – Welch, D. (2013): *Understanding Global Conflict and Cooperation: An Introduction to Theory and History.* Cambridge: Pearson. 2013, 384s. ISBN 978-12-920-2318-2.

OBERNDÖRFER, D. (2001): Integration der Ausländer im demokratischen Verfassungsstaat: Ziele und Aufgaben. In Rat für Migration (RfM) (ed.): *Integration und Illegalität in Deutschland.* Osnabrück: Selbstverlag, pp. 11-29.

OBŠITNÍK, L. (2016): *Migrácia potrebuje pravicový prístup. Opozícia má čo dobiehať.* (Migration needs a right-wing approach. Opposition has much to catch up). [online] Available at: https://www.postoj.sk/11174/migracia-potrebuje-pravicovy-pristup-opozicia-ma-co-dobiehat.

OFFICIAL JOURNAL OF THE EUROPEAN UNION (1997): *Resolution on the case of Frantisek Gaulieder, Member of the Slovak Parliament.* B4-1389 and 1419/96. In Official Journal C 020, 20/01/1997 P. 0145. [online] Available at: http://eur-law.eu/EN/Resolution-case-Frantisek-Gaulieder-member-Slovak-Parliament,168400,d.

OFFICIAL JOURNAL OF THE EUROPEAN UNION (2016): *Action brought on 2 December 2015 – Slovak Republic v Council of the European Union* (Case C-643/15) (2016/C 038/55) [online] Available at: http://eur-lex.europa.eu/legal-content/ENG/TXT/PDF/?uri=CELEX:62015CN0643&from=ENG.

OKS (2006): *Štíhla vláda.* Program OKS – Správna vec. Volebný program Občianskej konzervatívnej strany pre voľby do NR SR 2006.

OKS (2002): *Výzva pre Slovensko.* Volebný program OKS pre parlamentné voľby 2002.

OĽaNO (2016): *Program za ľudské a rozumné Slovensko.* (A program for humane and sane Slovakia) Available at: http://www.obycajniludia.sk/wp-content/uploads/2016/02/program-olano.pdf.

ÖLLÖS, L. (2008): *Az egyetértés konfliktusa.* Somorja: Fórum, 2008. 159 s. ISBN 978-80-89249-22-0.

Oslavy Slovanstva a štátnosti na Jankovom vŕšku (2017): (Celebrations of Slavism and statehood on the Jankov Vŕšok Mountain) 29 August 2017. [online] Available at: https://www.facebook.com/events/2011442062420335/?active_tab=about.

PAJTINKA, E. (2007): *Hospodárska diplomacia a jej úloha v 21. storočí.* In: Mezinárodní vztahy 4/2007, roč. 42, s.52-72. ISSN 0323-1844.

PALATA, Ľ. (2015): *Slavkov, bermudský trojúhelník české diplomacie.* (Slavkov: The Bermuda Triangle of Czech diplomacy) Zahraničná politika, 20 February 2015.

PALKO, V. (2000): *Poznámky k národno-štátnemu záujmu.* Domino Fórum, 19. 10. 2000 – 25. 10. 2000.

PAYTON, P. (1999): Ethnicity in Western Europe. In: Cordell, K. (ed.) *Ethnicity an democratization in the new Europe.* London – New York: Routledge, 1999. 214 s. ISBN 9780-415-17312-4. s. 21-32.

PEREZ DE CUELLAR, J. et al. (eds.) (1996): *Our creative diversity. Report of the World Comission on Culture and Development.* Paris: UNESCO, 1996. 399 s. ISBN 92-3-103282-8.

PETRIČ, E. (2013): *Foreign Policy: From Conception to Diplomatic Practice.* Leiden: Matinus Nijhoff, 2013. 302s. ISBN 978-90-042-4549-5.

PIŠKO, M. (2014): *Lipšic rečnil na Majdane, Ukrajincom sľúbil rokovať o pomoci.*(Lipšic speaks at Maidan, promising the Ukrainians negotiations on help) Sme, 7 February 2014. [online] Available at: https://svet.sme.sk/c/7095139/lipsic-recnil-na-majdane-ukrajin com-slubil-rokovat-o-pomoci.html.

PLUSKA (2015a): *Prieskum: prijmeme utečencov za svojich takýto je postoj Slovákov.* (A survey: We will accept refugees – such is the position of the Slovaks.) [online] Available at: http://www.pluska.sk/spravy/z-domova/prieskum-prijmeme-utecencov-za-svojich-takyto-je-postoj-slovakov.html.

PLUSKA (2015b): *V zahraničí pracuje vyše 300 tisíc Slovákov.* (More than 300,000 Slovaks work abroad.) [online] Available at: http://www.pluska.sk/spravy/ekonomika/v-zahranici-pracuje-vyse-300-tisic-slovakov-domov-vratit-nechcu.html.

POLÁČKOVÁ, Z – BRHLÍKOVÁ, R. a kol. (2017): *Národnoštátne záujmy v postintegračnom období.* – 1. vyd. – Nitra: Univerzita Konštantína Filozofa, 2017. 350 s. ISBN 978-80-558-1246-5.

POPÉLY, Á. (2003): *A kolonializáció területi vonatkozásai és etnikai következményei.* Fórum Társadalomtudományi Szemle. [online] Available at: http://forumszemle.eu/2003/06/08/popely-arpad-a-kolonizacio-teruleti-vonatkozasai-es-etnikai-kovetkezmenyei/.

PRAVDA (2014a): *Do vojny na Ukrajine sa vtiahnuť nenecháme, tvrdí premiér.* (We will not be drawn into the war in Ukraine, says Prime Minister). Pravda, 6 September 2014.

PRAVDA (2014b): *Európa je nervózna. Na Ukrajine hrozí veľký vojenský konflikt.* Pravda, 2 December 2014. [online] Available at: https://spravy.pravda.sk/domace/clanok/338203-fico-europa-je-nervozna-na-ukrajine-hrozi-velky-vojensky-konflikt/.

PRAVDA (2015): *Fico: Diktát odmietame, kvóty nebude Slovensko rešpektovať.* Pravda, 22 Septembre 2015. [online] Available at: http://spravy.pravda.sk/domace/clanok/368428-fico-povinne-kvoty-slovensko-nebude-respektovat/.

PRAVDA (2015): *Fico: Kvótam hovorím nie. Nechcem niesť zodpovednosť za teroristický útok.* Pravda, 09 September 2015. [online] Available at: http://spravy.pravda.sk/domace/clanok/367102-fico-kvotam-hovorim-nie-nechcem-niest-zodpovednost-za-teroristicky-utok/.

PRAVDA (2016a): *Fico na summite EÚ označil sankcie voči Rusku za nezmyselné a nefunkčné.* (Fico at the EU summit: Sanctions against Russia are pointless and useless). Pravda, 21 October 2016.

PRAVDA (2016b): *Fico: Podozrenia o predsedníctve v Rade EÚ sú nezmyselné a vymyslené.* Pravda, 26 November 2016. [online] Available at: https://spravy.pravda.sk/domace/clanok/412101-fico-podozrenia-o-predsednictve-v-rade-eu-su-nezmyselne-a-vymyslene/.

PRAVDA (2017): *Kiska sa obul do Fica kvôli Rusku.* (Kiska snaps at Fico for Russia). Pravda, 17 March 2017.

PRAVDA (2018): *Hrnkovi neprešiel návrh, aby parlament nerokoval o bezpečnostných dokumentoch.* Pravda, 13 November 2018.

PREAMBULA. Ústava Slovenskej republiky. (Preamble. Constitution of the Slovak Republic) [online] Available online: http://www.slpk.sk/dokumenty/ustava.pdf.

PREZIDENT.SK (2017a): *Prezident Kiska: Bude to rok pravdy aj pre zahraničnú politiku.* (President Kiska: This will be a year of truth for foreign policy). Andrej Kiska – President of the Slovak Republic – official website, 16 March 2017. [online] Available at: https://www.prezident.sk/article/prezident-kiska-bude-to-rok-pravdy-aj-pre-zahranicnu-politiku/.

PREZIDENT.SK (2017b): *Vyhlásenie prezidenta, predsedu Národnej rady a predsedu vlády k EÚ a NATO.* (Statement of the President, Chairman of the National Council and Prime Minister on the EU and NATO. Andrej Kiska — President of the Slovak Republic [online], 23 October 2017. Available at: https://www.prezident.sk/article/vyhlasenie-prezidenta-predsedu-narodnej-rady-a-predsedu-vlady-k-eu-a-nato/ [cit. 2018-11-20].

PROFANT, T. (2015): *Konštrukcia Slovenska ako darcu a jej mocenské dopady.* In: Mezinárodní vztahy, 50, č. 2.

PROGRAMOVÉ VYHLÁSENIE VLÁDY SR NA ROKY 2016-2020 [Policy Statement of the Government of the Slovak Republic for 2016 to 2020]. [online] Available at: https://www.vlada.gov.sk/data/files/7179.pdf.

PSL.PL: *Sankcje wobec Rosji podtrzymane. Tracimy miliardy.* Polskie Stronnictwo Ludowe — official website, 3 July 2017. [online] Available at: http://www.psl.pl/sankcje-rosja-podtrzymane/.

PŠEJA, P. (ed.) (2005): *Přehled teorií mezinárodních vztahů.* Brno: Masarykova univerzita.

RADA EURÓPSKEJ ÚNIE: *Európska bezpečnostná stratégia — Bezpečná Európa v lepšom svete.* Luxemburg: Úrad pre vydávanie publikácií Európskej únie, 2009. 43 s. ISBN 978-92-824-2432-2.

RAFAJ, R. (2014): *Ruky preč od agresie proti Rusku.* (Hands off aggression against Russia) Bratislava: Slovak National Party — official website, 16 May 2014. [online] Available at: http://www.sns.sk/aktuality/rafael-rafaj-ruky-prec-od-agresie-voci-rusku/.

REUTERS (2016): *EU should drop Russia sanctions, Slovak PM says after meeting Putin.* Reuters, 26 Aug. 2016. [online] Available at: http://www.reuters.com/article/us-ukraine-crisis-slovakia/eu-should-drop-russia-sanctions-slovak-pm-says-after-meeting-putin-idUSKCN1111A1.

RÍMSKA DEKLARÁCIA. 2017. [online] Available at: http://www.consilium.europa.eu/sk/press/press-releases/2017/03/25-rome-declaration/.

RING, É. (2004): *Államnemzet és kultúrnemzet válaszútján.* Budapest: ELTE — Eötvös, 2004. 212 s. ISBN 963-463-660-8.

RINGMAR, E. (2008): *Identity, interest and action. A cultural explanation of Sweden's intervention in the Thirty Years War.* Cambridge: Cambridge University Press 2008.

ROGALSKA, K. (2016): *Misslungener Poker mit der Flüchtlingskrise.* In Osteuropa, vol. 66, 2016, No. 3, pp. 43-50.

ROHE, K. (1996): Politische Kultur. Zum Verständnis eines theoretischen Konzepts. In NIEDERMEYER, O. – BEYME, K. v. (eds.). *Politische Kultur in Ost- und Westdeutschland*. Opladen: Leske + Budrich, 1996, pp. 1-21.

ROUGEMONT, D. (2004): Nyílt levél az európaiakhoz. In: SZÉNÁSI Éva (eds.): *Elméletek az európai egységről*. L´Harmattan, Zsigmond Király Főiskola, Budapest, 2004.

ROZHODNUTIE RADY EURÓPSKEJ ÚNIE Č. 472/2014/EU ZO 16. APRÍLA 2014. [online] Available at: http://www.europarl.europa.eu/meetdocs/2014_2019/documents/deve/dv/eyd2015_/eyd2015_sk.pdf.

RTVS (2016): *RTVS dostalo žiadosť*. (Radio and Television of Slovakia received a request), Available online: http://www.hlavnespravy.sk/rtvs-dostalo-ziadost-odvysielat-film-11-september-1683-bitka-priviedni-ktorou-nasi-predkovia-zachranili-europu-pred-islamom/816203/.

RUSIŇÁK P. (2005): *K teoretickým prístupom skúmania zahraničnej politiky*. In: Medzinárodné vzťahy, 3, 2005, č. 2.

RUŽIČKA, F. (2013): *Slovenská diplomacia 3.0*. [online] Available at: http://zahranicnapolitika.dennikn.sk/slovenska-diplomacia-3-0/.

RÚŽIČKA, F – KARVAŠOVÁ, Ľ.: *Európska diplomacia*, Bratislava: EPOS, 2012. 270 s. 270 ISBN 978-80-8057-963-0.

RUŽINSKÁ, V. (2016): *Plynovod Nord Stream nechce deväť krajín*. (Nine countries against the Nord Stream pipeline) Pravda, 22 March 2016.

SALAT, L. (2001): *Etnopolitika*. Marosvásárhely: Mentor, 2001. 346 s. ISBN 973-599-002-4.

SAMSON, I. (1999): *Der widerspruchsvolle Weg der Slowakei in die Europäische Union. Die Slowakei vor der Marginalisierung in Zentraleuropa?* Bonn: Zentrum für europäische Integrationsforschung, 1999.

SAMSON, I. (2000): *Die Sicherheits- und Außenpolitik der Slowakei in den ersten Jahren der Selbständigkeit*. Baden-Baden, Nomos Verlagsgesellschaft 2000.

SaS (2014): *Fico je pre národnú bezpečnosť riziko*. (SaS: Fico poses a threat to national security). Bratislava: Sloboda a Solidarita, 24 March 2014.

SaS (2016): *Sloboda a solidarita: Volebný program Parlamentné voľby 2016*. (Freedom and Solidarity Party: Election manifesto Parliamentary elections 2016.) Available online: http://sulik.sk/wp-content/uploads/2016/11/volebny-program-sas-nr-sr-2010.pdf.

SCRUTON, R. (2005): *A nemzetek szükségességéről*. Budapest: Helikon, 2005. 224 s. ISBN 963-208-989-8.

SDK: *Spolu za lepšie Slovensko*. Volebný program. Slovenská demokratická koalícia.

SECURITY STRATEGY OF THE SLOVAK REPUBLIC (2005). Available online: https://www.mod.gov.sk/data/files/795.pdf.

SDĽ: REPUBLIKOVÝ VÝKONNÝ VÝBOR STRANY DEMOKRATICKEJ ĽAVICE. 5. zjazd SDĽ. Súbor podkladových materiálov pre rokovanie výročných členských schôdzí SDĽ a straníckych konferencií v roku 1998. Informačný bulletin č. 1. Bratislava, december 1997.

SHO (2016): *Vyhlásenie delegátov Snemu SHO k politickej budúcnosti nášho hnutia*. (Statement of the delegates of the SHO Congress on the political future of our movement) — official website, 1 June 2016. [online] Available at: http://sho.sk/clanok/1762/vyhlasenie-delegatov-snemu-sho-k-politickej-buducnosti-nasho-hnutia.

SCHOLZ, A. (2011): *Migrationspolitik zwischen moralischem Anspruch und strategischem Kalkül Der Einfluss politischer Ideen in Deutschland und Frankreich*. Wiesbaden: Verlag für Sozialwissenschaften. ISBN 3-9803401-1-2.

SCHÖPFLIN. G. (2003): *Vytváranie európskej kultúrnej identity? Stredná Európa v rozšírenej Európskej únii*. (Creating European cultural identity? Central Europe in an extended European Union) [online] Available at: https://euractiv.sk/analyzy/uncategorized/vytvaranie-europskej-kulturnej-identity-stredna-europa-v-roz/.

SCHUBERTH, M. (2016): *Die Nichtigkeitsklagen der Slowakei und Ungarns gegen die Notfallumsiedlung aus Italien und Griechenland — Eine rechtliche Erörterung der EuGH-Rechtssachen C-643/15 und C-647/15*. Saar Blueprints, 11/2016 DE. [online] Available at: http://jean-monnet-saar.eu/?page_id=6.

SIMON, A. (2014): *Magyar idők a Felvidéken*. Budapest: Jaffa, 2014. 248 s. ISBN 978-615-5418-91-4.

SITA (2015): *Fico: EÚ je do seba taká zamilovaná, že nič iné neexistuje*. (EU is so much enamored with itself that there is nothing else except it). SITA, 3 December 2015.

SLOVAK SPECTATOR (2015a): *Pro-Russia conference to open in Košice*. Slovak Spectator, 5 March 2015.

SLOVAK SPECTATOR (2015b): *The Košice conference about Ukraine ended vaguely*. Slovak Spectator, 9 March 2015.

SLOVAK SPECTATOR (2016a): *Fico: Russian sanctions are pointless, but EU unity more important*. Slovak Spectator, 24 Oct. 2016. [online] Available at: https://spectator.sme.sk/c/20365554/fico-russian-sanctions-are-pointless-but-eu-unity-more-important.html.

SLOVAK SPECTATOR (2016b): *Lajčák still failing to provide answers to key questions about Evka*. Slovak Spectator, 20 Dec. 2016. [online] Available at: https://spectator.sme.sk/c/20414836/lajcak-still-failing-to-provide-answers-to-key-questions-about-evka.html.

SLOVAK SPECTATOR (2016c): *Scandal persists as Kaliňák leaves questions unanswered*. Slovak Spectator, 15 June 2016. [online] Available at: https://spectator.sme.sk/c/20191278/scandal-persists-as-kalinak-leaves-questions-unanswered.html.

SLOVAK SPECTATOR (2016d): *Slovakia is the second most corrupt country in Europe, a report shows*. Slovak Spectator, 3 Oct. 2016. [online] Available at: https://spectator.sme.sk/c/20342765/slovakia-is-the-second-most-corrupt-country-in-europe-a-report-shows.html.

SLOVAK SPECTATOR (2017a): *EU Presidency Seen as a Success*. Slovak Spectator, 10 Jan. 2017. [online] Available at: https://spectator.sme.sk/c/20427404/eu-presidency-seen-as-a-success.html.

SLOVAK SPECTATOR (2017b): *Chinese are closer to taking over Košice steelworks*. Slovak Spectator, 26 Sept. 2017. [online] Available at: https://spectator.sme.sk/c/20658123/chinese-are-closer-to-taking-over-kosice-steelworks.html. Accessed: 24 Oct. 2017.

SLOVAK SPECTATOR (2017c): *Is Visegrad on its way out of Europe?* Slovak Spectator, 15 March 2017. [online] Available at: https://spectator.sme.sk/c/20483131/is-visegrad-on-its-way-out-of-europe.html.

SLOVAK SPECTATOR (2017d): *PM Fico wants Education Minister's resignation*. Slovak Spectator, 16 August 2017. [online] Available at: https://spectator.sme.sk/c/20627915/education-minister-will-depart.html.

SLOVAK SPECTATOR (2017e): *Will the new Silk Road pass through Slovakia?* Slovak Spectator, 15 May 2017. [online] Available at: https://spectator.sme.sk/c/20533493/will-the-new-silk-road-pass-through-slovakia.html.

SLOVENSKÝ EXPORTÉR (2016): *Obchodovanie s Ruskom*. (Trading with Russia). Slovenský exportér. Internetové noviny Slovenskej asociácie exportérov a importérov — SAEI, 7 August 2016. [online] Available at: http://www.slovakexporter.sk/2016/08/07/obchodovanie-s-ruskom/.

SME (1998): *Jeľcin Mečiarovi: Chceme, veľmi-veľmi chceme, aby ste vyhrali voľby*. (Yeltsin to Mečiar: We wish, very-very much, for you to win the elections) Sme, 29 May 1998.

SME (2001): *Podľa exprezidenta Kováča by štátnu doktrínu mala prijať ústavná väčšina*. Sme, 5 January 2001.

SME (2001a): *Štátna doktrína zaujala okrem prezidenta aj opozíciu*. Sme, 30 April 2001.

SME (2014): *Fico si vyhradil právo odmietnuť európske sankcie voči Rusku.* (Fico reserves his right to reject Europe's sanctions against Russia). Sme, 31 August 2014.

SME (2015a): *Fico: Nikto ma nezastaví, ak pôjde o národné záujmy.* Sme, 7 June 2015.

SME (2015b): *O širokorozchodnej trati rozhodne štúdia realizovateľnosti.* (A feasibility study will decide the fate of the broad-gauge railway line) Sme, 8 June 2015.

SME (2016): *Robert Fico tvrdí, že nič nebolo predražené. Lajčák má jeho dôveru.* Sme, 26 November 2016, [online] Available at: http://domov.sme.sk/c/20394032/robert-fico-tvrdi-ze-nic-nebolo-predrazene-miroslav-lajcak- ma-jeho-doveru.html.

SME (2017): *Fico sa chválil: Môžeme byť v jadre Európskej únie.* (Fico boasts: We may be part of the EU's core). Sme, 22 August 2017.

SME (2018): *Danko prijal na hrade veľvyslancov. Dbajte na záujmy Slovenska, hovorí.* Sme, 21. 8. 2018.

SMER (2001): *Štátna doktrína Slovenskej republiky.* Bratislava: Smer 2001.

SME-RODINA (2016): *Sme-Rodina: Program Sme Rodina – Boris Kollár 2016.* (Sme-Rodina: Party programme of Sme Rodina – Boris Kollár 2016). [online] Available at: http://hnutie-smerodina.sk/Program-Hnutia-Sme-Rodina.pdf.

SMER-SD: *Programové zameranie strany SMER – Sociálna demokracia pre volebné obdobie 2010-2014.*

SMITH, A. D. (2004): *The Antiquity of Nations.* Cambridge: Polity Press, 2004.

SMOLEC, M. (2014): *Sú prezidentovi cudzie záujmy bližšie?* Slovenské národné novny, 5. 9. 2014.

SNS (1992): *Slovensko,* 1992.

SNS (1994): *Program Slovenskej národnej strany,* 1994.

SNS (1998): *127. výročie založenia SNS. 8. výročie znovuobnovenia činnosti SNS. 1871 – 1998. Hej, Slováci, ešte naša slovenská reč žije...* Program Slovenskej národnej strany.

SNS (2006): *Sme Slováci. Slovákom slovenskú vládu.* Volebný program Slovenskej národnej strany, Rok 2006.

SNS (2012): *Vernosť Slovensku.* Programové memorandum SNS. Odsúhlasené rozšíreným Predsedníctvom SNS v Žiline 21. 1. 2012. (Allegiance to Slovakia. SNS election memorandum. Approved by the extended SNS Presidium in Zilina in 21 January 2012) [online] Available at: https://is.muni.cz/el/1423/jaro2016/EVS187/um/Volebne-memorandum-2012.pdf.

SNS (2013): *Petícia slovenských vlastencov adresovaná Bruselu. Popradské memorandum z 29. júna 2013.* (Petition of Slovak patriots addressed to Brussels. Poprad Memorandum of 29 June 2013.) [online] Available at: http://www.popradskememorandum.sk/.

SNS (2015): *Košické programové tézy pre Slovensko.* (Slovak National Party: Košice program propositions for Slovakia) [online] Available at: http://www.sns.sk/engine/assets/uploads/2015/06/kosicke_tezy.pdf.

SNS (2015a): *Slovenská národná strana, 1871. Hrdo, odborne, slušne.* Volebný program pre silný štát 2016-2020 [online] Available at: http://sns.sk/wp-content/uploads/2017/04/volebny_program_2016.pdf.

SNS (2018): *A. Danko – prejav v Štátnej Dume RF* (A. Danko – Address in the RF State Duma). Slovak National Party [online], 19 December 2017. [online] Available at: https://www.sns.sk/a-danko-prejav-v-statnej-dume-rf/.

SOLANA, J. (2003): *A secure Europe in a better world. European security strategy.* [online] Brussels: December 2003. [10.3.2017] Available at: http://www.consilium.europa.eu/uedocs/cmsUpload/78367.pdf.

SOP (1998): *Voľte číslo 7. Dvanásť bodov pre SOP.* Strana občianskeho porozumenia.

SOSNOWSKA, A. (2016): *Mitteleuropa versus Central Europe.* In Aspen Review, Vol. 5, 2016, No. 2, pp. 15-18.

SOTNÍK, A.: *Širokorozchodná – beh na dlhú trať* (Broad-guage line – a long-track run). Transport a logistika, 31 October 2013.

SPÁČ, P. (2016): Anti-Europeanism and Euroskepticism in Slovakia, in: MOREAU, P.; WASSERBERG, B. (eds.): European Integration and New Anti-Europeanism II. The 2014 European Election and New Anti-European Forces in Southern, Northern and Eastern Europe, Stuttgart: Steiner-Verlag, 2016, pp. 163-180.

STAŠKO, J. (1982): Slovenská národná ideológia (Slovak national ideology), in: STAŠKO, J. (ed.): *Tvorcovia nového Slovenska – The shaping of modern Slovakia,* Cambridge-Ontario: Friends of good books, 1982, pp. 63-138.

STATISTA (2016): *The rise of nationalism across Europe.* Statista, 26 May 2016. Dostupné na: https://www.statista.com/chart/4901/the-rise-of-nationalism-across-europe/.

STATISTIA (2014): *Corruption is widespread across Europe.* Statistia, 4 Feb. 2014. https://www.statista.com/chart/1853/corruption-is-widespread-across-europe/.

STRATEGIA NACIONALNOJ BEZOPASNOSTI ROSSIJSKOJ FEDERACII DO 2020 GODA (2009): (Utverždena ukazom prezidenta RF ot 12 maja 2009 No 537). (The strategy of national security of the Russian federation till 2020). [online] Available at: http://www.scrf.gov.ru/documents/99.html

STRATEGIA NACIONAĽNOJ BEZOPASNOSTI ROSSIJSKOJ FEDERACII. Prezident Rossii (2015): (The strategy of national security of the Russian federation. Russia's President). 31 December 2015. [online] Available at: http://kremlin.ru/acts/bank/40391/page/1.

STRATFOR.COM: Population Growth and Control in Africa. 2013. Stratfor. Partner Perspectives. [online] Available at: https://www.stratfor.com/the-hub/population-growth-and-control-africa.

STREDOEURÓPSKA IDENTITA — Central European Identity, Stredoeurópska nadácia, Bratislava 2002.

STUPŇAN, I. — RUŽINSKÁ, V. (2016): *O telefonát s Ficom prejavil záujem Putin.* (Putin shows interest in the telephone call with Fico). Pravda, 16 June 2016.

STÝSKALÍKOVÁ (STOJAROVÁ), V. (2005): Der Einfluss des EU-Beitrittes auf die tschechische Integrations- und Migrationspolitik. In Salimi-Asl, C., Wrasse, E., Schuch, G. (ed.). *Die Transformation nationaler Politik. Europäisierungsprozesse in Mitteleuropa.* Budapest DGAP. ISBN 978-398-10553-0-6, s. 137-156.

SULÍK, R. (2015): *Es gibt keine Pflicht, Flüchtlinge aufzunehmen.* [online] Available at: www.deutschlandfunk.de/fluechtlingsdebatte-es-gibt-keine-pflicht-fluechtlinge.694.de.html?dram:article_id=328736.

SULÍK, R. (2016): *Mohamedov život* (Life of Muhammad). [online] Available at: https://dennikn.sk/594122/mohamedov-zivot/.

SULÍK, R.: *Národní sebci v Európskej únii. Richard Sulík — Spravme Slovensko lepším,* 14 July 2016. [online] Available at: http://sulik.sk/slovenske-zaujmy-v-europskej-unii/.

SURJÁN, L. (2016): Perbeszéd, párbeszéd [online] 2016. Tények.sk, www.tenyek.sk/2016/08/23/perbeszed-parbeszed.

SZENTANDRÁSI, T. (2009): Situace maďarských menšin ve státech sousedících s Maďarskem. In: Hirtlová, P., Srb, V. (eds.) *Menšiny a integrující se Evropa.* Kolín: Nezávislé centrum pro studium politiky, 2009. ISBN 978-80-86879-23-9, s. 395-411.

SZENTANDRÁSI, T. (2011): Šance multikulturality a pluralitnej demokracie v národných štátoch. In: Németh Š. (ed.) 2011. *Politika, etnopolitika a identita.* Nitra: UKF, 2011. 112 s. ISBN 978-80-8094-931-0. s. 73-83.

SZENTANDRÁSI, T. (2016): A megoldás az autonómia. Andó Krisztina (ed.) In: *Új Nő* roč. 22, 2016, č. 9, ISSN 1335-938X s. 38-9 [online] Available at: http://www.ujno.sk/megoldas-az-autonomia.

ŠEBEJ, F. (2000): *Ďalšie poznámky o národných záujmoch*. Domino Fórum, 26.10.2000.

ŠEBESTA, Š. – ROTH, V. (eds.) (2016): *Suverénne európske Slovensko. Nad dielom a činnosťou Svetoslava Bombíka*. Bratislava: VEDA, vydavateľstvo SAV – ÚPV SAV.

ŠKVARNA, D. – MOJŽITA, M. (1992): Národné záujmy Slovenskej republiky. In: VALENTA Jiří a kol.: *Máme národní zájmy?* Praha: Ústav mezinárodních vztahů.

ŠKVARNA, D. (2001): Zvláštna cesta Slovenska. Moderné slovenské dejiny a súčasná polarizácia našej spoločnosti (A peculiar path of Slovakia. Modern Slovak history and current polarization of our society) In SZIGETI, László (ed.). *Slovenská otázka dnes*. Bratislava: Kalligram, 2007, pp. 254-262.

ŠKVRNDA, F. – POLONSKÝ.(2003): *Terorizmus a medzinárodná bezpečnosť po skončení studenej vojny*. Liptovský Mikuláš: Vojenská akadémia, 2003. 86 s. ISBN 80-8040-21-3.

ŠKVRNDA, F. (2001): *Mäkká bezpečnosť a nevojenské bezpečnostné hrozby*, In: Mezinárodní politika 12/2001, Praha: IIR, 2001, p. 16.

ŠNÍDL, V. (2016): *Europoslanci prvýkrát varovali pred ruskou propagandou, Sulík a Flašíková-Beňová sa zdržali* (Euro-deputies first warn against the Russian propaganda, Sulík and Flašíková-Beňová refrain). DenníkN, 25 November 2016.

ŠTATISTICKÚ ÚRAD (2016): *Zahraničný obchod SR – za rok 2015 (v porovnaní s rokom 2014)* (Slovakia's foreign trade for 2015 (as compared with 2014)). Bratislava: Statistical Office of the Slovak Republic 2016.

ŠTATISTICKÚ ÚRAD (2017): *Celkový dovoz a celkový vývoz podľa kontinentov a ekonomických zoskupení krajín (2016, 2017)* (Total imports and total exports by continents and economic blocs). Bratislava: Statistical Office of the Slovak Republic 2017.

ŠTATISTICKÝ ÚRAD (2003): *Referendum on Accession of the Slovak Republic to the European Union 2003. Results on voting of participant citizen in referendum*. [online] Available at: http://volby.statistics.sk/ref/ref2003/webdata/sk/graf/graf3.htm.

ŠTATISTICKÝ ÚRAD (2014): *Voľby prezidenta Slovenskej republiky.*Marec 2014. (Slovak Republic presidential elections) Bratislava: Statistical office of the Slovak Republic 2014.

ŠTEFANČÍK, R.—LENČ, J. (2012): *Mladí migranti v slovenskej spoločnosti. Medzinárodná migrácia, moslimovia, štát a verejná mienka.* (Young migrants in Slovak society. International migration, Muslims, state and public opinion.) Brno: Tribun EU, 2012.

ŠTEFANČÍK, R. (2011): *Úrovne migračnej politiky.* In: Politické vedy, roč. XIV, č. 3, 2011. ISSN 1335-2741, s. 6-34.

ŠTEFANČÍK, R. (2016): Kam kráčaš demokracia, keď k tebe kráčajú migranti? Politizácia medzinárodnej migrácie vo výstupoch slovenských politických strán. In Dobiaš, D.—Eštok, G.—Bzdilová, R. (eds.). *Medzi jednotlivosťou a pospolitosťou. Kam kráčaš demokracia.* Košice: UPJŠ v Košiciach, 2016. ISBN 978-80-8152-450-9, s. 317-334.

ŠTEFANČIK. R. (2010): *Prenikanie témy migrácie do politiky straníckych subjektov v Českej republike a na Slovensku.* (Permeation of the theme of migration in the policies of party organizations in the Czech Republic and Slovakia.) In Studia Politica Slovaca, vol. 3, 2010, No. 1, pp. 3-22.

ŠTEFANČIK. R. (2011) *Islamofóbny populizmus v stranickej politike.* (Islamophobic populism in party politics.), in Rexter—Časopis pro výzkum radikalismu, extremismu a terorismu, vol. 9, 2011, No. 2, ISSN 1214-7737, pp. 1-30.

ŠTÚR, L. (1848): *Štúrova reč pred slovenskými dobrovoľnými.* In Dokumenty slovenskej národnej identity a štátnosti I. Bratislava: Nár. Lit. Centrum, 1998, p. 313.

TAMO (2014): *Turci idú.* (The Turks are coming) [online] Available at: http://www.tamo.sk/spravy/.

TAYLOR, CH. (2001): Politika uznání. In Gutmanová, A. (ed.). *Multikulturalismus. Zkoumání politiky uznání.* Praha: Filosofia. 2001. ISBN 80-7007-161-3.

TERAZ.SK (2015): *G. Schröder: EÚ potrebuje jednotu i schopnosť väčšej koordinácie.* (G. Schröder: EU needs integrity and better coordination). Teraz.sk, 2 December 2015. [online] Available at: http://www.teraz.sk/slovensko/sr-schroder-eu-konferencia-fico/169167-clanok.html.

TERAZ.SK (2016): *F. Šebej: Na Slovensku pôsobí ruská propaganda.* (Russian propaganda at work in Slovakia). Teraz.sk, 11 June 2016. [online] Available at: http://www.teraz.sk/slovensko/sebej-ruska-propaganda-dezinformacie/201184-clanok.html.

TERAZ.SK (2018): *A. Kiska: Problémom strednej Európy je bezškrupulózna politika.* Teraz.sk, 17. 5. 2018.

THE FINANCIAL TIMES (2012): *Slovaks protest over corruption claims.* The Financial Times, 10 Feb. 2012. [online] Available at: https://www.ft.com/content/6fc1858c-48cd-11e1-954a-00144feabdc0.

THE FUTURE OF THE UNION – THE LAEKEN DECLARATION. (PRESIDENCY CONCLUSIONS).

THE GLOBAL ECONOMIC CRIME SURVEY. 2009. [online] Available at:https://www.pwc.com/gx/en/economic-crime-survey/pdf/global-economic-crime-survey-2009.pdf.

THE WALL STREET JOURNAL (2015): *Russia's Sergei Lavrov Says Cease-Fire Is Only Solution to Ukraine Conflict*. The Wall Street Journal, 4 April 2015. [online] Available at: https://www.wsj.com/articles/russias-sergei-lavrov-says-cease-fire-is-only-solution-to-ukraine-conflict-1428157689.

THIBAULT, P. (2006): A nemzetek Európája és Európa nemzetei. In.: FERRY, Jean Marc – THIBAULT, Paul: *Vita Európáról*, L´Harmattan, Zsigmond Király Főiskola, Budapest, 2006.

THRÄNHARDT, D. (2003): Der Nationalstaat als migrationspolitischer Akteur. In: Thränhardt, D., Hunger, U. (ed.). *Migration im Spannungsfeld von Globalisierung und Nationalstaat*. Sonderheft 22. 2003. ISBN 3-531-13807-3, pp. 8-34.

THRÄNHARDT, D. (2005): *Integrationspolitik richtet sich nach der Tradition*. In Tera cognita, 7/2006, 2005 pp. 88-93.

TOPKY.SK: *Podľa Fica nemá islam na Slovensku priestor*. [online] Available at: http://www.topky.sk/cl/100535/1549827/Podla-Fica-nema-islam-na-Slovensku-priestor--Moslimovia-su-pobureni--toto-je-ich-reakcia.

TRAUNER, F. (2016): *Wie sollen Flüchtlinge in Europa verteilt werden? Der Streit um einen Paradigmenwechsel in der EU-Asylpolitik*. In: Integration. Vierteljahreszeitschrift des Instituts für Europäische Politik. Vol. 39, 2016, No. 2, pp. 93-106.

TREATY EU 2012. *Consolidated Version of the Treaty on the Functioning of the European Union.* [online] Available at: http://eur-lex.europa.eu/legal-content/SK/TXT/PDF/?uri=CELEX:12012E/TXT&from=EN.

TRINITAS.RU (2017): *Obraščenije učastnikov Jubilejnogo vseslavianskogo sjezda k glavam gosudarstv, praviteľstvam i parlamentam slavianskih gosudarstv.* (Address of the participants in the anniversary Pan-Slavic Congress to the heads of states, governments and parliaments of Slavic states). In: Glavnyje itogi Jubilejnogo vseslavianskogo sjezda. Moskva – St. Peterburg 26 May 2017 - 3 June 2017. [online] Available at: http://trinitas.ru/rus/doc/0001/005c/1975-slv.pdf.

ÚRADNÝ VESTNÍK (2015): *Rozhodnutie Rady (EÚ) 2015/1601 z 22. septembra 2015 o zavedení dočasných opatrení v oblasti medzinárodnej ochrany v prospech Talianska a Grécka*. [online] Available at: http://eur-lex.europa.eu/legal-content/SK/TXT/PDF/?uri=CELEX:32015D1601&from=SK.

ÚRADNÝ VESTNÍK (2016): *Žaloba podaná 2. decembra 2015 – Slovenská republika/Rada Európskej únie*. [online] Available at: http://eur-lex.europa.eu/legal-content/SK/TXT/PDF/?uri=CELEX:62015CN0643&from=SK.

V ENERGETIKE.SK (2016): *Premiéri na novom Nord Streame kritizujú viacero vecí.* (Prime Ministers criticize the new Nord Stream over a number of issues) V energetike.sk, 18 March 2016. [online] Available at: http://venergetike.sk/premieri-na-novom-nord-streame-kritizuju-viacero-veci/.

VALENTA J. a kol. (1992): *Máme národní zájmy?* Praha: Ústav mezinárodních vztahů.

VALENTA, J. (1992a): Národní zájmy, demokratické principy a postkomunistické Československo. In: VALENTA Jiří a kol.: *Máme národní zájmy?* Praha: Ústav mezinárodních vztahů. Praha: ÚMV 1992, s. 12-24.

VAŠEČKA, M. (2009): *Postoje verejnosti k cudzincom a zahraničnej migrácií v Slovenskej republike* (Attitudes of the public to foreigners and foreign migration in the Slovak Republic), Bratislava: IOM 2009.

VAUBEL, R. (2004): *Az unió árnyéka – az európai intézmények gőgje*. Budapest: Allprint, 2004. 250 s. ISBN 963-9575-01-1.

VECZÁN, Z. (2015): *Itt a vége a szlovák történelemhamisításnak?* [online] 2015. MNO. Available at: https://mno.hu/hatarontul/itt-a-vege-a-szlovak-tortenelemhamisitasnak-1278968.

VÍGH, K.: *A szlovákiai magyarság sorsa*. Budapest: Bereményi. 181 p. (no date).

VISEGRÁD GROUP (2014a): *Joint Statement of V4 Foreign Ministers on Ukraine*. Visegrad Group – official website, 24 February 2014. [online] Available at: http://www.visegradgroup.eu/joint-statement-of-v4.

VISEGRÁD GROUP (2014b): *Statement of the Prime Ministers of the Visegrad Countries on Ukraine*. Visegrad Group – official website, 4 March 2014. [online] Available at: http://www.visegradgroup.eu/calendar/2014/statement-of-the-prime.

VISEGRÁD GROUP (2014c): *V4 Interior Ministers' Joint Statement on Ukraine*. Visegrad Group – official website, 25 February 2014. [online] Available at: http://www.visegradgroup.eu/documents/official-statements/v4-interior-ministers.

VISEGRÁD GROUP (2014d): *Bratislava Declaration of the Visegrad Group Heads of Government on the Deepening V4 Defence Cooperation* — official website, 9 December 2014. [online] Available at: http://www.vise gradgroup.eu/deepening-v4-defence.

VLÁDA SR (1992): *Programové vyhlásenie vlády Slovenskej republiky.* (Program Statement of the Government of SR). 1992.

VLÁDA SR (2012): *Programové vyhlásenie vlády Slovenskej republiky.* (Program Statement of the Government of SR). May 2012.

VLÁDA SR (2016): *Fico o novom postoji vlády k téme migrácie.* [online] Available at: http://www.vlada.gov.sk/tlacova-konferencia-predse du-vlady-sr-roberta-fica-o-novom-postoji-vlady-k-teme-migracie-po -udalostiach-v-nemeckom-koline-nad-rynom/.

VLÁDA SR (2016a): *Premiér SR Róbert Fico rokoval s ruským prezidentom Vladimírom Putinom* (SR Prime Minister Róbert Fico holds talks with the Russian president Vladimir Putin). Bratislava: Office of the government of the Slovak Republic — official website, 25 August 2016. [online] Available at: http://www.vlada.gov.sk/premier-sr-robert-fico-rokoval-s-ruskym-prezidentom-vladimirom-putinom/.

VLÁDA SR (2016b): *Programové vyhlásenie vlády SR* (Program Statement of the Government of SR), Bratislava 2016. [online] Available at: www.vlada.gov.sk/data/files/6483programove-vyhlasenie-vlady-slovenskej-republiky.pdf.

VLČEJ, J. (2016): *Ako volia Slováci. Politický vývoj Slovenskej republiky v období 1989-2016.* (How Slovaks vote. Political development of the Slovak Republic in 1989-2016.) Brno: Tribun EU 2016.

VOEGELIN, E. (1991): *Die neue Wissenschaft der Politik. Eine Einführung,* Freiburg: Alber.

VOGEL, D. (1994): *Sozialpolitische Integration als zuwanderungspolitisches Steuerungsinstrument.* In: Forum Demographie und Politik, No. 5. 1994. ISBN 3-9265-709-2-X, pp. 132-155.

VOĽBYSR.SK: *Voľby do Národnej rady Slovenskej republiky 2016. Definitívne výsledky hlasovania.* (Elections to the National Council of the Slovak Republic 2016. Official voting results.) Available at: http://volbysr.sk/sk/data02.html.

VOLNER, Š. (2007): *Nová teória bezpečnosti.* Zvolen 2007, ISBN 978-80-89241-12-5.

VRAŽDA, D. (2014): *Kotleba píše list ukrajinskému prezidentovi Janukovyčovi: Neustupujte.* (Kotleba writes a letter to Ukraine's president Yanukovych: Do not yield. Sme, 31 January 2014.

WAISOVÁ, Š. (2011): *Tíha volby. Česká zahraniční politika mezi principy a zájmy*. Praha: Ústav mezinárodních vztahů (Institute of International Relations) 2011, pp. 9–10.

WALKER, N. (2003): Late Sovereignty in the European Union. In: WALKER, N. (ed.): *Sovereignty in Transition*. Oxford: Hart, 2003, pp. 3–32.

WALT, S.(2014): *No-bluff Putin*. Foreign Policy. 4. June 2014, [online] Available at: http://www.foreignpolicy.com/articles/2014/06/04/no_bluff_putin_russia_ukraine_obama_tom_friedman.

WALTZ, K. (1979): *Theory of International Politics*. Columbia University. Waveland Press. ISBN 978-1-57766-670-7.

WALTZ, K. (2001): *Man, the State and War*. New York. Columbia University Press. ISBN 978-0-231-12537-6.

WEBNOVINY (2014a): *Fico a Jaceňuk spustili reverzný tok plynu na Ukrajinu*. (Fico and Yatsenyuk launch reverse gas flow to Ukraine). Webnoviny.sk, 2 September 2014. [online] Available at: https://www.webnoviny.sk/fico-a-jacenuk-spustili-reverzny-tok-plynu-na-ukrajinu/.

WEBNOVINY (2014b): *Flašíková odsúdila, že krajiny neuznali referendum na Kryme*. (Flašíková slams countries for not recognising the Crimea referendum) Webnoviny.sk, 17 March 2014. [online] Available at: https://www.webnoviny.sk/flasikova-odsudila-ze-krajiny-neuznali-referendum-na-kryme/.

WEBNOVINY (2015a): *Premiér Fico sa rozhodol, pôjde do Moskvy na oslavy* (Prime Minister Fico decides to attend the Moscow celebrations). Webnoviny.sk, 27 April 2015. [online] Available at: http://www.webnoviny.sk/slovensko/clanok/946651-premier-fico-sa-rozhodol-pojde-do-moskvy-na-oslavy/.

WEBNOVINY (2015b): *SaS žiada Lajčáka, aby sa vyjadril k Ficovej ceste do Moskvy*. (SaS demands that Lajčák explain Fico's visit to Moscow).Webnoviny.sk, 28 April 2015. [online] Available at: http://www.webnoviny.sk/slovensko/clanok/947071-sas-ziada-lajcaka-aby-sa-vyjadril-k-ficovej-ceste-do-moskvy/.

WEBNOVINY (2015c): *Slováci nechcú, aby utečenci našli v našej krajine domov*. (Slovaks do not want refugees to find a home in our country.) [online] Available at: www.webnoviny.sk/slovensko/clanok/993247-slovaci-nechcu-aby-utecenci-nasli-v-nasej-krajine-domov/.

WEBNOVINY (2016): *Slováci majú z utečencov obavy*. (Slovaks are afraid of refugees) [online] Available at: www.webnoviny.sk/slovaci-maju-z-utecencov-obavy-v-prieskume-povedali-dovody/.

WEBNOVINY (2017): *Pozitívne vnímanie Európskej Únie na Slovensku rastie.* (Positive image of the European Union increases in Slovakia.) [online] Available at: http://www.webnoviny.sk/pozitivne-vnimanie-europskej-unie-na-slovensku-rastie/.

WEISS, P. (2008): *On the definition of categories. The position and role of the state in international relations.* Politické vedy, Vol. 11, 2008, No. 1–2, pp. 103-126.

WEISS, P. (2009): *Národný záujem a zodpovednosť v slovenskej zahraničnej politike.* Bratislava: Kalligram 2009.

WEISS, P. (2010): Národný záujem a zahraničná politika štátu. In: MARUŠIAK, Juraj a kol.: *Za zrkadlom politiky.* Bratislava: Veda 2010, s. 42-83.

WEISS, P. (2013): *Szomszédságban – Nemzeti érdek és felelősség a szlovák külpolitikában.* Pozsony: Kalligram, 2013. 264 s. ISBN 978-80-8101-743-8.

WENDEKAMM, M. (2015): *Die Wahrnehmung von Migration als Bedrohung. Zur Verzahnung der Politikfelder Innere Sicherheit und Migrationspolitik.* Wiesbaden: Springer, 2015. 978-3-658-08073-0.

WHEATCROFT, A. 2006. *Nevěřící. Střety křesťanstva s islámen v letetch 638-2002.* (Infidels. A History of the Conflict between Christendom and Islam 638-2002.), Praha: BB/art, 2006.

WOLF, K. (1997a): *Od Žirinovského k Le Penovi.* (From Zhirinovsky to Le Pen) Domino fórum, 15–21 August 1997.

WOLF, K. (1997b): *Žiadne NATO, žiadna druhá vlna. Slovensko vyradené z procesu integrácie do civilizovaného sveta.* (No NATO, no second wave. Slovakia excluded from the process of integration into the civilised world). Domino fórum, 2-8 May 1997.

WOYKE, W. (1993): *Handwörterbuch Internationale Politik,* 5. Auflage, Oplanden: Leske und Budrich, 1993.

WRÓBEL, A. (2018): *Who's expelling Russian diplomats (and who isn't).* Politico, March 26, 2018.

ZARTMAN, I. W. (ed.), (2007): *Peacemaking in international conflict.* Washington: US Institute of Peace, 2007. 511 p. ISBN 978-1-929223-66-4.

ZEIDLER, M. (2002): *A magyar irredenta kultusz a két világháború között.* Budapest: Teleki László Alapítvány, 2002. 138 p. ISBN 963-85774-3-6. [online] Available at: http://mek.oszk.hu/06000/06030/06030.pdf.

ZEMKO, M. (1998): Moderný politický národ (A modern political nation). In SZIGETI, L. (ed.). *Slovenská otázka dnes.* Bratislava: Kalligram, 2007, pp. 188-192.

ŽIADOSTI 1848. *Žiadosti slovenského národa*. (Claims of the Slovak nation) In Dokumenty slovenskej národnej identity a štátnosti I. Bratislava: Nár. Lit. Centrum, 1998, pp. 307-310.

Authors

Mgr. Juraj Marušiak, PhD. — Independent researcher, Institute of Political Sciences of the Slovak Academy of Sciences, Bratislava, juraj.marusiak@savba.sk

Doc., Mgr. László Öllös, PhD. — Assistant Professor, Department of Political Science and Eurasian Studies of Constantine the Philosopher University in Nitra, lollos@ukf.sk

Mgr. Radoslava Brhlíková, Ph.D. — Assistant Professor, Department of Political Science and Eurasian Studies of Constantine the Philosopher University in Nitra, rbrhlikova@ukf.sk

Mgr. Norbert Kmeť, Ph.D. — Independent researcher, Institute of Political Sciences of the Slovak Academy of Sciences, Bratislava, norbert.kmet@savba.sk

Doc. PhDr. Radoslav Štefančík, MPol., Ph.D. — Dean, Department of Intercultural Communication, Faculty of Applied Languages, University of Economics in Bratislava, radoslav.stefancik@euba.sk

Dirk Mathias Dalberg, Dr. phil. — Independent researcher, Institute of Political Sciences of the Slovak Academy of Sciences, Bratislava, dirk.dalberg@savba.sk

Mgr. Tibor Szentandrási, Ph.D. — Assistant professor, Department of Political Studies and Eurasian Studies in Constantine the Philosopher University in Nitra, tszentandrasi@ukf.sk

Dr. David Reichardt — Assistant Professor, Faculty of Social and Economic Sciences, Comenius University in Bratislava, dr0608@gmail.com

ibidem.eu